# Entrepreneurship & Startup Growth Strategies

Dr. Gaurav Kumar

**ISBN:** 978-93-344-3446-0

**Published by:**
SB Knowledge Press
Patna, Bihar, India

**Disclaimer:**
This book is intended solely for educational, academic, and informational purposes. The contents are designed to support learning, research, and discussion in the fields of entrepreneurship, startups, innovation, and business strategy. While every effort has been made to ensure accuracy and reliability, the author and publisher do not assume any legal responsibility or liability for errors, omissions, or outcomes arising from the use or application of the information presented. The case studies, examples, and scenarios included are for illustrative purposes only and should not be construed as professional, legal, financial, or investment advice.

**First Edition:** 2026
**Printed in India**

*The views expressed in this book are those of the author and do not necessarily reflect the views of the publisher or affiliated institutions.*

# DEDICATION

I lovingly dedicate this book to my **parents**, whose unconditional love, guidance, and lifelong sacrifices have been the foundation of my personal and professional journey. I dedicate it to my **wife** and my **son**, whose constant support, patience, encouragement, and love give meaning to my work and strength to my aspirations. I am deeply grateful to my **teachers**, whose wisdom, discipline, and inspiration have shaped my thinking, values, and commitment to learning. I also dedicate this work to my **students**, whose curiosity, energy, and aspirations continually motivate me to learn, innovate, and share knowledge. This book stands as a reflection of their influence and an expression of my enduring gratitude.

CONTENTS

# ACKNOWLEDGMENTS

I express my profound gratitude to the leadership and administration of Galgotias University for providing a nurturing academic environment that encourages innovation, scholarship, and entrepreneurship. I respectfully acknowledge the guidance and support of the Hon'ble Chancellor, **Shri Suneel Galgotia**, whose visionary leadership continues to inspire academic excellence and institutional growth. I am sincerely thankful to the Hon'ble CEO, **Dr. Dhruv Galgotia**, for his dynamic outlook and unwavering commitment to fostering innovation, research, and startup culture within the university.

I extend my sincere thanks to the Hon'ble Director – Operations, the Hon'ble Vice Chancellor, the Hon'ble Pro Vice Chancellor, the Hon'ble Advisor to the Chancellor, and the Registrar of Galgotias University for their continuous administrative support, encouragement, and facilitation of academic and research initiatives.

I am especially grateful to the Dean, School of Biosciences & Technology, **Prof. Abhimanyu Kumar Jha**, for his constant encouragement, academic guidance, and confidence in my work, which have been instrumental throughout this journey.

I owe my deepest gratitude to my PhD Supervisor, **Prof. Ranjana Patnaik,** whose scholarly guidance, critical insights, and unwavering mentorship have profoundly shaped my academic growth and research orientation. Her support and inspiration have been invaluable in both my professional development and intellectual pursuits.

I also acknowledge my colleagues, students, mentors, and members of the academic and startup ecosystem who, directly or indirectly, contributed through discussions, feedback, and shared experiences that enriched this work.

Finally, I express my heartfelt appreciation to my family for their patience, understanding, and constant support, which made the completion of this book possible. This work is a collective outcome of the guidance, encouragement, and goodwill of all those acknowledged herein.

# PREFACE

Entrepreneurship has emerged as a powerful driver of economic growth, technological advancement, and social transformation in the twenty-first century. Across the globe, startups are redefining industries, creating new markets, and offering innovative solutions to complex societal challenges. In India, this momentum has been further strengthened by progressive policies, expanding incubation and innovation ecosystems, and an increasing convergence of academia, industry, and government. Against this backdrop, *Entrepreneurship & Startup Growth Strategies* has been conceived to serve as a structured, practical, and academically rigorous guide for understanding and applying entrepreneurship in real-world contexts.

This book is the outcome of my academic experience, research engagement, interactions with startup founders, incubators, investors, and students, and my involvement in entrepreneurship education and innovation-led programs. While numerous texts address entrepreneurship either from a purely theoretical perspective or as fragmented practitioner guides, there remains a need for an integrated resource that connects entrepreneurial thinking with validation, business modeling, funding, scaling, and investment readiness. This book seeks to bridge that gap.

The primary objective of this book is to guide readers through the complete startup lifecycle—from opportunity identification and ideation to market validation, business model development, funding, scaling, and commercialization. Special emphasis has been placed on contemporary frameworks such as Lean Startup, Minimum Viable Product (MVP), Business Model Canvas, and market-driven innovation. At the same time, advanced concepts such as Manufacturing Readiness Levels (MRL) and Investment Readiness Levels (IRL) have been incorporated to address the needs of deep-tech, biotech, and manufacturing-oriented startups, which often face unique commercialization challenges.

The book adopts a learner-centric and application-oriented approach. Each chapter integrates key concepts, definitions, mini case studies, practical activities, review questions, and startup lab exercises to reinforce experiential learning. Indian startup examples are used extensively to contextualize global concepts within local realities, while global case studies provide comparative insights and broader perspectives.

This book is intended for undergraduate and postgraduate students of entrepreneurship, management, engineering, life sciences, and allied disciplines; doctoral scholars and researchers; startup founders and early-stage teams; faculty members and trainers; incubation and innovation professionals; and ecosystem stakeholders involved in policy, mentoring, and startup support. It can be effectively used as a core textbook, a supplementary reference, or a practical handbook for entrepreneurship development programs.

I hope this book not only enhances conceptual understanding but also empowers readers to think critically, act strategically, and build sustainable ventures with confidence, responsibility, and ethical awareness. If this work contributes in any measure to nurturing entrepreneurial mindsets, strengthening startup ecosystems, and translating ideas into impactful enterprises, it will have fulfilled its purpose.

**Dr. Gaurav Kumar**

# HOW TO USE THIS BOOK

*Entrepreneurship & Startup Growth Strategies* is designed as a flexible, application-oriented resource that can be effectively used by diverse stakeholders within the entrepreneurship and innovation ecosystem. The structure of the book allows readers to progress sequentially through the startup lifecycle or selectively engage with specific chapters based on their learning or practical needs.

**For Students:** Students of entrepreneurship, management, engineering, life sciences, and allied disciplines are encouraged to read the chapters sequentially to develop a comprehensive understanding of the startup journey—from opportunity identification to scaling and investment readiness. Each chapter begins with conceptual foundations and progresses toward applied frameworks. Students should actively engage with the key concepts, review questions, and practical activities to reinforce learning outcomes. Mini case studies, field assignments, and startup lab exercises are particularly useful for project-based learning, internships, and capstone projects aligned with academic curricula and the National Education Policy (NEP) 2020.

**For Faculty Members and Trainers:** Faculty and trainers may use this book as a core or supplementary textbook for courses in entrepreneurship, innovation management, startup development, and technology commercialization. Chapters are modular and can be assigned independently based on course objectives. The inclusion of case studies, worksheets, canvas tools, and evaluation rubrics enables outcome-based education, flipped classrooms, experiential learning, and continuous assessment. The book also supports certification programs, faculty development programs, and entrepreneurship development initiatives.

**For Startup Founders and Early-Stage Teams:** Founders can use this book as a practical playbook to navigate real-world startup challenges. The Lean Startup, MVP, market validation, business model, funding, pitching, and scaling chapters can be consulted at different stages of venture development. Tools such as the Lean Canvas, growth playbooks, funding roadmaps, and readiness assessment frameworks are intended for direct application in incubators, accelerators, and startup studios.

**For Incubators, Accelerators, and Mentors:** Incubation managers and mentors may use the book as a structured mentoring framework. The chapters on validation, funding, MRL–IRL readiness, and ecosystem support can guide cohort-based programs, review meetings, and milestone tracking. Case studies and ecosystem mapping sections are useful for benchmarking and best-practice discussions.

**For Researchers, Policymakers, and Ecosystem Stakeholders:** Researchers and policymakers can selectively use chapters addressing the startup ecosystem, academic entrepreneurship, incubation models, and commercialization pathways to support policy formulation, program design, and impact assessment. The Indian ecosystem focus, complemented by global perspectives, provides valuable contextual insights.
Readers are encouraged to combine conceptual reading with hands-on execution of activities, reflection on case studies, and collaborative discussions. Used in this manner, the book serves not only as a source of knowledge but as a practical guide for building entrepreneurial competence and creating sustainable, innovation-driven ventures.

# LEARNING OUTCOMES & COMPETENCY MAPPING

This book is designed to support outcome-based and competency-driven learning in entrepreneurship and startup development. On successful completion of *Entrepreneurship & Startup Growth Strategies*, readers will acquire integrated knowledge, practical skills, and professional competencies required to ideate, validate, launch, scale, and sustain innovation-driven ventures in academic, industrial, and societal contexts.

**Learning Outcomes:** After studying this book, the reader will be able to:

1. Explain the evolution, types, and role of entrepreneurship in economic and social development, with particular reference to the Indian startup ecosystem.
2. Apply entrepreneurial mindset frameworks to identify opportunities, analyze problems, and design innovative solutions.
3. Implement Lean Startup principles, including customer discovery, hypothesis testing, MVP development, and iterative learning.
4. Conduct structured market analysis using market sizing, segmentation, competitive assessment, and customer validation tools.
5. Design, test, and refine viable business models using the Business Model Canvas and Lean Canvas frameworks.
6. Demonstrate startup literacy through appropriate use of business, funding, legal, technology, and growth-related terminology.
7. Evaluate and select suitable digital and e-commerce business models based on market and operational requirements.
8. Plan startup funding strategies, understand valuation methods, interpret term sheets, and prepare for investor due diligence.
9. Formulate growth and scaling strategies addressing customer acquisition, partnerships, team development, and global expansion.
10. Assess technology commercialization, manufacturability, and investment preparedness using MRL and IRL frameworks.
11. Analyze startup success, failure, and turnaround cases to derive actionable managerial and strategic insights.

**Competency Mapping**

The learning outcomes of this book are aligned with the following core competency domains:

- **Entrepreneurial Competency:** Opportunity recognition, innovation, risk awareness, and resilience.
- **Analytical Competency:** Market assessment, financial reasoning, and data-driven decision-making.
- **Practical Competency:** Canvas design, MVP development, validation, pitching, and scaling execution.
- **Communication Competency:** Professional articulation, persuasion, negotiation, and leadership communication.
- **Ecosystem Competency:** Engagement with incubators, investors, regulatory systems, and commercialization pathways.

This competency mapping ensures that readers develop both conceptual understanding and practical, industry-relevant entrepreneurial skills aligned with academic and startup ecosystem needs.

# LIST OF ABBREVIATIONS

AI – Artificial Intelligence
AIM – Atal Innovation Mission
API – Application Programming Interface
B2B – Business to Business
B2C – Business to Consumer
BIRAC – Biotechnology Industry Research Assistance Council
C2C – Consumer to Consumer
CAC – Customer Acquisition Cost
CSR – Corporate Social Responsibility
D2C – Direct to Consumer
EDP – Entrepreneurship Development Programme
ESOP – Employee Stock Ownership Plan
FDI – Foreign Direct Investment
IPO – Initial Public Offering
IP – Intellectual Property
IRL – Investment Readiness Level
KPI – Key Performance Indicator
LTV – Customer Lifetime Value
MoU – Memorandum of Understanding
MRL – Manufacturing Readiness Level
MVP – Minimum Viable Product
NEP – National Education Policy
NGO – Non-Governmental Organization
PE – Private Equity
PR – Public Relations
R&D – Research and Development
ROI – Return on Investment
SaaS – Software as a Service
SAM – Serviceable Available Market
SOM – Serviceable Obtainable Market
STP – Segmentation, Targeting, and Positioning
TAM – Total Addressable Market
TRL – Technology Readiness Level
TTO – Technology Transfer Office
UVP – Unique Value Proposition
VC – Venture Capital

# CHAPTER-1

# STARTUP & ENTREPRENEURSHIP

**Abstract**: This chapter provides a comprehensive foundation of startup and entrepreneurship studies by examining the evolution, concepts, and contemporary dimensions of entrepreneurial activity. It traces the historical development of entrepreneurship from classical economic interpretations to modern innovation-driven and technology-based venture creation. The chapter classifies different types of entrepreneurs and startups, emphasizing the entrepreneurial mindset and competency frameworks required for successful venture development. Core processes such as opportunity recognition, problem identification, and innovation commercialization are discussed in detail. Special focus is given to academic entrepreneurship, university spin-offs, and the growing relevance of research-driven enterprises. The role of entrepreneurship in economic growth, employment generation, and social development is highlighted, alongside an overview of the Indian startup ecosystem, including key policies and institutional support mechanisms. The chapter also analyzes barriers, risks, and common causes of startup failure, and concludes by outlining emerging global trends shaping the future of entrepreneurship.

**Keywords:** Entrepreneurship; Startups; Innovation; Entrepreneurial Ecosystem; Academic Entrepreneurship; Economic Development

## 1.1 EVOLUTION AND CONCEPT OF ENTREPRENEURSHIP

Entrepreneurship is a dynamic and evolving discipline that mirrors transformations in economic structures, technological progress, and societal aspirations. Rather than being confined to the act of starting a business, entrepreneurship represents a broader process of value creation under conditions of uncertainty. The term "entrepreneur" is derived from the French word ***entreprendre***, meaning "**to undertake**," reflecting the fundamental nature of entrepreneurial activity as the willingness to initiate, organize, and lead new ventures.

The intellectual foundations of entrepreneurship can be traced to the eighteenth century, when economist **Richard Cantillon** described the entrepreneur as a risk bearer who operates in uncertain market conditions, purchasing inputs at known costs and selling outputs at unpredictable prices. This early view emphasized uncertainty and risk as the defining characteristics of entrepreneurial behavior. Subsequently, **Jean-Baptiste** Say expanded this perspective by highlighting the entrepreneur's economic function of reallocating resources from areas of lower productivity to more productive and profitable uses. Here, entrepreneurship began to be associated not merely with risk, but with coordination, judgment, and economic efficiency (Fig. 1.1).

A major conceptual shift occurred in the twentieth century with the work of Joseph Schumpeter, who positioned the entrepreneur as an innovator and a central agent of economic development. Schumpeter introduced the concept of "creative destruction," describing entrepreneurship as a disruptive force that continuously transforms industries through new products, new production methods, new markets, and new forms of organization. In this view, entrepreneurs do not merely respond to markets; they actively reshape them. Entrepreneurship thus became inseparable from innovation and technological change.

In contemporary scholarship and practice, entrepreneurship extends well beyond the creation of small businesses. It encompasses the systematic recognition of opportunities, the development and commercialization of innovations, the construction of scalable business models, and the pursuit of sustainable impact. Modern entrepreneurial activity is visible across diverse contexts, including technology startups that leverage digital, biological, and engineering advances; social enterprises that combine commercial logic with social and environmental missions; corporate entrepreneurship or intrapreneurship, where innovation is driven from within established organizations; and academic and research-based ventures that translate scientific knowledge into marketable solutions.

Accordingly, entrepreneurship is best understood not as a single event, but as an ongoing process—one that involves identifying meaningful opportunities, mobilizing human, financial, and technological resources, and creating economic and social value amid uncertainty. This process-oriented view captures the essence of entrepreneurship as a catalyst for innovation, competitiveness, and long-term development.

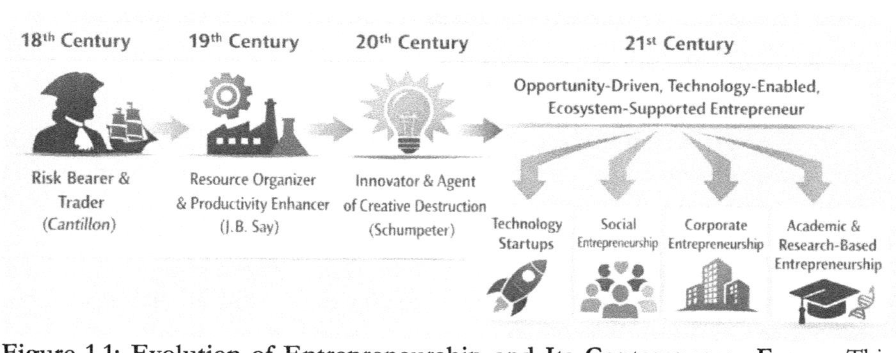


**Figure 1.1: Evolution of Entrepreneurship and Its Contemporary Forms.** This figure illustrates the historical evolution of entrepreneurship from the eighteenth-century conception of the entrepreneur as a risk bearer and trader (Cantillon), through the nineteenth century role of resource organizer and productivity enhancer (J.B. Say), to the twentieth century view of the entrepreneur as an innovator and agent of creative destruction (Schumpeter). It further presents the modern twenty-first century entrepreneur as opportunity-driven, technology-enabled, and ecosystem-supported, branching into technology startups, social entrepreneurship, corporate entrepreneurship, and academic and research-based ventures.

## 1.2 TYPES OF ENTREPRENEURS AND STARTUPS

Entrepreneurship manifests in multiple forms, shaped by the motivations of founders, the nature of opportunities pursued, and the intended scale and impact of ventures. Understanding the different types of entrepreneurs and startups is essential for appreciating the diversity of entrepreneurial activity and for aligning entrepreneurial strategies with appropriate goals, resources, and ecosystems.

Traditionally, entrepreneurs were often associated with small business ownership, where the primary objective was to establish a stable source of income and long-term self-employment. Such entrepreneurs typically operate local or regional enterprises in retail, services, manufacturing, or trading. While these ventures may not pursue rapid expansion, they play a vital role in employment generation, community development, and economic stability. Their success is usually measured in terms of sustainability, customer loyalty, and steady profitability rather than exponential growth.

In contrast, scalable startup entrepreneurs are driven by innovation and growth. These entrepreneurs design ventures around novel technologies, products, or platforms with the intention of serving large markets and achieving rapid expansion. Their business models are built for replication and scale, often supported by venture capital, angel investment, and global market access. Technology startups in domains such as artificial intelligence, biotechnology, financial technology, and clean energy exemplify this category, where uncertainty is high but potential impact and valuation are substantial.

Another important category is corporate entrepreneurship, commonly referred to as intrapreneurship. Here, entrepreneurial activity takes place within established organizations. Employees or internal teams act as entrepreneurs by developing new products, services, or processes that renew organizational capabilities and competitiveness. Intrapreneurship enables large firms to remain innovative, responsive, and resilient in rapidly changing environments, blending the agility of startups with the resources of corporations.

Social entrepreneurs represent a mission-driven form of entrepreneurship. Their primary objective is to address societal challenges such as poverty, healthcare access, education quality, environmental sustainability, and inclusion. While financial viability remains essential, profit is treated as a means to sustain and scale impact rather than as an end in itself. Social enterprises often operate at the intersection of the public, private, and non-profit sectors, applying entrepreneurial tools to achieve measurable social outcomes.

Academic entrepreneurs form another distinct category, particularly relevant in knowledge-based economies. These entrepreneurs emerge from universities and research institutions, where scientific discoveries and technological innovations are transformed into commercial ventures. University spin-offs, faculty-founded startups, and student-led technology enterprises exemplify this type. Such ventures are especially prominent in biotechnology, pharmaceuticals, advanced materials, medical devices, and information technology, where research intensity and intellectual property form the core assets.

Correspondingly, startups themselves may be classified according to their underlying models and sectors. Some are product-based startups focused on developing tangible or digital products; others are service-based, delivering specialized expertise or solutions. Platform startups create digital or physical infrastructures that connect multiple user groups, while deep-technology startups are rooted in advanced scientific research and long-term innovation cycles. What distinguishes startups from conventional businesses is not merely their youth, but their fundamental orientation toward experimentation, innovation, scalability, and the search for repeatable and high-impact business models.

Together, these varied forms demonstrate that entrepreneurship is not a singular pathway but a spectrum of approaches through which individuals and teams create value. Recognizing these distinctions enables aspiring entrepreneurs, educators, and policymakers to design more targeted strategies, support systems, and performance expectations across the entrepreneurial landscape.

## 1.3 ENTREPRENEURIAL MINDSET AND COMPETENCY FRAMEWORK

At the core of entrepreneurial activity lies a distinct way of thinking and acting commonly described as the entrepreneurial mindset. This mindset is not limited to founders of startups; rather, it is a cognitive and behavioral orientation that enables individuals to recognize opportunities, respond creatively to challenges, and function effectively in environments characterized by ambiguity and rapid change. Unlike routine managerial thinking, which often focuses on optimization within existing structures, the entrepreneurial mindset emphasizes exploration, innovation, and proactive value creation.

An entrepreneurial mindset is marked by opportunity orientation rather than problem fixation. Entrepreneurs view unmet needs, inefficiencies, and emerging trends as potential starting points for innovation. They demonstrate a tolerance for uncertainty and risk, coupled with resilience in the face of failure. Since entrepreneurial processes rarely follow linear paths, persistence, adaptability, and learning agility become critical psychological attributes. Creativity and curiosity drive the search for novel solutions, while ethical awareness and social responsibility guide sustainable decision-making, especially in sectors with significant societal impact such as healthcare, biotechnology, and environmental technology.

While mindset shapes orientation, entrepreneurial effectiveness depends on the systematic development of competencies. Contemporary entrepreneurship research increasingly adopts competency-based frameworks that integrate knowledge, skills, and attitudes required across the venture lifecycle. These competencies evolve from opportunity recognition to venture creation and scaling (Fig 2.2).

Opportunity-related competencies form the foundation of entrepreneurship. They include environmental scanning, customer discovery, market sensing, and problem framing. Entrepreneurs must be able to interpret technological signals, social trends, and regulatory changes, and translate them into viable venture ideas. Strategic competencies then enable entrepreneurs to articulate vision, design value propositions, and construct business and revenue models. This strategic layer aligns innovation with market realities and long-term positioning.

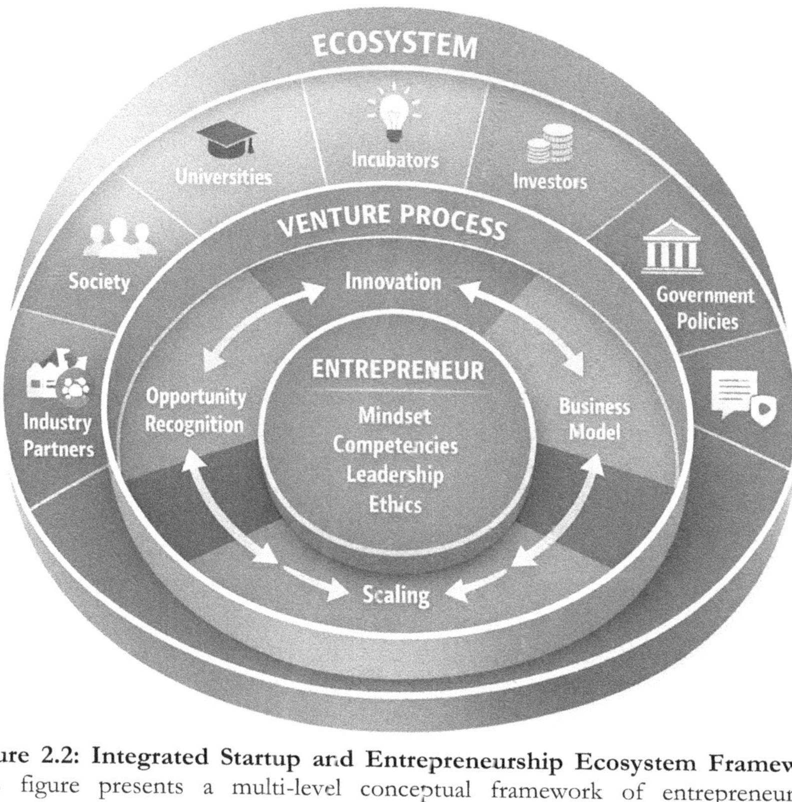


**Figure 2.2: Integrated Startup and Entrepreneurship Ecosystem Framework.** This figure presents a multi-level conceptual framework of entrepreneurship, highlighting the entrepreneur at the core (mindset and competencies), surrounded by the venture development process (opportunity recognition, innovation, business modeling, resource mobilization, and scaling), and embedded within the broader entrepreneurial ecosystem comprising universities, incubators, investors, government policies, industry partners, markets, and society. The figure emphasizes the systemic and interconnected nature of startup development.

Technical and functional competencies support venture execution. These include product and service development, intellectual property management, regulatory awareness, quality systems, and digital literacy. In technology-intensive and life-science ventures, the ability to integrate scientific rigor with commercialization pathways is particularly critical. Financial competencies—such as budgeting, valuation, fundraising, and cash-flow management—ensure resource sustainability and investor confidence.

Equally important are leadership and relational competencies. Team formation, talent management, negotiation, stakeholder engagement, and organizational culture building directly influence venture resilience and growth. As startups transition from small founding teams to structured organizations, execution competencies related to project management, operations, performance measurement, and scaling strategies become increasingly central. Thus, entrepreneurship emerges from the interaction between mindset and capability. The entrepreneurial mindset initiates action, while the competency framework sustains and amplifies impact. Developing both dimensions through education, experiential learning, and mentorship is essential for preparing individuals to navigate complex entrepreneurial ecosystems and to transform ideas into sustainable, high-value ventures.

## 1.4 OPPORTUNITY RECOGNITION AND PROBLEM IDENTIFICATION

Opportunity recognition constitutes the foundational phase of the entrepreneurial process. Every successful venture begins not with a product, but with a deep understanding of a problem worth solving. Entrepreneurs distinguish themselves by their ability to observe unmet needs, inefficiencies, or emerging demands and reinterpret them as opportunities for value creation. This process is both analytical and intuitive, drawing upon domain knowledge, market awareness, and creative insight.

Entrepreneurial opportunities often emerge from multiple sources. Technological advancement creates new capabilities that enable novel solutions, as seen in artificial intelligence–driven platforms, genomic diagnostics, and digital health systems. Market gaps arise when existing products or services fail to meet customer expectations in terms of affordability, accessibility, performance, or user experience. Regulatory and policy changes can open entirely new sectors, such as renewable energy, medical devices, and fintech. Demographic transitions, lifestyle shifts, and global challenges further generate demand for innovative products and services. Academic research and industrial R&D represent particularly powerful opportunity engines, where new knowledge can be translated into commercial applications.

However, not all ideas represent genuine entrepreneurial opportunities. A critical distinction exists between a creative idea and a validated problem. Effective problem identification requires systematic engagement with end users and stakeholders to understand pain points, behaviors, and constraints. Methods such as customer discovery interviews, ethnographic observation, and field immersion allow entrepreneurs to move beyond assumptions and capture authentic needs. Design thinking frameworks support this process by emphasizing empathy, problem definition, ideation, prototyping, and iterative testing.

Analytical tools further strengthen opportunity evaluation. Value chain and ecosystem analyses reveal inefficiencies and coordination gaps. Technology scouting helps assess the maturity and applicability of emerging innovations. Market research and competitive mapping clarify whether a problem is widespread, urgent, and inadequately addressed. Through these approaches, entrepreneurs refine broad problem statements into specific, actionable opportunity spaces.

Opportunity recognition is therefore not a single moment of insight but a continuous, evidence-based learning process. Entrepreneurs progressively shape and reshape their understanding of the problem as they interact with customers, partners, and markets. Ventures gain traction not by offering attractive solutions alone, but by demonstrating a strong problem–solution fit and the potential for scalable impact. In this sense, rigorous problem identification becomes the most strategic investment in the entrepreneurial journey.

## 1.5 INNOVATION-DRIVEN AND TECHNOLOGY-BASED ENTREPRENEURSHIP

Innovation-driven and technology-based entrepreneurship represents the most transformative form of modern venture creation. Unlike traditional enterprises that often compete through incremental improvements or operational efficiency, innovation-driven ventures are built around the development and commercialization of novel products, processes, or business models. Their competitive advantage arises from new knowledge, proprietary technology, or disruptive approaches that redefine how value is created and delivered.

Technology-based entrepreneurship is deeply rooted in scientific discovery and engineering advancement. Breakthroughs in areas such as biotechnology, artificial intelligence, advanced materials, medical devices, and renewable energy continually generate opportunities for new ventures. These startups typically originate from research laboratories, corporate R&D centers, or interdisciplinary innovation hubs, where experimentation, prototyping, and validation form the early stages of venture development. Consequently, such enterprises are characterized by high research and development intensity, strong reliance on intellectual property, and extended gestation periods before market entry.

A defining feature of innovation-driven startups is uncertainty across multiple dimensions. Technical uncertainty surrounds feasibility and performance; market uncertainty concerns adoption, pricing, and competition; regulatory uncertainty is particularly significant in healthcare, pharmaceuticals, and environmental technologies; and financial uncertainty reflects long development cycles and capital-intensive operations. To navigate these conditions, entrepreneurs adopt structured innovation processes that integrate lean experimentation with scientific rigor. Proof-of-concept studies, minimum viable products, pilot deployments, and iterative prototyping enable early validation while controlling risk.

Innovation-driven entrepreneurship also requires the orchestration of complex ecosystems. Strategic partnerships with universities, hospitals, manufacturing organizations, and regulatory bodies are often essential. Venture capital, corporate venture arms, and public funding agencies play a critical role in supporting early-stage development, while incubators and accelerators provide mentorship, infrastructure, and market access. In this context, the entrepreneur functions not only as a founder, but as a translator between science, markets, and institutions.

Ultimately, technology-based startups serve as mechanisms for knowledge translation and economic modernization. They transform research outputs into societal solutions, stimulate high-value employment, and enhance national competitiveness. By converting innovation into scalable ventures, such entrepreneurship becomes a cornerstone of contemporary development, linking scientific progress directly to economic and social impact.

## 1.6 ROLE OF ENTREPRENEURSHIP IN ECONOMIC AND SOCIAL DEVELOPMENT

Entrepreneurship is widely recognized as a central driver of economic growth, structural transformation, and social progress. By introducing new products, services, and business models, entrepreneurs stimulate competition, enhance productivity, and catalyze innovation across industries. New ventures not only create economic value for founders and investors, but also generate broader developmental outcomes that extend to employment, regional development, and social well-being.

From an economic perspective, entrepreneurship contributes directly to job creation and income generation. Startups and small enterprises collectively account for a significant proportion of new employment, particularly in emerging economies. Entrepreneurial activity also promotes industrial diversification by introducing new sectors and revitalizing traditional ones through technology integration. As innovative firms challenge incumbents, they compel continuous improvement, leading to efficiency gains and the diffusion of new technologies throughout the economy. Over time, this process strengthens national competitiveness and export potential.

Entrepreneurship further supports regional and inclusive development. Local ventures harness indigenous resources, address context-specific needs, and reduce dependency on centralized economic structures. In rural and semi-urban regions, entrepreneurship enables the development of agribusinesses, healthcare services, educational platforms, and clean energy solutions tailored to community realities. Such ventures stimulate local supply chains, build skills, and encourage youth engagement in productive economic activities.

Beyond economics, entrepreneurship plays a vital social role. Social and impact-oriented enterprises address challenges such as poverty, public health, environmental degradation, gender inequality, and educational access. By applying entrepreneurial principles to social problems, these ventures create sustainable models that combine financial viability with measurable social outcomes. In sectors such as healthcare and biotechnology, entrepreneurial innovation expands access to diagnostics, therapeutics, and preventive solutions, directly improving quality of life.

In the contemporary global context, entrepreneurship is increasingly aligned with sustainable development imperatives. Climate-tech ventures, circular economy models, and inclusive digital platforms demonstrate how entrepreneurship can reconcile profitability with responsibility. Thus, entrepreneurship functions not merely as a mechanism of wealth creation, but as an institutional force for societal transformation—one that mobilizes creativity, resources, and human capital toward long-term economic resilience and social advancement.

## 1.7 ACADEMIC ENTREPRENEURSHIP AND UNIVERSITY SPIN-OFFS

Academic entrepreneurship represents the convergence of knowledge creation and venture formation. It refers to entrepreneurial activities originating within universities and research institutions, where scientific discoveries, technological innovations, and intellectual property are transformed into commercial and societal applications. As economies increasingly depend on knowledge and innovation, universities have evolved from being centers of education and research to becoming active participants in entrepreneurial ecosystems.

University spin-offs constitute a primary mechanism of academic entrepreneurship. These are companies formed specifically to commercialize technologies developed through academic research. Faculty members, research scholars, and students often collaborate to translate laboratory findings into products, platforms, or services with market potential. Such ventures are especially prominent in biotechnology, pharmaceuticals, medical devices, advanced materials, and information technology, where the path from discovery to application requires specialized expertise, infrastructure, and long-term development.

The academic entrepreneurial ecosystem is supported by a range of institutional structures. Technology Transfer Offices facilitate patenting, licensing, and industry partnerships. Intellectual Property cells guide researchers in protecting and managing innovations. Incubation and acceleration centers provide startups with physical infrastructure, mentoring, business development support, and access to funding networks. University–industry collaboration platforms further enable joint research, pilot testing, and early market engagement.

Academic entrepreneurship offers multiple benefits. It accelerates the societal impact of publicly funded research, diversifies university revenue streams, and enhances experiential learning opportunities for students. It also strengthens national innovation capacity by creating high-technology enterprises and skilled employment. However, successful academic entrepreneurship requires a cultural shift toward interdisciplinary collaboration, entrepreneurial education, and supportive institutional policies.

In this framework, universities are no longer viewed solely as knowledge producers, but as entrepreneurial hubs—nurturing innovation pipelines that connect discovery, development, and deployment. University spin-offs thus function as critical bridges between science and society, transforming intellectual capital into engines of economic growth and technological advancement.

## 1.8 INDIAN STARTUP ECOSYSTEM: POLICIES AND INSTITUTIONAL SUPPORT

Over the past decade, India has emerged as one of the world's most vibrant startup ecosystems, driven by a combination of demographic advantage, expanding digital infrastructure, policy reforms, and a growing culture of innovation. The Indian entrepreneurial landscape today spans metropolitan hubs and emerging regional centers, encompassing sectors such as information technology, biotechnology, healthcare, agritech, fintech, education technology, clean energy, and advanced manufacturing. This transformation reflects a deliberate national effort to position entrepreneurship as a strategic instrument of economic development and technological self-reliance.

A critical catalyst in this evolution has been the role of government policy. National initiatives such as Startup India have sought to simplify regulatory procedures, facilitate ease of doing business, provide tax incentives, and improve access to early-stage funding. The Atal Innovation Mission has promoted innovation and entrepreneurship across schools, universities, and incubation centers, fostering a pipeline of problem-solvers and venture creators. In the life sciences and biotechnology sectors, dedicated institutional mechanisms have strengthened translational research and enterprise formation, enabling academic discoveries to move toward commercialization.

Institutional support structures form the backbone of the Indian startup ecosystem. University-based incubators, research parks, biotechnology parks, and technology business incubators provide physical infrastructure, technical facilities, mentorship, and business development services. Accelerators and corporate innovation programs offer market access, pilot opportunities, and strategic partnerships. Public and private funding mechanisms—including seed funds, angel networks, venture capital firms, and government-backed funds—support startups across stages of growth, from ideation to scale-up.

Equally important is the expanding network of ecosystem enablers: intellectual property facilitation centers, regulatory advisory platforms, startup exchanges, and innovation clusters. Together, these institutions reduce entry barriers, enhance survival rates, and promote a culture of experimentation. For students and researchers, this ecosystem creates structured pathways from classroom and laboratory environments to entrepreneurial careers.

Thus, the Indian startup ecosystem represents a coordinated model of policy, institutions, and culture. It demonstrates how systematic support can transform entrepreneurial intent into scalable ventures, positioning entrepreneurship as a central pillar of national innovation, employment generation, and global competitiveness.

## 1.9 BARRIERS, RISKS, AND CAUSES OF STARTUP FAILURE

Despite the growing sophistication of entrepreneurial ecosystems, startups continue to operate in environments characterized by high uncertainty and elevated failure rates. Understanding the barriers and risks inherent in the entrepreneurial process is essential for realistic venture planning and for developing resilience-oriented strategies. Failure in entrepreneurship should not be viewed solely as a negative outcome, but as a learning-intensive phase that informs subsequent innovation and venture design.

Startups commonly encounter structural and contextual barriers at early stages. Limited access to seed and pre-seed capital constrains product development, team formation, and market validation. Regulatory complexity, particularly in sectors such as biotechnology, healthcare, and financial services, can delay commercialization and increase compliance costs. Infrastructure limitations, including inadequate laboratory facilities, manufacturing capabilities, or digital connectivity, further restrict operational efficiency. Additionally, challenges in attracting and retaining skilled talent often impede technical progress and organizational stability.

Entrepreneurial risk is multidimensional. Technological risk arises when innovations fail to achieve intended performance or scalability. Market risk reflects uncertainty regarding customer adoption, competitive response, and pricing viability. Financial risk involves cash-flow instability, funding dependency, and valuation pressures. Operational risk emerges from weak internal processes, supply-chain disruptions, and execution inefficiencies. Legal and regulatory risks encompass intellectual property disputes, licensing delays, and compliance failures.

Empirical studies consistently identify a set of recurring causes behind startup failure. The most prominent is the absence of a genuine problem–solution fit, where ventures develop products for which there is insufficient or misjudged demand. Weak or unsustainable business models, poor financial management, and premature scaling frequently exacerbate resource depletion. Founder conflicts, governance deficiencies, and lack of complementary skills undermine organizational cohesion. In technology-based ventures, inadequate regulatory planning and overestimation of technological readiness often prove decisive.

By systematically analyzing these barriers and failure mechanisms, entrepreneurs can design ventures that are more adaptive, evidence-driven, and risk-aware. Structured experimentation, milestone-based financing, mentorship engagement, and ecosystem integration significantly enhance survival probabilities. In this sense, the disciplined management of uncertainty becomes a defining competence of successful entrepreneurship.

## 1.10 FUTURE TRENDS IN GLOBAL ENTREPRENEURSHIP

The landscape of entrepreneurship is undergoing rapid transformation, shaped by technological convergence, global connectivity, and the growing urgency of sustainable development. Future entrepreneurial activity will be less constrained by geography and more influenced by the ability to integrate interdisciplinary knowledge, digital infrastructures, and ethical responsibility into scalable venture models. As economies transition toward knowledge- and innovation-driven paradigms, entrepreneurship will increasingly function at the intersection of science, society, and global markets.

One of the most significant trends is the rise of artificial intelligence–enabled and data-centric startups. AI-driven analytics, automation, and decision-support systems are redefining healthcare, finance, manufacturing, and education. In parallel, biotechnology, synthetic biology, and precision medicine are generating new venture opportunities focused on personalized healthcare, regenerative solutions, and bio-industrial applications. Climate technology and sustainability-oriented entrepreneurship are also expanding rapidly, addressing renewable energy, carbon management, circular economy systems, and resource-efficient production.

Digital platforms and creator economies continue to lower entry barriers, enabling individuals and small teams to access global markets. Decentralized and blockchain-based ventures are introducing alternative organizational and financial architectures, influencing areas such as supply-chain management, digital identity, and intellectual property governance. These developments are complemented by the increasing prominence of hybrid enterprises that blend commercial objectives with social and environmental missions.

Institutionally, the future of entrepreneurship will be characterized by stronger university–industry–government integration, where innovation ecosystems operate as coordinated networks rather than isolated entities. Entrepreneurial education will emphasize experiential learning, interdisciplinary fluency, and ethical leadership. In this evolving environment, successful entrepreneurs will be those who can navigate complexity, leverage emerging technologies responsibly, and align innovation with long-term societal value.

## KEY CONCEPTS & DEFINITIONS

**Business Model:** A structured representation of how a startup creates value for customers, delivers that value through appropriate mechanisms, and captures revenue in a sustainable manner.
**Startup Business Model:** A set of testable assumptions that define how a new venture intends to operate, grow, and achieve scalability under conditions of uncertainty.
**Business Model Innovation:** The process of modifying or redesigning one or more elements of a business model—such as value proposition, revenue logic, or delivery mechanisms—to achieve competitive advantage.
**Business Model Canvas (BMC):** A strategic visual framework consisting of nine building blocks that collectively describe the logic of value creation, delivery, and capture within an organization.
**Customer Segments:** Clearly defined groups of customers or users that a startup aims to serve.
**Value Proposition:** The bundle of products or services that solve customer problems or satisfy specific needs, creating value for the target segment.
**Channels:** The communication, distribution, and sales pathways through which a startup reaches and delivers value to its customers.
**Customer Relationships:** The types of interactions a startup establishes with its customer segments to acquire, retain, and grow customers.
**Revenue Streams:** The various ways through which a startup generates income from its customers.
**Cost Structure:** The major costs incurred in operating a business model, including fixed and variable expenses.
**Key Resources:** The essential assets—human, intellectual, physical, or financial—required to deliver the value proposition.
**Key Activities:** The most important actions a startup must perform to operate successfully and deliver value.
**Key Partnerships:** External organizations or individuals that help optimize the business model, reduce risk, or access critical resources.
**Lean Canvas:** A startup-focused adaptation of the Business Model Canvas that emphasizes problem–solution fit, rapid experimentation, and validated learning.
**Problem–Solution Fit:** The degree to which a proposed solution effectively addresses a clearly defined and validated customer problem.

**Unique Value Proposition (UVP):** A clear statement explaining why a startup's offering is distinct and worth choosing over alternatives.
**Key Metrics:** Quantitative indicators used to track performance, learning, and traction in a startup.
**Unfair Advantage:** A defensible capability or asset that is difficult for competitors to replicate, such as proprietary knowledge, data, or expertise.
**Minimum Viable Product (MVP):** The simplest version of a product or service developed to test core assumptions and gather customer feedback with minimal resources.
**Validated Learning:** Evidence-based insights gained from systematic experimentation that guide decisions to pivot or persevere.
**Pivot:** A strategic change in one or more components of a business model based on learning from market feedback.
**Unit Economics:** Financial metrics that evaluate profitability at the level of a single customer or transaction, commonly using measures such as customer acquisition cost and lifetime value.
**Scalability:** The ability of a business model to increase revenue at a faster rate than costs as the venture grows.
**Sustainability:** The capacity of a business model to remain economically viable over the long term while responsibly managing social and environmental impacts.

---

**Mini Case Study 1: Zerodha – Building India's Largest Retail Stockbroking Startup**

Zerodha was founded in 2010 by Nithin and Nikhil Kamath with the objective of solving a clear market inefficiency in the Indian stockbroking industry: high brokerage costs, poor technology platforms, and limited transparency. Traditional brokers relied heavily on commission-based advisory models and outdated trading systems, which discouraged young and small investors from entering the market.

The founders adopted a technology-first and customer-centric approach. Zerodha introduced a flat-fee, discount brokerage model supported by an advanced online trading platform. By investing heavily in in-house technology development, the company created fast, reliable, and intuitive tools for retail traders. This innovation-driven model significantly reduced transaction costs while improving user experience.

Without external venture capital in its early years, Zerodha focused on sustainable growth, operational efficiency, and community-based learning initiatives such as Varsity and Rainmatter. Today, Zerodha is India's largest retail stockbroker by active clients.

---

**Mini Case Study 2: Biocon – From Enzymes to Global Biopharmaceutical Leadership**

Biocon was founded in 1978 by Kiran Mazumdar-Shaw as a small industrial enzymes company operating out of a garage in Bengaluru. At a time when biotechnology entrepreneurship was almost non-existent in India, Biocon faced major barriers including lack of investor confidence, regulatory ambiguity, and minimal technical infrastructure.

Recognizing the long-term potential of biotechnology, Biocon strategically transitioned from industrial enzymes to biopharmaceuticals, focusing on insulin, monoclonal antibodies, and biosimilars. The company invested heavily in R&D capabilities, regulatory compliance, and international quality standards. Partnerships with global pharmaceutical firms enabled technology access, market expansion, and credibility building.

Over time, Biocon evolved into a globally recognized biopharmaceutical enterprise, delivering affordable biologics to international markets and contributing significantly to healthcare accessibility.

**Mini Case Study 3: Paytm – Opportunity Recognition in the Digital Economy**

Paytm was founded in 2010 by Vijay Shekhar Sharma to address a clear opportunity arising from low credit card penetration and limited access to digital payments in India. Initially launched as a mobile recharge platform, Paytm progressively expanded into digital wallets, payments banking, and financial services.

A major inflection point occurred during India's 2016 demonetization initiative, which accelerated adoption of cashless transactions. Paytm leveraged this external policy shock by rapidly scaling its platform, onboarding merchants, and enhancing user trust. The company exemplifies how **environmental change, policy shifts, and technology convergence** can create entrepreneurial opportunities.

---

## REVIEW QUESTIONS AND EXERCISES

## REVIEW QUESTIONS

### A. Short Answer Questions

1. What is a business model, and why is it critical for startups operating under uncertainty?
2. Explain the difference between a business model and a business plan.
3. Define business model innovation with an example.
4. List the nine building blocks of the Business Model Canvas.
5. What is the primary purpose of the Lean Canvas framework?
6. Explain the concept of problem–solution fit.
7. What is meant by unit economics in the context of startups?
8. Define Customer Acquisition Cost (CAC) and Customer Lifetime Value (LTV).

**B. Descriptive Questions**

9. Explain the role of customer segments and value propositions in shaping a startup business model.
10. Describe the nine building blocks of the Business Model Canvas and their interrelationships.
11. Discuss how the Lean Canvas differs from the Business Model Canvas in terms of focus and application.
12. Explain various revenue models commonly adopted by startups.
13. Discuss the importance of key activities, key resources, and key partnerships in executing a business model.
14. Describe the process of testing and iterating business models using validated learning.

**C. Analytical / Essay-Type Questions**

15. Critically analyze the role of business model innovation in achieving competitive advantage.
16. Compare and contrast the Business Model Canvas and Lean Canvas as tools for startup development.
17. Discuss the significance of platform, subscription, and freemium business models in digital startups.
18. Explain how unit economics influence decisions related to startup scalability and sustainability.
19. Evaluate the importance of experimentation and iteration in reducing startup failure.
20. Explain the process of translating a validated business model canvas into a formal business plan.

**EXERCISES**

**Exercise 1: Business Model Canvas Development:** Identify a startup idea of your choice and develop a complete **Business Model Canvas**. Clearly explain each of the nine building blocks and justify your choices.

**Exercise 2: Lean Canvas Application:** Using the same startup idea, construct a **Lean Canvas** highlighting the problem, solution, unique value proposition, key metrics, and unfair advantage. Compare the insights gained from both canvases.

**Exercise 3: Revenue Model Analysis:** Select a startup operating in the digital or technology sector. Identify its revenue model and cost structure. Analyze whether the model supports long-term scalability.

**Exercise 4: Unit Economics Calculation:** Assume the following data for a startup:

- Customer Acquisition Cost (CAC): ₹1,200
- Average Monthly Revenue per Customer: ₹400
- Average Customer Lifetime: 10 months

Calculate the Customer Lifetime Value (LTV) and evaluate the sustainability of the business model.

**Exercise 5: Pivot or Persevere Decision:** A startup observes strong customer interest but low revenue conversion. Using the business model testing and iteration framework, recommend whether the startup should pivot or persevere, providing justification.

**Exercise 6: Mini Case Analysis:** Choose one mini case study discussed in the chapter (Airbnb, Netflix, or Dropbox).

- Identify the core business model type
- Map the business model using either BMC or Lean Canvas
- Discuss the key factors contributing to its success

# CHAPTER-2

# LEAN STARTUP & MINIMUM VIABLE PRODUCT (MVP)

**Abstract**: This chapter introduces the lean startup methodology as a systematic, experimentation-driven approach to venture creation in uncertain environments. It explains the core principles of lean entrepreneurship, emphasizing validated learning, customer discovery, and hypothesis-driven decision-making. The chapter explores the central role of problem–solution fit and the Build–Measure–Learn feedback loop in reducing risk and accelerating innovation. It further integrates design thinking to highlight the importance of human-centered problem framing and rapid prototyping. A detailed discussion of the concept and types of Minimum Viable Products (MVPs) is presented, along with sector-specific MVP development strategies across technology, product, and service-based ventures. The chapter also examines prototyping tools, rapid validation techniques, and traction metrics essential for evidence-based entrepreneurship. It concludes by analyzing strategic decision pathways—pivoting, persevering, or exiting—demonstrating how lean methodology transforms uncertainty into structured learning and guides startups toward scalable and sustainable business models.

**Keywords:** Lean Startup; Minimum Viable Product (MVP); Validated Learning; Customer Discovery; Innovation Experimentation; Startup Metrics

## 2.1 PRINCIPLES OF LEAN STARTUP METHODOLOGY

The Lean Startup methodology emerged in response to the high failure rates of new ventures and the limitations of traditional business planning in uncertain environments. Popularized by **Eric Ries**, the lean startup approach reframes entrepreneurship as a process of systematic experimentation rather than linear execution. It draws upon principles from lean manufacturing, customer development, and agile product design to minimize waste, accelerate learning, and improve the probability of building ventures that customers genuinely need.

At its core, lean startup methodology emphasizes validated learning—the process of empirically testing assumptions about customers, markets, and technologies. Instead of investing extensive time and capital in fully developed products, entrepreneurs are encouraged to test ideas early, cheaply, and iteratively. This approach treats every startup as a temporary organization whose primary objective is not immediate growth, but the discovery of a scalable and repeatable business model.

Key principles include rapid experimentation, customer-centric development, continuous iteration, and evidence-based decision-making. Lean startups prioritize learning over planning, insight over intuition, and data over assumptions. By embedding experimentation into the entrepreneurial process, the methodology reduces uncertainty and aligns innovation more closely with real-world needs.

## 2.2 CUSTOMER DISCOVERY AND PROBLEM–SOLUTION FIT

Customer discovery represents the first operational stage of the lean startup process. Its purpose is to deeply understand potential users, their problems, behaviors, constraints, and motivations. Rather than starting with solutions, lean entrepreneurship begins with structured inquiry into whether a meaningful problem exists and for whom.

Through interviews, field observations, surveys, and immersion studies, entrepreneurs test whether the problem they seek to address is real, significant, and frequent enough to justify venture creation. This stage emphasizes empathy and listening over pitching. Insights generated during customer discovery often challenge founder assumptions and lead to reformulation of both problem statements and target segments (Fig 2.1).

Problem–solution fit is achieved when a proposed solution demonstrably addresses a clearly defined and validated customer problem. At this point, early adopters recognize value, express willingness to engage, and participate in pilot testing. Without problem–solution fit, further investment in product development, branding, or scaling remains premature. Establishing this fit ensures that innovation is anchored in demand rather than in technological novelty alone.

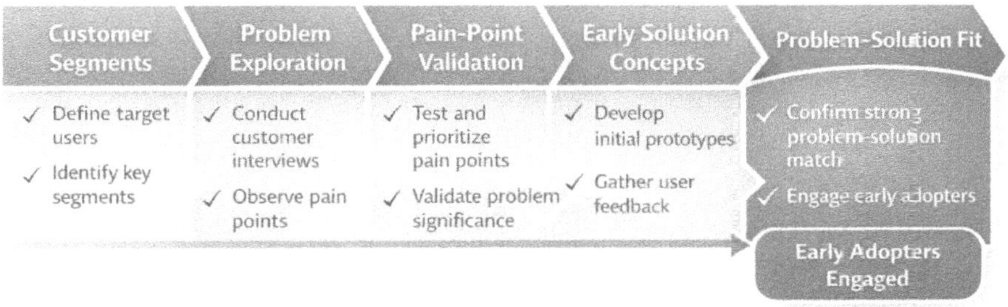


**Figure 2.1: Customer Discovery and Problem–Solution Fit Framework.** Stage-wise framework depicting the progression from customer segmentation and problem exploration to pain-point validation, early solution development, and confirmation of problem–solution fit with early adopters.

## 2.3 HYPOTHESIS-DRIVEN ENTREPRENEURSHIP

Lean startups conceptualize entrepreneurship as a hypothesis-testing process. Every startup idea embodies a set of assumptions regarding customer needs, value propositions, channels, revenue mechanisms, and operational feasibility. These assumptions, if untested, represent risk rather than strategy.

Hypothesis-driven entrepreneurship requires founders to explicitly articulate their beliefs in testable form. Typical hypotheses include statements such as: a specific customer segment experiences a defined problem; a proposed solution alleviates that problem; customers are willing to pay; and the solution can be delivered sustainably. These hypotheses are then prioritized based on risk and uncertainty.

Experiments are designed to test the most critical assumptions first. Interviews validate problem existence, prototypes test usability, landing pages assess demand, and pilot deployments evaluate behavioral response. Learning generated from these experiments informs iteration, refinement, or strategic redirection. In this framework, failure is not operational collapse, but informative feedback that improves venture design.

## 2.4 BUILD–MEASURE–LEARN FEEDBACK LOOP

The Build–Measure–Learn loop constitutes the operational engine of the lean startup methodology. It represents a continuous cycle through which ideas are transformed into testable artifacts, evaluated through real-world interaction, and refined based on evidence.

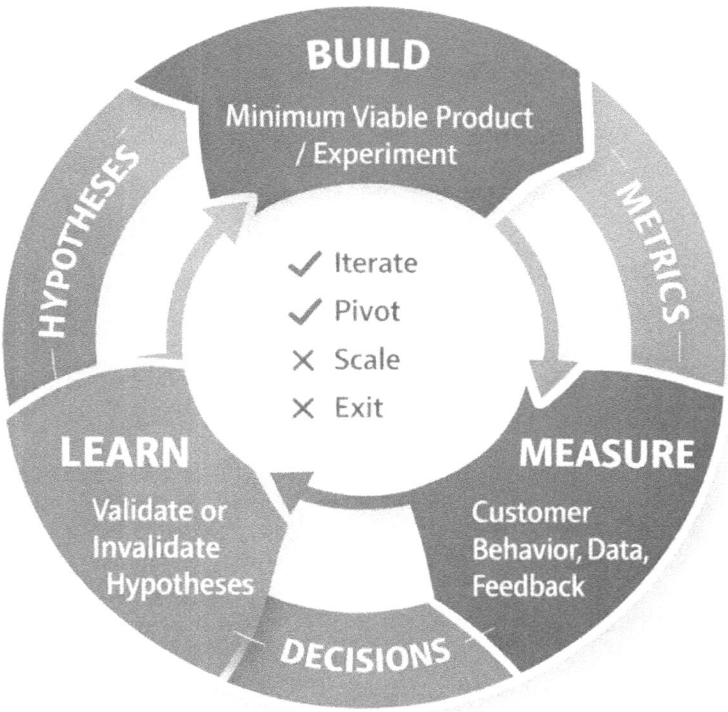


**Figure 2.2: Lean Startup Build–Measure–Learn Cycle.** Core feedback loop of lean entrepreneurship illustrating how startups iteratively build experimental solutions, measure customer responses, and learn through validated evidence to guide decisions such as iteration, pivoting, scaling, or exit.

The build phase involves developing a minimum set of features or representations necessary to test a hypothesis. This may include prototypes, mock-ups, service simulations, or digital products. The objective is not product perfection, but learning optimization.

The measure phase focuses on collecting actionable data. Metrics are designed to capture user behavior, engagement, conversion, retention, or satisfaction. Importantly, lean measurement prioritizes learning metrics over vanity metrics. Downloads, page views, or media attention are secondary to indicators that reveal whether value is being created.

The learn phase integrates results into decision-making. Entrepreneurs assess whether hypotheses are supported or invalidated. Supported hypotheses are refined and expanded; invalidated ones trigger redesign or strategic shifts. This iterative loop enables startups to evolve rapidly while conserving resources and aligning development with validated insights (Fig 2.2).

## 2.5 DESIGN THINKING INTEGRATION IN LEAN STARTUPS

Design thinking complements lean startup methodology by strengthening the human-centered dimension of venture creation. While lean startup emphasizes experimentation and validation, design thinking contributes tools for empathy, creativity, and reframing (Fig 2.3).

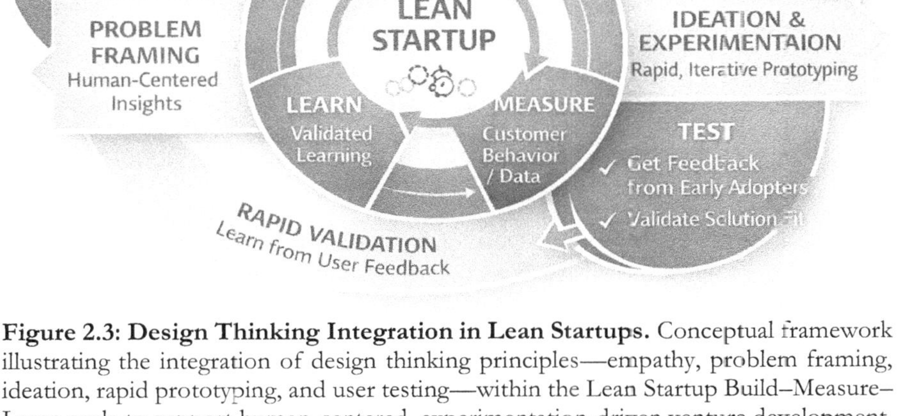


**Figure 2.3: Design Thinking Integration in Lean Startups.** Conceptual framework illustrating the integration of design thinking principles—empathy, problem framing, ideation, rapid prototyping, and user testing—within the Lean Startup Build–Measure–Learn cycle to support human-centered, experimentation-driven venture development.

Design thinking begins with deep user understanding. Through observation, immersion, and narrative mapping, entrepreneurs capture emotional, functional, and contextual dimensions of user experience. This insight supports problem reframing, often revealing latent needs not evident through surveys alone.

The ideation phase generates a wide range of solution concepts before narrowing through prototyping and testing. Rapid prototyping enables early visualization and interaction, reducing ambiguity and accelerating feedback. When integrated with lean principles, design thinking ensures that experimentation remains grounded in user meaning, usability, and desirability. Together, lean startup and design thinking form a powerful innovation system—one that balances analytical validation with creative exploration, enabling startups to build solutions that are not only viable and feasible, but also desirable.

## 2.6 CONCEPT AND TYPES OF MVP

The Minimum Viable Product (MVP) is a central construct in lean entrepreneurship. It refers to the simplest version of a product, service, or system that allows entrepreneurs to test critical hypotheses and gather validated learning with minimal investment (Fig 2.4).

An MVP is not a reduced-quality product; rather, it is a strategically scoped experiment. Its purpose is to test assumptions regarding problem relevance, solution effectiveness, user behavior, and value perception.

| | Digital Ventures | Product Ventures | Service Ventures | Deep-Ventures | Deep-Tech Ventures |
|---|---|---|---|---|---|
| Concierge MVP | | ✓ | | ✓ | ✓ |
| Wizard-of-Oz MVP | ✓ | | ✓ | | ✓ |
| Landing Page MVP | | ✓ | | | ✓ |
| Prototype MVP | ✓ | ✓ | ✓ | | |
| Piecemeal MVP | | | ✓ | | |
| Proof-of-Concept MVP | | | | | ✓ |

Classification of MVP types and their application across different startup models.

**Figure 2.4: MVP Typology and Development Pathways.** Classification of major MVP types—including concierge, Wizard-of-Oz, landing page, prototype, piecemeal, and proof-of-concept MVPs—and their applicability across digital, product, service, and deep-technology startup models.

MVPs may take multiple forms. Concierge MVPs deliver services manually to test demand before automation. Wizard-of-Oz MVPs simulate full functionality while operations remain internal. Prototype MVPs demonstrate form and usability without full engineering. Landing page MVPs test interest and conversion. Piecemeal MVPs integrate existing tools to replicate functionality. In scientific and engineering domains, proof-of-concept MVPs validate technical feasibility prior to commercialization.

The appropriate MVP form depends on sector, risk profile, regulatory context, and development cost. What remains constant is the objective: maximize learning while minimizing waste.

## 2.7 MVP DEVELOPMENT STRATEGIES (TECH, PRODUCT, AND SERVICE MODELS)

MVP development strategies vary significantly across technological, product-based, and service-oriented startups. In digital technology ventures, MVPs often take the form of functional software prototypes, alpha versions, or limited-feature applications deployed to controlled user groups. Agile development methods enable rapid iteration, modular releases, and real-time analytics integration.

In product-based startups, especially hardware, medical device, and biotechnology ventures, MVPs frequently focus on proof-of-concept, laboratory prototypes, and functional demonstrators. These MVPs prioritize technical validation, usability testing, and regulatory alignment over immediate market scale. Rapid fabrication, modular design, and simulation tools accelerate development cycles.

Service-based startups employ experiential MVPs. Pilot programs, manual service delivery, or limited geographic rollouts allow entrepreneurs to test workflows, pricing, customer interaction models, and operational feasibility. These MVPs generate insight into customer satisfaction, cost structures, and scalability challenges.

Across all models, MVP strategy requires careful alignment between learning objectives, resource constraints, and risk exposure. An effective MVP answers the most critical questions before capital-intensive commitments are made.

## 2.8 PROTOTYPING TOOLS AND RAPID VALIDATION TECHNIQUES

Prototyping tools and rapid validation techniques operationalize lean experimentation. Digital prototyping platforms enable interface simulation, user flow modeling, and usability testing without full-scale development. No-code and low-code environments support rapid deployment and iteration. In physical product domains, 3D printing, microfabrication, and rapid tooling facilitate fast prototyping.

Validation techniques extend beyond prototypes. A/B testing compares alternative features or messages. Smoke tests assess demand through pre-orders

or sign-up pages. Pilot studies enable real-world evaluation. Crowdfunding platforms function as both funding mechanisms and validation environments. In research-intensive startups, laboratory assays, preclinical models, and technical benchmarking provide early evidence of feasibility.
Together, these tools shorten feedback cycles, reduce uncertainty, and support evidence-based venture design.

## 2.9 MEASURING TRACTION AND KEY VALIDATION METRICS

Measurement in lean startups focuses on learning and traction rather than vanity indicators. Traction reflects meaningful customer engagement and behavioral validation. It demonstrates that a startup is moving from assumption to evidence.

Key validation metrics vary by venture type but often include customer acquisition rates, activation and engagement levels, retention and churn, conversion to paid usage, unit economics, and customer lifetime value. In platform and digital ventures, cohort analysis reveals behavioral patterns over time. In product and healthcare startups, pilot adoption, clinical endpoints, and regulatory milestones function as critical validation indicators.

Actionable metrics inform decisions. They connect experiments to strategic outcomes and guide resource allocation. Effective measurement frameworks integrate quantitative analytics with qualitative insight, ensuring that growth is driven by validated value creation.

## 2.10 PIVOTING, PERSEVERING, OR EXITING DECISIONS

The ultimate purpose of lean experimentation is informed strategic decision-making. Based on accumulated learning, startups must periodically determine whether to pivot, persevere, or exit (Fig 2.5).

**Pivoting** involves a structured change in one or more fundamental elements of the business model—customer segment, value proposition, revenue mechanism, technology, or channel—while retaining validated components.

**Perseverance** reflects continued execution along a validated trajectory, supported by evidence of traction and alignment. Exit decisions occur when experiments consistently invalidate core assumptions or when external constraints render the venture nonviable.

These decisions are not intuitive judgments but learning-driven conclusions. They require disciplined analysis, founder alignment, and ecosystem consultation. Effective entrepreneurs view pivots not as failures, but as evolutionary adaptations.
Through systematic experimentation, lean startups transform uncertainty into

knowledge. In doing so, they replace speculative entrepreneurship with evidence-based venture creation, significantly improving the probability of building scalable, impactful, and sustainable enterprises.

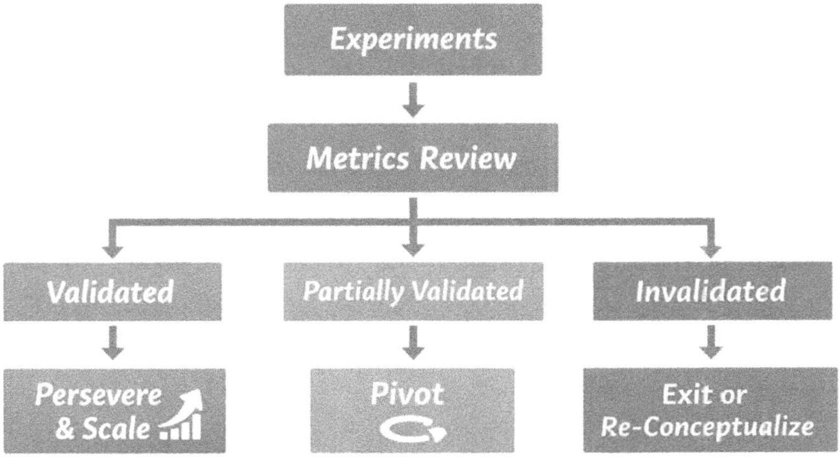


**Figure 2.5 Pivot–Persevere–Exit Decision Framework.** Lean decision model illustrating how validated learning and traction metrics guide strategic choices between pivoting the business model, persevering with the current strategy, or exiting the venture.

---

## KEY CONCEPTS & DEFINITIONS

**Lean Startup:** A methodology for developing startups through rapid experimentation, iterative product releases, and validated learning, with the objective of discovering a scalable and repeatable business model under conditions of uncertainty.

**Validated Learning:** A systematic process of testing entrepreneurial assumptions through real-world experiments to generate evidence-based insights about customers, markets, and technologies.

**Customer Discovery:** An early-stage process of engaging with potential users and stakeholders to understand their problems, needs, behaviors, and contexts before building full solutions.

**Problem–Solution Fit:** The stage at which a startup demonstrates that a proposed solution meaningfully addresses a clearly defined and validated customer problem.

**Hypothesis-Driven Entrepreneurship:** An approach that treats business ideas as testable hypotheses about customers, value propositions, and business models, which must be empirically examined through structured experiments.

**Build–Measure–Learn Loop:** The core feedback cycle of lean startups in which entrepreneurs build experimental solutions, measure user responses, and learn whether to refine, pivot, or scale.

**Minimum Viable Product (MVP):** The simplest version of a product, service, or system designed to test critical assumptions and generate validated learning with minimal time, effort, and resources.

**Pivot:** A strategic shift in one or more fundamental elements of a startup's business model—such as customer segment, value proposition, or technology—based on validated learning.

**Traction:** Demonstrable evidence of meaningful customer engagement or adoption that indicates a startup is creating real value and progressing toward product–market fit.

**Rapid Prototyping:** The use of fast, low-cost methods and tools to create early versions of products or services for testing, feedback, and iterative refinement.

---

**Mini Case Study 1: Dropbox – Validating Demand Before Building the Product**

Dropbox was founded in 2007 by Drew Houston to solve a personal frustration: unreliable file synchronization across devices. Rather than immediately developing a full product, the founding team adopted a lean validation approach to test whether the problem was widespread and whether users would trust a cloud-based solution.

Instead of releasing a complex MVP, Dropbox created a simple three-minute explainer video demonstrating how the product would work. The video was shared on a technology forum frequented by early adopters. Within a short period, sign-ups increased from 5,000 to over 75,000, providing strong evidence of unmet demand.

Only after validating interest did the team invest heavily in engineering development. Early beta versions were released to a limited audience, and feedback was continuously integrated using the Build–Measure–Learn loop. Dropbox later implemented referral-based experiments to optimize growth.

---

**Mini Case Study 2: Zomato – Iterative MVP Evolution from a Simple Problem**

Zomato was founded in 2008 by Deepinder Goyal and Pankaj Chaddah as a modest internal project to digitize restaurant menus for office colleagues. The initial MVP was a simple website that hosted scanned menus, addressing a specific and immediate user problem: lack of accessible dining information.

Early traction revealed strong demand, prompting continuous iteration. Customer feedback highlighted the need for searchable listings, reviews, location-based discovery, and mobile access. Zomato incrementally built these features, transforming the platform into a comprehensive food discovery and delivery ecosystem.

The company tested expansions city by city, refined monetization models through experiments with restaurant partnerships and advertising, and pivoted its offerings based on user behavior. Each major strategic shift was supported by real usage data and controlled pilots.

---

**Mini Case Study 3: Netflix – Subscription-Based Business Model Evolution**

Netflix illustrates the strategic evolution of a **subscription-based business model**. Originally operating as a DVD-by-mail service, the company transitioned to digital streaming in response to technological change and shifting consumer preferences. Its core value proposition centers on on-demand access to diverse content supported by personalized recommendations. Revenue is generated through recurring subscription fees, emphasizing customer retention and lifetime value. While content acquisition and production represent significant costs, scale and global subscriber growth enable financial sustainability.

---

## REVIEW QUESTIONS AND EXERCISES

## REVIEW QUESTIONS

### A. Short Answer Questions

1. What is meant by the Lean Startup methodology?
2. Define validated learning and explain its importance in startup development.
3. What is customer discovery, and why does it precede product development?
4. Explain the concept of problem–solution fit.
5. What is hypothesis-driven entrepreneurship?
6. Describe the Build–Measure–Learn feedback loop.
7. Define a Minimum Viable Product (MVP).
8. What is the difference between an MVP and a fully developed product?
9. What are actionable metrics, and how do they differ from vanity metrics?
10. Define pivot in the context of lean startups.

### B. Descriptive Questions

11. Explain the key principles of the Lean Startup methodology.
12. Discuss the role of customer discovery in reducing startup risk.
13. Describe the stages involved in achieving problem–solution fit.
14. Explain how hypotheses are formulated and tested in lean entrepreneurship.
15. Describe the Build–Measure–Learn cycle with suitable examples.
16. Discuss how design thinking complements the Lean Startup approach.
17. Explain different types of MVPs and their applications across sectors.

18. Describe MVP development strategies for technology-based, product-based, and service-based startups.
19. Discuss the importance of measuring traction in lean startups.

**C. Analytical / Essay-Type Questions**

20. Critically analyze how the Lean Startup methodology differs from traditional business planning.
21. Evaluate the role of MVPs in accelerating innovation while minimizing waste.
22. Discuss the integration of design thinking and lean startup principles in human-centered innovation.
23. Analyze the significance of hypothesis testing in evidence-based entrepreneurship.
24. Explain how validated learning guides decisions to pivot, persevere, or exit.
25. Assess the role of experimentation and metrics in transforming uncertainty into structured learning.

**EXERCISES**

**Exercise 1: Problem–Solution Fit Analysis:** Identify a real-world problem faced by a specific customer segment. Conduct a brief customer discovery exercise and describe how you would validate problem–solution fit.

**Exercise 2: Hypothesis Formulation:** For a startup idea of your choice, list at least five key hypotheses related to:

- Customer segment
- Problem relevance
- Solution effectiveness
- Willingness to pay
- Delivery feasibility

Indicate how each hypothesis can be tested.

**Exercise 3: MVP Design:** Design an appropriate MVP for:
a) A digital application
b) A physical product
c) A service-based venture
Justify the choice of MVP type for each case.

**Exercise 4: Build–Measure–Learn Application:** Using a hypothetical startup, outline one complete Build–Measure–Learn cycle, clearly specifying:

- What will be built
- What metrics will be measured
- What learning is expected

**Exercise 5: Metrics and Traction:** Identify five actionable metrics suitable for:

- A mobile application startup
- A service-based startup

Explain how each metric contributes to validated learning.

**Exercise 6: Pivot–Persevere–Exit Decision Scenario:** A startup observes high user engagement but low retention after three months. Using the Pivot–Persevere–Exit framework, recommend a strategic decision and justify it using lean principles.

**Exercise 7: Case-Based Exercise:** Based on the Dropbox or Zomato mini case studies presented in the chapter:

- Identify the initial MVP
- Describe how validated learning influenced product evolution
- Explain how experimentation reduced risk

# CHAPTER-3

# MARKET ANALYSIS & SEGMENTATION

**Abstract**: Market analysis and segmentation are critical foundations for developing sustainable and scalable business models in entrepreneurial and innovation-driven ventures. This chapter presents a structured and evidence-based approach to understanding markets by systematically assessing opportunities, customers, and competitive environments before product commercialization. It begins with market opportunity assessment, emphasizing problem significance, customer willingness to pay, and market readiness. The chapter then explores customer profiling and buyer persona development to translate heterogeneous customer needs into actionable insights for product and marketing strategy. Primary and secondary market research methods are discussed as complementary tools for generating reliable market intelligence. The chapter further explains market size estimation using Total Addressable Market (TAM), Serviceable Available Market (SAM), and Serviceable Obtainable Market (SOM) frameworks to quantify commercial potential and support strategic decision-making. Segmentation, Targeting, and Positioning (STP) are presented as essential mechanisms for focusing resources and achieving differentiation. Competitive and industry analyses highlight the importance of understanding rivalry, substitutes, and entry barriers. The chapter also introduces value proposition design and customer journey mapping to align offerings with customer expectations across touchpoints. Finally, methods for validating market demand and common errors in market assessment are discussed, reinforcing the need for data-driven decisions. Collectively, this chapter equips learners and practitioners with practical tools to reduce uncertainty, improve product–market fit, and enhance venture success.

**Keywords:** Market Analysis; Customer Segmentation; Buyer Personas; Market Sizing (TAM–SAM–SOM); Value Proposition; Market Validation

## 3.1 MARKET ANALYSIS & SEGMENTATION

Market analysis and segmentation form the analytical foundation of effective business planning and strategic decision-making. Market analysis involves the systematic examination of external market conditions to understand demand dynamics, customer needs, industry structure, and competitive forces. It enables entrepreneurs and managers to assess whether a proposed product or service addresses a real market problem and whether the opportunity is commercially viable. Without rigorous market analysis, ventures risk building solutions that lack relevance, scalability, or economic sustainability.

Segmentation complements market analysis by recognizing that markets are inherently heterogeneous. Customers differ in their needs, purchasing power, usage behavior, and decision-making criteria. Market segmentation therefore divides a broad market into distinct, identifiable groups that share similar characteristics or needs. These segments may be based on demographic, geographic, psychographic, behavioral, or firmographic variables, depending on whether the context is consumer or business-to-business oriented. Effective segmentation allows firms to prioritize attractive customer groups rather than attempting to serve the entire market with a uniform offering.

Together, market analysis and segmentation enable more precise targeting, resource allocation, and value creation. They support informed decisions related to product design, pricing, distribution channels, and promotional strategies. In innovation-driven and technology-intensive sectors, such as biotechnology and digital startups, these processes are particularly important due to high development costs and uncertain adoption patterns. By grounding strategic choices in empirical market insights, market analysis and segmentation reduce uncertainty, enhance customer alignment, and significantly increase the likelihood of achieving a strong product–market fit (Fig 3.1).

## 3.2 MARKET OPPORTUNITY ASSESSMENT

Market opportunity assessment is a critical step in determining whether an identified problem represents a viable and sustainable business opportunity. It goes beyond recognizing unmet needs and systematically evaluates the economic, strategic, and contextual feasibility of addressing those needs through a market offering. A strong market opportunity exists when a significant problem affects a clearly identifiable customer group that is both willing and able to pay for an effective solution.

The assessment process begins with evaluating the **magnitude and relevance of the problem**, including its frequency, intensity, and consequences for the target customer. Problems that are persistent, costly, or mission-critical are more likely to generate demand. This is followed by an analysis of **existing solutions**, identifying gaps in performance, accessibility, cost, or user experience that create room for innovation. Understanding why current alternatives fail to fully satisfy customers provides direction for differentiation. Market opportunity assessment also considers **market trends and external drivers**, such as technological advancements, regulatory changes, demographic shifts, and socio-economic factors that may accelerate or constrain adoption. Equally important is the evaluation of **customer readiness and timing**, as even well-designed solutions may fail if introduced prematurely or into an unreceptive market.

Finally, scalability and long-term growth potential must be examined. Opportunities that allow expansion across customer segments, geographies, or adjacent applications are more attractive than narrowly confined markets.

Through systematic opportunity assessment, entrepreneurs and organizations can prioritize high-potential ideas, avoid resource misallocation, and build ventures on a foundation of market reality rather than assumption.

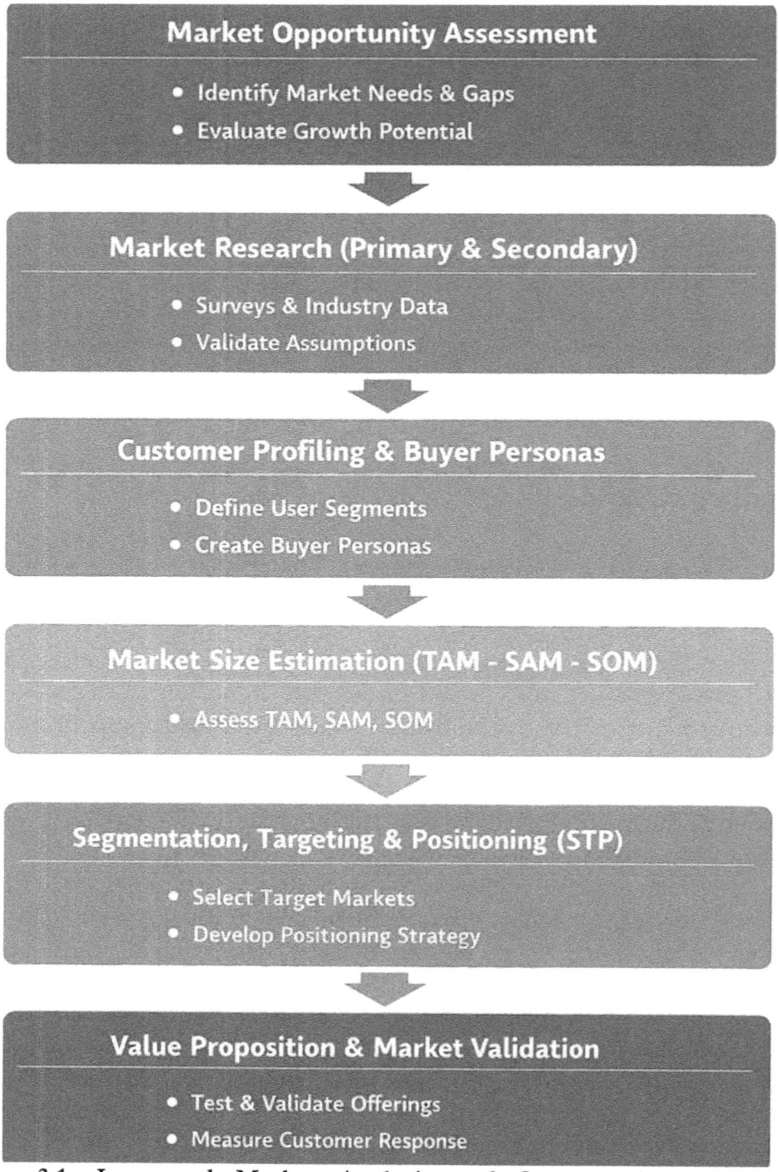


**Figure 3.1. Integrated Market Analysis and Segmentation Framework.** Illustrating the sequential and interrelated stages from market opportunity assessment and empirical market research to customer profiling, market size estimation (TAM–SAM–SOM), strategic segmentation–targeting–positioning (STP), and final value proposition development with market validation.

## 3.3 CUSTOMER PROFILING AND BUYER PERSONAS

Customer profiling and buyer persona development are essential for translating broad market insights into a deep understanding of actual users and decision-makers. Customer profiling focuses on identifying and categorizing customers based on observable characteristics, while buyer personas provide a richer, behavior-oriented representation of how customers think, decide, and act in purchasing situations.

Customer profiling typically includes demographic and geographic variables in consumer markets, and firmographic variables such as industry type, organization size, purchasing authority, and regulatory constraints in business-to-business contexts. Behavioral attributes, including usage patterns, adoption readiness, price sensitivity, and brand loyalty, further refine customer understanding. Psychographic factors—values, motivations, risk perception, and attitudes toward innovation—add depth to the profile and are particularly relevant for novel or high-involvement products.

Buyer personas build upon these profiles by synthesizing data into semi-fictional yet realistic archetypes. A well-constructed buyer persona captures the customer's goals, pain points, decision triggers, evaluation criteria, and perceived risks. It also reflects the customer's journey, including information sources, influencers, and barriers that may delay or prevent adoption. In complex purchasing environments, multiple personas may exist, such as users, technical evaluators, and final decision-makers.

By grounding product development, pricing, communication, and channel strategy in clearly defined customer profiles and personas, organizations can avoid generic offerings and misaligned messaging. This customer-centric approach enhances relevance, improves engagement, and increases the probability of achieving sustained market acceptance.

## 3.4 PRIMARY AND SECONDARY MARKET RESEARCH METHODS

Market research provides the empirical foundation for informed market analysis and reduces reliance on assumptions or intuition. It involves the systematic collection and interpretation of data to understand customer needs, preferences, behaviors, and market dynamics. Market research methods are broadly classified into primary and secondary research, each serving distinct but complementary purposes.

Primary market research involves the direct collection of original data from potential or existing customers. Common techniques include surveys, structured questionnaires, in-depth interviews, focus group discussions, observational studies, and pilot testing of prototypes or minimum viable products. Primary research is particularly valuable for exploring unmet needs, testing hypotheses, validating assumptions, and gaining contextual insights that are specific to the target market. However, it can be time-intensive and resource-demanding, requiring careful design to ensure reliability and validity. Secondary market research relies on data that has already been collected and published by external sources. These include government reports, industry and market analysis reports, academic publications, trade journals, company annual reports, and databases maintained by professional or regulatory bodies. Secondary research is cost-effective and useful for understanding macro-level trends, industry structure, regulatory environments, and benchmark metrics. Its main limitation lies in the lack of customization and potential issues with data timeliness.

An effective market analysis integrates both primary and secondary research. Secondary data helps frame the market context and identify key questions, while primary research provides targeted, up-to-date insights. Together, they enable evidence-based decision-making and strengthen the credibility of market assessments.

## 3.5 MARKET SIZE ESTIMATION (TAM, SAM, SOM)

Market size estimation quantifies the commercial potential of a business opportunity and plays a crucial role in strategic planning, investment decisions, and resource allocation. It provides a structured understanding of how large a market is, how much of it can realistically be served, and what share can be captured within a defined time frame. The most widely used framework for this purpose is the TAM–SAM–SOM model (Fig 3.2).

**Total Addressable Market (TAM)** represents the total demand for a product or service if a firm were to achieve 100 percent market share under ideal conditions. It reflects the maximum revenue opportunity and is useful for understanding the long-term potential of an industry. **Serviceable Available Market (SAM)** is the portion of the TAM that falls within the firm's target segments and operational scope, considering factors such as geography, regulatory constraints, and product capabilities. **Serviceable Obtainable Market (SOM)** refers to the realistically achievable market share in the short to medium term, given competitive intensity, capacity limitations, and go-to-market strategy.

Market size can be estimated using a **top-down approach**, which starts with broad industry data and narrows it to relevant segments, or a **bottom-up approach**, which aggregates revenues based on unit price and the number of target customers. The bottom-up method is generally more accurate and defensible.

Accurate market sizing prevents overestimation, supports credible business planning, and helps align growth expectations with market realities.

**Figure 3.2. Market Size Estimation Funnel.** Illustrating the progressive narrowing of market potential from the Total Addressable Market (TAM) to the Serviceable Available Market (SAM) and the Serviceable Obtainable Market (SOM), incorporating geographic scope, customer segmentation, and competitive constraints to estimate realistic market capture.

**Example: Market Size Estimation for a Face Wash**

**Product:** Face wash
**Geographic scope:** India
**Target segment:** Urban consumers using herbal/ayurvedic personal care products

**Step 1: Key Assumptions**

1. **Population of India:** ~1.43 billion
2. **Relevant age group (15–60 years):** ~60% → **858 million**
3. **Urban population share:** ~36% → **309 million**
4. **Face wash usage penetration (urban):** ~70% → **216 million users**
5. **Average consumption:** 3 face wash units/person/year
6. **Average price per unit:** ₹200

**Step 2: TAM (Total Addressable Market)**

TAM represents the **entire face wash market** in urban India.

$$\textbf{TAM} = 216 \text{ million users} \times 3 \times ₹200$$

$$\textbf{TAM} = ₹129,600 \text{ million} = \textbf{₹12,960 crore per year}$$

**Step 3: SAM (Serviceable Available Market)**

SAM is the portion of TAM relevant to **herbal/ayurvedic face wash users,** VLCC's core category. Assume: Herbal/ayurvedic share of face wash market = **30%**

$$\textbf{SAM} = 30\% \times ₹12,960 \text{ crore}$$

$$\textbf{SAM} = \textbf{₹3,888 crore per year}$$

**Step 4: SOM (Serviceable Obtainable Market)**

SOM is the **realistically achievable market share** for VLCC. Assume: **Company** market share in herbal face wash segment = **8%**

$$\textbf{SOM} = 8\% \times ₹3,888 \text{ crore}$$

$$\textbf{SOM} = \textbf{₹311 crore per year}$$

| Market Level | Description | Estimated Value |
|---|---|---|
| **TAM** | Total urban face wash market | ₹12,960 crore |
| **SAM** | Herbal/ayurvedic face wash market | ₹3,888 crore |
| **SOM** | VLCC's obtainable share | ₹311 crore |

## 3.6 SEGMENTATION, TARGETING, AND POSITIONING (STP)

Segmentation, Targeting, and Positioning (STP) is a strategic framework that enables organizations to focus their efforts on the most attractive and relevant customer groups (Fig 3.3). It recognizes that attempting to serve the entire market with a single offering often leads to diluted value and ineffective resource utilization.

**Figure 3.3. Segmentation–Targeting–Positioning (STP) Strategic Model.** This figure illustrates the strategic decision flow from market segmentation to target selection and finally to positioning. It demonstrates how markets are first divided based on customer needs and characteristics, followed by the evaluation and selection of attractive segments, and culminates in the development of a clear value proposition and differentiated position in the customer's mind.

**Market segmentation** involves dividing a heterogeneous market into smaller, homogeneous groups based on shared characteristics. Segmentation variables may include demographic and geographic factors in consumer markets, and firmographic, operational, or regulatory factors in business-to-business contexts. Behavioral and needs-based segmentation is particularly valuable, as it reflects actual usage patterns and customer expectations rather than surface-level attributes.

**Targeting** refers to the evaluation and selection of one or more market segments to serve. Target segments are chosen based on criteria such as segment size, growth potential, profitability, competitive intensity, and alignment with organizational capabilities. Effective targeting ensures that limited resources are directed toward segments where the firm can create and capture the most value.

**Positioning** defines how a product or service is perceived by the target customers relative to competing alternatives. It involves articulating a clear value proposition, identifying key differentiators, and consistently communicating these elements across all customer touchpoints. Strong positioning simplifies customer decision-making and strengthens brand identity. Together, STP enables strategic clarity, competitive differentiation, and improved market performance by aligning offerings with well-defined customer needs.

## 3.7 COMPETITIVE LANDSCAPE AND INDUSTRY ANALYSIS

Competitive landscape and industry analysis provide a comprehensive understanding of the external forces that influence a firm's ability to enter, compete, and sustain itself within a market. This analysis examines both direct competitors offering similar solutions and indirect competitors that address the same customer need through alternative means. Understanding the competitive environment helps organizations anticipate market responses and identify areas for differentiation.

A thorough competitive analysis evaluates competitors on parameters such as product or service features, pricing strategies, quality standards, distribution channels, customer segments served, and brand positioning. It also considers competitors' strengths, weaknesses, and strategic intent. Such insights enable firms to benchmark their offerings and identify unmet needs or underserved segments within the market.

Industry analysis focuses on the broader structural characteristics of the market. Key factors include entry barriers, such as capital requirements, regulatory approvals, intellectual property protection, and economies of scale. The degree of rivalry among existing players, the availability of substitute solutions, and the bargaining power of suppliers and customers also shape competitive dynamics. High competitive intensity or strong substitute threats may compress margins, while favorable industry structures can support sustainable profitability.

By systematically analyzing both competitors and industry conditions, organizations can assess risk, refine their strategic positioning, and develop defensible advantages. This analysis supports informed decision-making and enhances the likelihood of long-term market success.

## 3.8 VALUE PROPOSITION DESIGN

Value proposition design articulates the fundamental reason why customers should choose a particular product or service over available alternatives. It represents the alignment between customer needs and the benefits delivered by the offering. A well-defined value proposition clearly communicates how a solution creates value by solving a specific problem or fulfilling an important need more effectively than competitors.

The process of value proposition design begins with a deep understanding of the customer, including their functional challenges, emotional concerns, and desired outcomes. Customer pains refer to problems, risks, or inefficiencies experienced before, during, or after using existing solutions, while customer gains represent the benefits, improvements, or positive outcomes customers seek. An effective value proposition explicitly addresses these pains and gains through clearly articulated features and benefits.

A strong value proposition is characterized by clarity, relevance, and differentiation. It avoids vague or generic claims and instead focuses on specific outcomes that matter to the target segment, such as cost reduction, improved performance, convenience, reliability, or compliance. Importantly, the value proposition must be credible and deliverable, aligning with the organization's capabilities and resources.

Value proposition design plays a critical role in product development, marketing communication, and sales strategy. When consistently reflected across branding, messaging, and customer touchpoints, it strengthens market positioning, enhances customer trust, and increases the likelihood of adoption and long-term loyalty.

## 3.9 CUSTOMER JOURNEY MAPPING

Customer journey mapping is a strategic tool used to visualize and analyze the complete experience of a customer as they interact with a product, service, or organization over time. It captures the sequence of steps a customer takes, from initial awareness of a need to post-purchase engagement, highlighting how customers perceive and respond at each stage (Fig 3.4).

Typically, the customer journey is divided into key phases such as awareness, consideration, purchase, usage, and retention or advocacy. For each phase, journey mapping identifies customer actions, decision points, touchpoints, and channels of interaction. It also considers customer emotions, expectations, and potential pain points that may influence satisfaction or lead to disengagement. This holistic perspective enables organizations to understand not only what customers do, but why they behave in certain ways.

Customer journey mapping helps uncover gaps between intended service delivery and actual customer experience. It reveals friction points such as information overload, complex purchasing processes, delays, or inadequate support, which may hinder adoption or retention. By addressing these issues, organizations can improve customer satisfaction and strengthen long-term relationships.

In market analysis and segmentation, customer journey mapping complements customer profiling by contextualizing behavior across time and touchpoints. It supports more effective channel selection, messaging, and service design. Ultimately, well-designed customer journeys enhance value delivery, reduce churn, and contribute to sustainable competitive advantage.

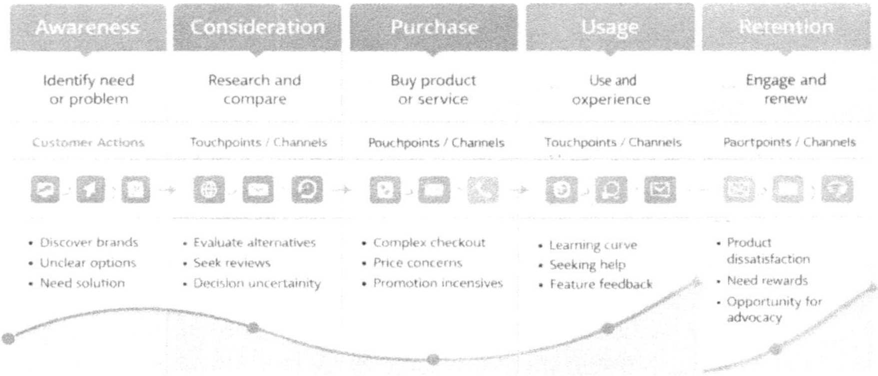


**Figure 3.4. Customer Journey Map Across Market Touchpoints.** This figure illustrates the end-to-end customer journey across key market stages—awareness, consideration, purchase, usage, and retention—mapping customer actions against major touchpoints, channels, pain points, and opportunity areas. It demonstrates how customer behavior evolves over time and how marketing and value delivery strategies can be aligned to optimize experience, engagement, and long-term retention.

## 3.10 VALIDATION OF MARKET DEMAND

Validation of market demand is the process of confirming that a sufficient number of customers are willing to pay for a proposed product or service under real market conditions. It serves as a critical checkpoint between market analysis and large-scale investment, ensuring that strategic decisions are based on evidence rather than assumptions or perceived interest.

Market demand validation involves testing key hypotheses related to customer needs, value proposition, pricing, and adoption behavior. Common validation methods include pilot launches, minimum viable product (MVP) testing, pre-orders, letters of intent, and controlled market experiments. These approaches generate observable customer actions—such as sign-ups, purchases, or repeat usage—that provide more reliable indicators of demand than stated preferences alone.

Quantitative metrics such as conversion rates, customer acquisition cost, retention levels, and willingness to pay are often used alongside qualitative feedback to assess demand strength. Negative or mixed results are equally valuable, as they highlight the need for refinement, repositioning, or strategic pivoting before scaling.

Validation is not a one-time activity but an iterative process that continues as markets evolve and offerings mature. By systematically validating demand at early and intermediate stages, organizations can minimize financial risk, improve product–market fit, and allocate resources more effectively. Strong market validation increases investor confidence and forms a robust foundation for sustainable growth.

## 3.11 COMMON ERRORS IN MARKET ASSESSMENT

Despite the availability of structured frameworks and analytical tools, market assessment is frequently compromised by conceptual and methodological errors. One of the most common mistakes is **equating customer interest with willingness to pay**. Expressions of curiosity or positive feedback do not necessarily translate into purchasing behavior, particularly when cost, switching barriers, or competing priorities are involved.

Another frequent error is **overestimating market size**, often by assuming that a product appeals to all users within a broad industry. This leads to inflated Total Addressable Market (TAM) estimates and unrealistic growth expectations. Closely related is the failure to clearly distinguish between users, influencers, and actual buyers, especially in business-to-business and regulated markets.

Reliance on **anecdotal evidence or limited samples** is another weakness. Decisions based on informal conversations or small, biased datasets can distort understanding of customer needs and market dynamics. Similarly, excessive dependence on outdated or generalized secondary data without validation through primary research reduces accuracy.

Organizations also err by **ignoring negative feedback** or selectively interpreting data to confirm pre-existing assumptions. This confirmation bias prevents timely pivots and increases the risk of market failure. Additionally, many ventures treat market analysis as a one-time activity, failing to reassess assumptions as technologies, regulations, or customer preferences evolve.

Avoiding these errors requires disciplined, evidence-based analysis, continuous learning, and a willingness to challenge assumptions. Rigorous market assessment strengthens strategic decisions and significantly improves the likelihood of long-term success.

---

## KEY CONCEPTS & DEFINITIONS

**Market Analysis**: A systematic process of examining market conditions, customer needs, industry structure, and competitive forces to determine the commercial feasibility of a product or service.
**Market Opportunity**: A favorable situation where a significant customer problem aligns with sufficient demand, purchasing power, and external conditions to support a viable business.
**Market Opportunity Assessment**: The evaluation of problem relevance, customer willingness to pay, market readiness, scalability, and growth potential before committing resources.
**Customer Profiling**: The classification of customers based on demographic, geographic, behavioral, psychographic, or firmographic characteristics to understand who the customers are.
**Buyer Persona**: A semi-fictional representation of an ideal customer based on

real data, capturing goals, motivations, pain points, and purchasing behavior.

**Primary Market Research**: The collection of original data directly from potential or existing customers through methods such as surveys, interviews, focus groups, and pilot studies.

**Secondary Market Research**: The use of existing data sources, including industry reports, government publications, academic literature, and market databases, to understand market trends and context.

**Total Addressable Market (TAM)**: The total market demand for a product or service if 100 percent market share were achieved under ideal conditions.

**Serviceable Available Market (SAM)**: The portion of the total market that can be served by a firm's products or services within its target segments and operational scope.

**Serviceable Obtainable Market (SOM)**: The realistic share of the market that a firm can capture in the short to medium term, considering competition and resource constraints.

**Market Segmentation**: The process of dividing a heterogeneous market into smaller, homogeneous groups with similar needs, characteristics, or behaviors.

**Targeting**: The strategic selection of one or more market segments that a firm chooses to serve based on attractiveness and strategic fit.

**Positioning**: The process of establishing a distinct and valued perception of a product or service in the minds of target customers relative to competitors.

**Competitive Landscape Analysis**: An assessment of direct and indirect competitors, their offerings, strengths, weaknesses, and strategic positioning within an industry.

**Value Proposition**: A clear statement describing the unique benefits a product or service delivers to customers and why it is preferable to competing alternatives.

**Customer Journey Map**: A visual representation of the stages a customer experiences when interacting with a product or service, from awareness to retention.

**Market Validation**: The process of confirming real customer demand through observable behaviors such as purchases, usage, or commitments rather than stated interest alone.

---

**Mini Case Study 1: Identifying the Right Market Opportunity**

A startup team developed a smart reusable water bottle capable of tracking hydration levels through a mobile application. Initial enthusiasm was high, driven by positive feedback from peers and technology enthusiasts. However, early market analysis revealed a critical issue: while many consumers appreciated the concept, only a small segment was willing to pay a premium price.

Further opportunity assessment showed that the general consumer market viewed hydration tracking as a "nice-to-have" feature rather than a necessity. In contrast, fitness trainers, athletes, and corporate wellness programs demonstrated stronger willingness to pay due to performance and health monitoring needs. By reassessing the market opportunity, the startup shifted its focus from mass consumers to institutional and professional segments, significantly improving product–market fit and revenue predictability.

---

**Mini Case Study 2: Market Sizing and Segmentation Errors**

An online education platform planned to offer skill-based certification courses and estimated its Total Addressable Market by assuming that all college students in the country were potential customers. This resulted in an inflated market size and unrealistic growth projections.

Upon conducting deeper segmentation, the company realized that only final-year students and early-career professionals actively sought paid certifications. Geographic access, internet availability, and affordability further reduced the serviceable market. By recalculating TAM, SAM, and SOM using a bottom-up approach, the firm aligned its marketing strategy with realistic demand and avoided overinvestment in low-conversion segments.

---

**Mini Case Study 3: Customer Journey Mapping for Market Validation**

A subscription-based healthy meal delivery service experienced high website traffic but low repeat purchases. Customer journey mapping revealed significant friction during the usage and retention stages. Customers struggled with unclear meal customization options and inconsistent delivery schedules.

By mapping customer actions, touchpoints, and pain points across the journey, the company redesigned its onboarding process, simplified menu selection, and introduced proactive customer support. These changes reduced churn and increased retention without major increases in marketing spend.

---

## REVIEW QUESTIONS AND EXERCISES

## REVIEW QUESTIONS

### Short Answer Questions

1. Define market analysis and explain its role in business model development.
2. What is market opportunity assessment? Why is willingness to pay a critical factor?
3. Differentiate between customer profiling and buyer personas.
4. Distinguish between primary and secondary market research with examples.
5. Define TAM, SAM, and SOM. Why is SOM considered the most realistic estimate?
6. What is market segmentation? List any four commonly used segmentation variables.
7. Explain the concept of positioning in the STP framework.

8. What is a value proposition, and how does it support competitive advantage?
9. Describe the purpose of customer journey mapping in market analysis.
10. What is market validation, and how does it differ from market research?

**Descriptive / Long Answer Questions**

1. Explain the process of market opportunity assessment with suitable examples.
2. Discuss the steps involved in developing buyer personas and their strategic relevance.
3. Compare primary and secondary market research methods, highlighting their advantages and limitations.
4. Explain the TAM–SAM–SOM framework with a numerical illustration.
5. Describe the Segmentation–Targeting–Positioning (STP) framework and its importance in competitive markets.
6. Analyze the role of competitive landscape and industry analysis in strategic decision-making.
7. Discuss the components of an effective value proposition and their linkage to customer needs.
8. Explain customer journey mapping and its role in improving customer experience and retention.
9. Describe methods used for validating market demand in early-stage ventures.
10. Critically examine common errors in market assessment and suggest strategies to avoid them.

## EXERCISES

**Exercise 1: Market Opportunity Analysis:** Identify a product or service of your choice and:

- Describe the problem it addresses
- Identify the target customer segment
- Assess customer willingness to pay
- Comment on market readiness and scalability

**Exercise 2: Customer Persona Development:** Select a consumer or business product and:

- Create one detailed buyer persona
- Identify the persona's goals, pain points, and decision criteria
- Explain how the product's value proposition addresses these factors

**Exercise 3: Market Size Estimation:** For a selected product:

- Estimate TAM using industry-level data
- Narrow it down to SAM using segmentation filters
- Calculate SOM based on realistic market share assumptions
- Justify all assumptions used

**Exercise 4: STP Strategy Design:** Choose a company or startup and:

- Segment its market using at least two variables
- Identify the most attractive target segment
- Propose a clear positioning statement for the product or service

**Exercise 5: Customer Journey Mapping:** Map the customer journey for an online or offline product by:

- Identifying key stages from awareness to retention
- Listing customer actions and touchpoints at each stage
- Highlighting pain points and improvement opportunities

**Exercise 6: Market Validation Plan:** Design a basic market validation plan for a new product idea:

- Define key assumptions to be tested
- Select appropriate validation methods
- Identify measurable indicators of demand

**Higher-Order Thinking Question:** "Market failure is often the result of flawed assumptions rather than poor execution." Critically evaluate this statement using concepts from market analysis and segmentation.

# CHAPTER-4

# BUSINESS MODEL CANVAS (BMC) & LEAN CANVAS

**Abstract**: This chapter examines the role of business models as foundational instruments for startup creation, validation, and growth under conditions of uncertainty. It systematically explores the conceptual evolution of business models in entrepreneurial contexts, emphasizing business model innovation as a strategic mechanism for competitive advantage. The chapter provides a detailed exposition of the **Business Model Canvas**, outlining its nine building blocks and their interdependencies in value creation, delivery, and capture. Complementing this, the Lean Canvas framework is discussed as a problem–solution–focused adaptation suited to early-stage ventures, highlighting hypothesis-driven experimentation and rapid iteration. Further, the chapter analyzes revenue models and cost structures, key activities, resources, and partnerships, illustrating how these elements influence scalability and operational efficiency. Contemporary business model patterns, including platform, subscription, and freemium models, are critically evaluated in relation to network effects, customer retention, and monetization dynamics. The chapter also introduces unit economics as a practical tool for assessing financial sustainability at the customer level. Finally, it explains how validated canvases can be translated into formal business plans for communication with investors and other stakeholders. Overall, the chapter integrates strategic frameworks with practical insights to support evidence-based entrepreneurial decision-making.

**Keywords:** Business Model Canvas; Lean Canvas; Startup Innovation; Revenue Models; Unit Economics; Business Planning

## 4.1 CONCEPT OF BUSINESS MODELS IN STARTUPS

In the context of startups, a **business model** represents a structured explanation of how an entrepreneurial venture creates value for customers, delivers that value through appropriate mechanisms, and captures economic returns in a sustainable manner. Unlike established organizations, startups operate under conditions of high uncertainty, where customer needs, market size, pricing logic, and even the final product are not fully known. Consequently, a startup's business model is not a fixed blueprint but a set of **testable assumptions** that evolve through experimentation and learning (Fig 4.1).

A well-defined business model clarifies **(i) who the customer is, (ii) what value is offered, (iii) how that value is delivered, and (iv) how the venture captures revenue in a sustainable manner**. These elements collectively define the internal logic of the venture and guide strategic and operational decisions. Frameworks such as the **Business Model Canvas** have been widely adopted because they enable entrepreneurs to visualize these components holistically and identify critical interdependencies.

Importantly, the primary objective of a startup business model is **validation rather than optimization**. Early-stage ventures focus on achieving problem–solution fit and product–market fit by continuously testing hypotheses with real customers. Market feedback informs iterative refinements to the value proposition, pricing mechanisms, channels, and cost structures.

Thus, in startups, the business model functions as a dynamic learning framework that aligns innovation, customer discovery, and financial sustainability. Its effective design and continuous refinement are essential for reducing uncertainty, attracting investment, and enabling scalable growth.

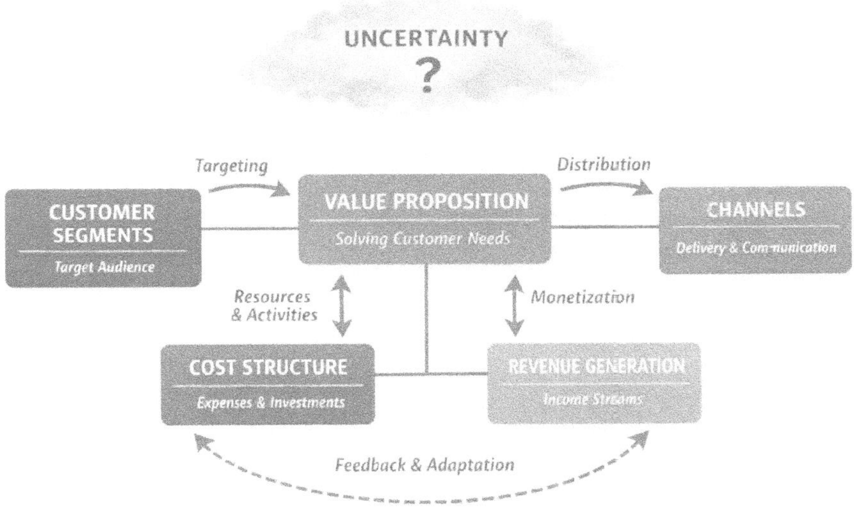


**Figure 4.1. Conceptual framework of a startup business model under conditions of uncertainty**. This figure illustrates the interdependent components of a startup business model—customer segments, value proposition, channels, cost structure, and revenue generation—operating under conditions of uncertainty. It highlights how value creation is shaped by targeting, distribution, resource deployment, and monetization, with continuous feedback and adaptation enabling entrepreneurs to refine assumptions, optimize performance, and progressively reduce uncertainty.

## 4.2 BUSINESS MODEL INNOVATION

**Business model innovation** refers to the purposeful modification or reconfiguration of one or more components of a business model to enhance value creation, delivery, or capture. In startup contexts, business model innovation is often more consequential than product or technological innovation because it directly shapes how a venture interacts with customers and generates sustainable revenue under conditions of uncertainty.

Rather than focusing solely on introducing new products or services, business model innovation involves questioning fundamental assumptions about target customers, value propositions, revenue mechanisms, channels, and cost structures. Startups frequently innovate by altering **who** they serve, **what** problem they solve, or **how** value is monetized. For example, a shift from one-time product sales to recurring subscription-based revenue represents a significant innovation in value capture logic, even if the core offering remains unchanged.

Business model innovation may be **incremental**, involving gradual refinements to existing components, or **radical**, resulting in entirely new configurations that disrupt established industry practices. Startups are particularly well positioned to pursue such innovation because they are not constrained by legacy systems, organizational inertia, or entrenched customer expectations. As a result, they can experiment with alternative pricing models, digital channels, asset-light structures, and partnership-driven ecosystems.

Frameworks such as the **Business Model Canvas** support business model innovation by enabling entrepreneurs to visualize interdependencies among components and systematically explore alternative configurations. Through iterative testing and market feedback, startups can assess the viability of innovative business model choices and refine them over time.

Ultimately, business model innovation enables startups to achieve differentiation, improve scalability, and respond effectively to changing market conditions. When grounded in validated learning and customer insight, it becomes a critical driver of long-term competitive advantage.

## 4.3 NINE BUILDING BLOCKS OF BUSINESS MODEL CANVAS

The **Business Model Canvas** is a widely adopted strategic framework that visually represents the logic of how an organization creates, delivers, and captures value. It consists of **nine interrelated building blocks**, each addressing a critical dimension of the business model. Together, these blocks provide a holistic view of the venture and support systematic analysis, comparison, and innovation (Fig 4.2).

1. **Customer Segments**: This block defines the specific groups of individuals or organizations the startup aims to serve. Clear identification of customer segments enables targeted value propositions and efficient resource allocation.
2. **Value Propositions**: The value proposition describes the bundle of products or services that create value for a particular customer segment by solving a problem or fulfilling a need. It is central to achieving problem–solution and product–market fit.
3. **Channels**: Channels outline how a startup communicates with, reaches, and delivers value to its customers. These include awareness, evaluation, purchase, delivery, and after-sales support channels.

4. **Customer Relationships**: This block specifies the type of relationship a startup establishes with each customer segment, such as personal assistance, self-service, automated services, or community-based interactions.
5. **Revenue Streams**: Revenue streams represent the ways in which a startup generates income from each customer segment. They may include transaction-based, recurring, or usage-based revenues, reflecting the value capture mechanism.
6. **Key Resources**: Key resources are the essential assets required to deliver the value proposition. These may be physical, intellectual, human, or financial in nature.
7. **Key Activities**: Key activities encompass the most important actions a startup must perform to operate successfully, such as product development, platform management, marketing, or customer support.
8. **Key Partnerships**: Key partnerships identify external organizations or individuals that help optimize the business model, reduce risk, or access complementary resources and capabilities.
9. **Cost Structure**: The cost structure summarizes the major costs incurred in operating the business model, including fixed and variable costs associated with resources, activities, and partnerships.

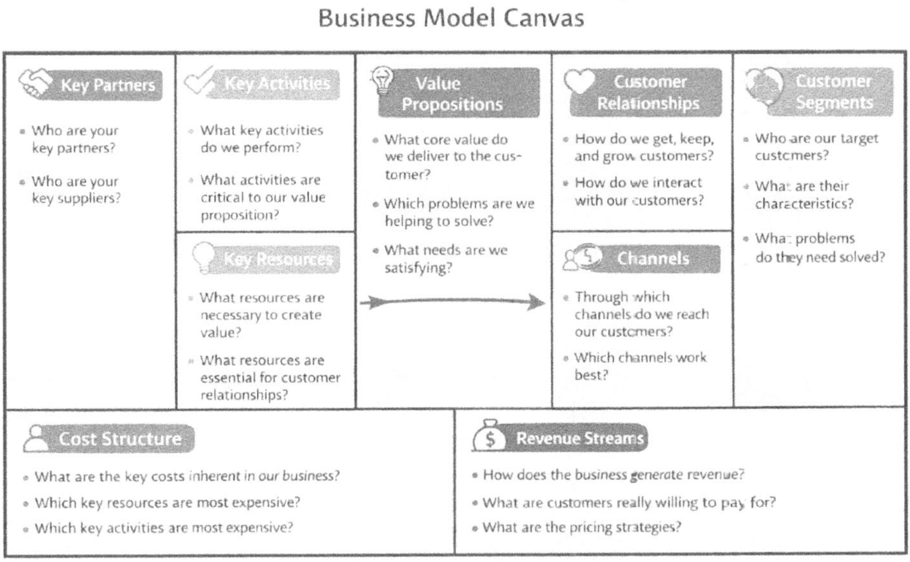


**Figure 4.2 Nine Building Blocks of the Business Model Canvas**

By organizing these nine building blocks into a single visual framework, the Business Model Canvas enables startups to articulate assumptions, identify interdependencies, and iteratively refine their business models through evidence-based learning.

## 4.4 LEAN CANVAS FRAMEWORK

The **Lean Canvas Framework** is a startup-focused adaptation of the Business Model Canvas designed to support ventures operating under extreme uncertainty. Developed by **Ash Maurya**, the Lean Canvas emphasizes rapid learning, hypothesis testing, and early validation, making it particularly suitable for early-stage and innovation-driven startups (Fig 4.3).

While the Business Model Canvas provides a comprehensive view of value creation and delivery, the Lean Canvas prioritizes **risk identification** by focusing on the most uncertain elements of a startup's business model. It retains the core logic of value creation, delivery, and capture but restructures certain building blocks to reflect startup realities.

The Lean Canvas consists of nine blocks: **Problem**, **Customer Segments**, **Unique Value Proposition**, **Solution**, **Channels**, **Revenue Streams**, **Cost Structure**, **Key Metrics**, and **Unfair Advantage**. The inclusion of the *Problem* and *Solution* blocks highlights the importance of problem–solution fit, while *Key Metrics* directs attention to measurable indicators of traction. The *Unfair Advantage* block encourages founders to articulate assets or capabilities that are difficult for competitors to replicate, such as proprietary data, domain expertise, or network effects.

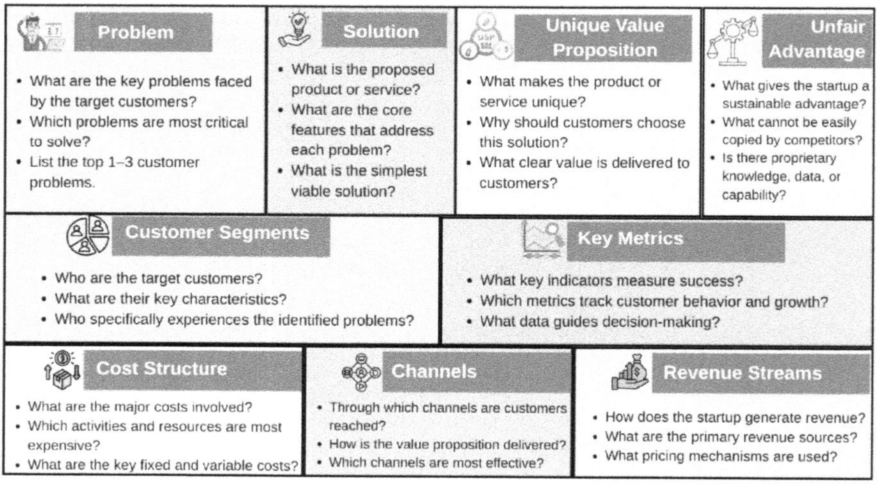


**Figure 4.3. Lean Canvas Framework for Startups.** This figure presents the Lean Canvas as a one-page, startup-oriented business modeling tool that captures the key assumptions underlying a new venture. It highlights nine core elements—Problem, Customer Segments, Unique Value Proposition, Solution, Channels, Revenue Streams, Cost Structure, Key Metrics, and Unfair Advantage—enabling entrepreneurs to systematically articulate, test, and refine their business model under conditions of uncertainty.

The Lean Canvas functions as a **living document**, evolving through continuous customer discovery, experimentation, and feedback. Assumptions documented in the canvas are translated into testable hypotheses and validated through minimum viable products, interviews, and pilot deployments. Insights gained from these experiments inform iterative refinement of the business model. Overall, the Lean Canvas complements the Business Model Canvas by providing a practical, execution-oriented framework that supports disciplined experimentation, reduces early-stage risk, and accelerates the path toward product–market fit.

**Table 4.1. Comparison between Business Model Canvas and Lean Canvas**

| Dimension | Business Model Canvas (BMC) | Lean Canvas |
|---|---|---|
| **Primary Purpose** | Provides a holistic view of how an organization creates, delivers, and captures value | Focuses on identifying and testing the riskiest assumptions in early-stage startups |
| **Target Users** | Startups, established firms, entrepreneurs, managers, and strategists | Early-stage startups, innovators, and entrepreneurial teams |
| **Conceptual Emphasis** | Value creation, delivery, and capture across the entire business system | Problem–solution fit, rapid validation, and learning |
| **Customer Focus** | Customer Segments and Customer Relationships | Problem, Customer Segments, and Unique Value Proposition |
| **Value Proposition** | Emphasizes the Value Proposition block within a balanced framework | Highlights Unique Value Proposition as a central differentiator |
| **Risk Orientation** | Suitable for relatively stable or validated business contexts | Designed for high-uncertainty and unvalidated environments |
| **Key Blocks Added or Modified** | Includes Key Partners, Key Activities, and Key Resources | Introduces Problem, Solution, Key Metrics, and Unfair Advantage |
| **Treatment of Metrics** | Implicit; metrics are not explicitly defined | Explicit focus on Key Metrics driving traction and growth |
| **Iteration Speed** | Supports iteration but often used for structured analysis | Optimized for rapid iteration and hypothesis testing |
| **Use in Business** | Commonly used as a precursor to formal business | Primarily used for experimentation before |

| | | |
|---|---|---|
| **Planning** | plans | detailed planning |
| **Typical Output** | Comprehensive visualization of the business model | Action-oriented snapshot of startup assumptions |
| **Strengths** | Holistic, versatile, and suitable for strategic alignment | Lean, focused, and effective for early-stage validation |
| **Limitations** | May be too broad for very early-stage startups | Less detailed on operations and partnerships |

## 4.5 REVENUE MODELS AND COST STRUCTURES

**Revenue models and cost structures** define the financial logic of a startup's business model and determine its ability to capture value sustainably. While value creation and delivery are essential for customer adoption, long-term viability depends on the alignment between how revenue is generated and how costs are incurred.

**Revenue models** describe the mechanisms through which a startup earns income from its customer segments. Common revenue models include one-time product sales, subscription-based pricing, licensing, advertising, transaction fees, and usage-based or pay-per-use models (Fig 4.4). The selection of an appropriate revenue model depends on customer willingness to pay, frequency of value realization, and competitive dynamics. Startups often experiment with multiple revenue mechanisms before identifying the most scalable and acceptable option.

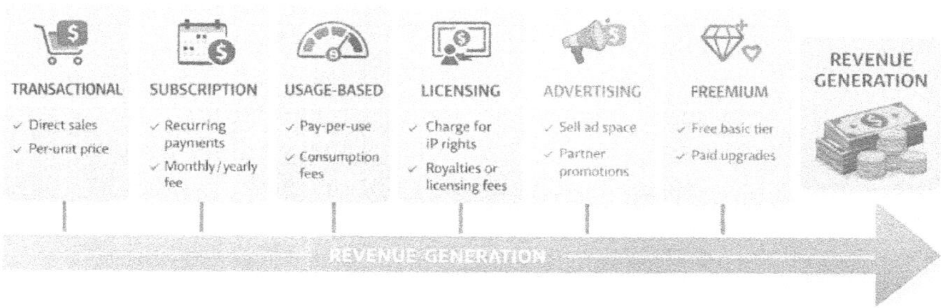


**Figure 4.4 Common Revenue Models in Startups.** This figure presents a schematic overview of major startup revenue models, including transactional, subscription-based, usage-based, licensing, advertising, and freemium models. It illustrates how startups select and structure income streams to align with customer value propositions, market behavior, and scalability objectives, ultimately guiding sustainable revenue generation.

**Cost structures** capture all significant expenses required to operate the business model. These typically include fixed costs such as salaries, infrastructure, and technology development, as well as variable costs linked to production, distribution, or customer acquisition. Early-stage startups frequently aim for cost structures that are flexible and scalable, minimizing upfront capital requirements and enabling rapid adjustment in response to market feedback.

The interaction between revenue models and cost structures directly influences profitability, scalability, and break-even timing. A mismatch—for example, high fixed costs paired with uncertain or delayed revenues—can threaten sustainability even when customer demand exists. Therefore, startups must continuously evaluate whether their revenue streams can support their cost base as the venture scales.

By systematically analyzing revenue models and cost structures within the canvas framework, entrepreneurs can assess financial feasibility, identify efficiency improvements, and make informed decisions that support sustainable growth.

## 4.6 KEY ACTIVITIES, RESOURCES, AND PARTNERSHIPS

**Key activities, key resources, and key partnerships** represent the operational backbone of a startup's business model. These components define how value propositions are executed in practice and how the venture organizes its internal and external capabilities to deliver value efficiently.

**Key activities** refer to the most critical actions a startup must perform to operate successfully. Depending on the nature of the business, these activities may include product or service development, platform maintenance, data analysis, marketing and customer acquisition, or customer support. Clear identification of key activities helps startups focus managerial attention and resources on functions that directly contribute to value creation and competitive advantage.

**Key resources** are the essential assets required to perform these activities and deliver the value proposition. They may be physical (equipment, infrastructure), intellectual (patents, software, data, brand), human (skills, expertise, leadership), or financial (capital, credit lines). In many startups, intellectual and human resources play a particularly important role, especially in knowledge-intensive and technology-driven ventures.

**Key partnerships** involve relationships with external organizations or individuals that support the business model. These may include suppliers, technology providers, distributors, research institutions, or strategic allies. Partnerships can help startups reduce risk, access complementary resources, lower costs, or accelerate market entry. For early-stage ventures with limited resources, well-structured partnerships are often critical for scaling operations. Together, key activities, resources, and partnerships ensure that the business model is operationally feasible. Their alignment with the value proposition and revenue logic is essential for efficiency, resilience, and sustainable growth.

## 4.7 TESTING AND ITERATING BUSINESS MODELS

In startup environments characterized by uncertainty, **testing and iterating business models** is essential for reducing risk and improving decision-making. Rather than assuming that initial business model assumptions are correct, startups adopt an experimental approach in which hypotheses about customers, value propositions, channels, and revenue mechanisms are systematically tested in the market (Fig 4.5).

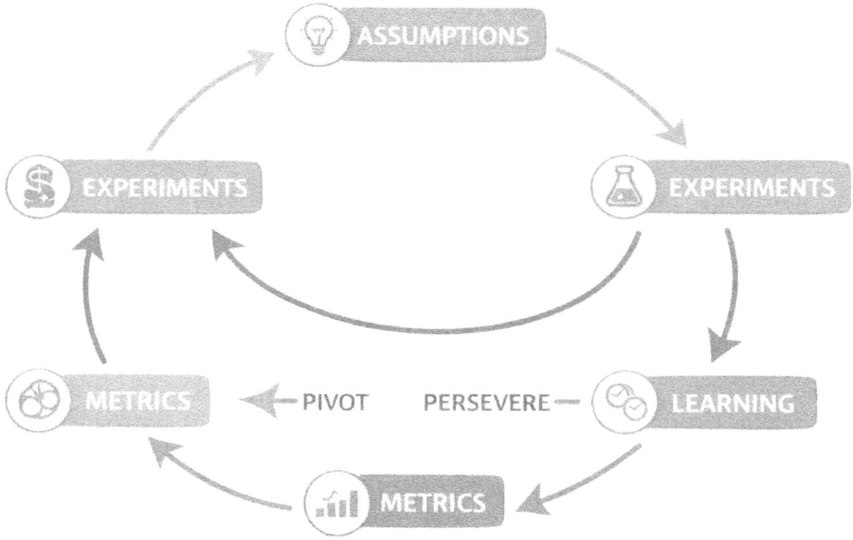


**Figure 4.5 Business Model Testing and Iteration Cycle.** This figure illustrates the iterative process through which startups refine their business models under conditions of uncertainty. Initial assumptions are translated into experiments, whose outcomes are evaluated using relevant metrics. Insights derived from these measurements lead to validated learning, informing strategic decisions to either pivot the business model or persevere with the current approach. The cyclical nature of the framework highlights continuous feedback, learning, and adaptation as essential mechanisms for achieving problem–solution fit and sustainable growth.

Testing typically begins by translating key assumptions documented in the canvas into **testable hypotheses**. These hypotheses are evaluated using methods such as customer interviews, surveys, prototypes, pilot projects, and minimum viable products (MVPs). The objective is to gather empirical evidence on customer behavior and preferences with minimal time and resource investment.

Iteration occurs when insights from testing lead to modifications in one or more components of the business model. Startups may refine their value proposition, adjust pricing strategies, change customer segments, or alter distribution channels based on validated learning. In some cases, evidence may indicate the need for a **pivot**, involving a substantial change in business model direction, while in others the appropriate response may be to persevere or discontinue an unviable approach.

A disciplined approach to testing and iteration relies on clearly defined metrics, feedback loops, and decision criteria. This prevents ad hoc changes and ensures that learning is cumulative and evidence-based. By continuously testing and iterating their business models, startups improve alignment with market needs, optimize resource allocation, and increase the likelihood of achieving product–market fit and sustainable growth.

## 4.8 PLATFORM, SUBSCRIPTION, AND FREEMIUM MODELS

**Platform, subscription, and freemium models** represent widely adopted business model patterns in contemporary startups, particularly in digital and technology-enabled markets. Each model embodies a distinct logic of value creation, delivery, and capture, with specific implications for scalability and sustainability.

**Platform models** facilitate interactions between two or more interdependent user groups, such as producers and consumers, service providers and users, or advertisers and audiences. Value is created by enabling efficient exchange and amplified through **network effects**, where the platform becomes more valuable as participation increases. Successful platform models require careful governance of pricing, access rules, trust mechanisms, and quality control to balance the interests of different user groups.

**Subscription models** generate revenue through recurring payments over a defined period. This model emphasizes customer retention, consistent value delivery, and long-term relationships rather than one-time transactions. Subscription-based startups focus on metrics such as churn rate, customer lifetime value, and engagement frequency, as sustained usage is critical for profitability.

**Freemium models** combine free access to basic features with paid premium offerings. Typically, a large base of non-paying users supports a smaller segment of paying customers. The effectiveness of this model depends on low marginal costs, clear differentiation between free and premium tiers, and efficient conversion strategies.

While these models offer strong scalability potential, they also present operational and financial challenges. Startups must align cost structures, customer acquisition strategies, and value propositions to ensure that growth translates into sustainable economic outcomes.

## 4.9 UNIT ECONOMICS AND SUSTAINABILITY

**Unit economics** provide a granular view of a startup's financial viability by evaluating profitability at the level of a single customer, transaction, or unit of output. Rather than focusing solely on aggregate revenues or costs, unit economics assess whether the core business model generates value on a per-unit basis, which is essential for scalable and sustainable growth.

Key unit economic metrics include **Customer Acquisition Cost (CAC)**, which represents the total cost of acquiring a new customer, and **Customer Lifetime Value (LTV)**, which estimates the total revenue a customer generates over the duration of their relationship with the venture. A sustainable business model typically demonstrates an LTV that significantly exceeds CAC, along with an acceptable payback period. When these conditions are not met, growth may amplify losses rather than create value.

Unit economics also incorporate contribution margins, churn rates, and usage intensity, depending on the nature of the business model. These metrics enable startups to identify inefficiencies in pricing, marketing, or cost structures and to make evidence-based adjustments before scaling operations. Beyond financial performance, sustainability increasingly encompasses **environmental and social considerations**. Resource efficiency, ethical sourcing, regulatory compliance, and long-term stakeholder impact are becoming integral to business model design. Startups that integrate sustainability principles into their unit economics are better positioned to manage risk, comply with evolving regulations, and build durable competitive advantage.

By systematically monitoring unit economics alongside broader sustainability goals, startups can ensure that growth is both economically viable and responsibly managed over the long term.

## 4.10 TRANSLATING CANVAS INTO BUSINESS PLAN

While the Business Model Canvas and Lean Canvas emphasize visualization, experimentation, and iteration, many stakeholders—such as investors, lenders, regulators, and institutional partners—require a **formal business plan** for evaluation and decision-making. Translating a validated canvas into a business plan involves expanding each building block into a structured and detailed narrative supported by evidence.

The process typically begins with the **value proposition and customer segments**, which are developed into comprehensive market analyses, including customer profiles, market size, and competitive positioning. **Channels and customer relationships** are translated into go-to-market strategies outlining marketing, sales, and distribution approaches. Similarly, **key**

**activities, resources, and partnerships** form the basis of the operational and organizational sections of the business plan.

**Revenue streams and cost structures** documented in the canvas are converted into financial projections, including income statements, cash flow forecasts, and break-even analyses. Assumptions underlying these projections should be explicitly stated and supported by data derived from customer validation and pilot testing. This ensures transparency and credibility.

Importantly, the business plan should reflect the **learning gained through iteration**, demonstrating how initial assumptions were tested and refined. In this way, the canvas serves as a strategic foundation, while the business plan functions as a formal communication document.

By systematically translating validated canvas elements into a coherent business plan, startups can present a compelling, evidence-based case for viability, scalability, and sustainable growth.

## KEY CONCEPTS & DEFINITIONS

**Business Model**: A conceptual framework that explains how a venture creates value for customers, delivers that value through appropriate channels, and captures revenue in a sustainable manner.

**Startup**: A temporary organization designed to search for a repeatable and scalable business model under conditions of high uncertainty.

**Business Model Innovation**: The process of redesigning one or more components of a business model—such as the value proposition, revenue logic, or delivery mechanisms—to achieve competitive advantage and improved performance.

**Business Model Canvas (BMC)**: A strategic management tool that visually represents a business model using nine interconnected building blocks covering value creation, delivery, and capture.

**Customer Segments**: Distinct groups of customers or users that a venture aims to serve with tailored value propositions.

**Value Proposition**: The bundle of products and services that create value by solving customer problems or fulfilling specific needs.

**Channels**: The communication, distribution, and sales pathways through which a venture reaches and serves its customers.

**Customer Relationships**: The types of interactions a venture establishes and maintains with its customer segments to acquire, retain, and grow customers.

**Revenue Streams**: The various ways in which a venture generates income from its customer segments.

**Cost Structure**: The major costs incurred in operating a business model, including fixed and variable expenses.

**Key Resources**: The essential assets—physical, intellectual, human, or financial—required to deliver the value proposition.

**Key Activities**: The critical actions a venture must perform to operate successfully and deliver value to customers.

**Key Partnerships**: Strategic relationships with external organizations that help optimize resources, reduce risk, or enhance value creation.

**Lean Canvas**: A startup-focused adaptation of the Business Model Canvas that emphasizes problem–solution fit, rapid experimentation, and validated learning.

**Problem–Solution Fit**: The degree to which a proposed solution effectively addresses a clearly defined customer problem.

**Unique Value Proposition (UVP)**: A clear and compelling statement that explains why a product or service is distinct and worth choosing over alternatives.

**Key Metrics**: Quantitative indicators used to measure startup performance, learning progress, and traction.

**Unfair Advantage**: A defensible capability or asset that is difficult for competitors to replicate, such as proprietary technology, data, or expertise.

**Minimum Viable Product (MVP)**: The simplest version of a product or service built to test key assumptions and gather customer feedback with minimal resources.

**Validated Learning**: Evidence-based insights gained through systematic experimentation that inform decisions to pivot or persevere.

**Pivot**: A strategic change in one or more elements of a business model based on learning from market feedback.

**Unit Economics**: Financial metrics that assess the profitability of a single customer or transaction, commonly expressed through measures such as customer acquisition cost and lifetime value.

**Scalability**: The ability of a business model to grow revenue faster than costs as customer demand increases.

**Sustainability**: The capacity of a business model to maintain long-term economic viability while responsibly managing environmental and social impacts.

---

**Mini Case Study 1: Airbnb – Platform-Based Business Model Innovation**

Airbnb disrupted the traditional hospitality industry by introducing a **two-sided platform business model** connecting hosts with travelers. Instead of owning physical assets such as hotels, Airbnb focused on enabling value creation through trust mechanisms, digital infrastructure, and community governance.

Using a platform-oriented business model, Airbnb's **value proposition** lies in offering affordable, diverse, and local accommodation experiences to travelers, while enabling hosts to monetize underutilized assets. Revenue is generated through service fees charged to both hosts and guests. The cost structure remains relatively asset-light, primarily involving platform development, marketing, and trust and safety operations.

Airbnb's success highlights how business model innovation—rather than product innovation alone—can create scalable growth and strong network effects.

---

**Mini Case Study 2: Netflix – Subscription-Based Business Model Evolution**

Netflix began as a DVD-by-mail service but transitioned into a **subscription-based digital streaming platform**, demonstrating strategic business model innovation. The core value proposition shifted from physical convenience to on-demand digital entertainment with personalized recommendations.

Netflix's recurring subscription revenue model emphasizes customer retention, lifetime value, and continuous content delivery. Significant costs arise from content acquisition and original production, making scale and subscriber growth critical to sustainability.

This case illustrates how aligning **revenue streams, cost structure, and customer relationships** is essential when scaling a subscription-based business model.

---

**Mini Case Study 3: Dropbox – Freemium Business Model and Lean Validation**

Dropbox adopted a **freemium business model**, offering basic cloud storage for free while charging for premium features such as increased storage and enterprise controls. In its early stages, Dropbox used a simple explainer video as a **minimum viable product** to validate demand before heavy infrastructure investment.

The company focused on key metrics such as user acquisition, activation, and conversion from free to paid users. Low marginal costs and high scalability enabled Dropbox to convert a small percentage of users into a sustainable revenue base.

This case demonstrates how the Lean Canvas approach supports hypothesis testing, rapid learning, and efficient scaling.

---

## REVIEW QUESTIONS AND EXERCISES

## REVIEW QUESTIONS

### Short-Answer Questions

1. Define a business model and explain why it is particularly important for startups.
2. Differentiate between a business model and a business plan.
3. What is meant by business model innovation, and how does it differ from product innovation?
4. List the nine building blocks of the Business Model Canvas.
5. Explain the concept of problem–solution fit in the context of startups.
6. What is the purpose of the Lean Canvas, and how does it address startup uncertainty?

7. Define unit economics and explain its relevance for startup sustainability.

**Descriptive Questions**

8. Describe the role of customer segments and value propositions in shaping a startup's business model.
9. Explain how revenue models and cost structures influence scalability.
10. Discuss the importance of key activities, resources, and partnerships in executing a business model.
11. Explain the testing and iteration cycle used for validating business models.
12. Compare platform, subscription, and freemium business models with suitable examples.
13. Discuss how unit economics can inform decisions to scale or pivot a startup.

**Analytical / Essay-Type Questions**

14. Critically analyze the Business Model Canvas as a strategic tool for startups.
15. Evaluate the Lean Canvas framework in comparison with the Business Model Canvas.
16. Discuss how business model innovation can create sustainable competitive advantage.
17. Explain the process of translating a validated canvas into a formal business plan.
18. Assess the role of experimentation and validated learning in reducing startup failure.

## EXERCISES

**Exercise 1: Business Model Canvas Design:** Select a startup idea of your choice and design a complete **Business Model Canvas**. Clearly describe each of the nine building blocks and explain how they are interrelated.

**Exercise 2: Lean Canvas Application:** Using the same startup idea, develop a **Lean Canvas**. Identify the key problems, proposed solution, unique value proposition, key metrics, and unfair advantage. Compare this with your Business Model Canvas and note the differences.

**Exercise 3: Revenue and Cost Analysis:** For a digital startup, identify at least two possible revenue models. Analyze the associated cost structures and discuss which combination offers better scalability and sustainability.

**Exercise 4: Unit Economics Calculation:** Assume the following:

- Customer Acquisition Cost (CAC) = ₹1,000
- Average Monthly Revenue per Customer = ₹300
- Average Customer Lifetime = 8 months

Calculate the Customer Lifetime Value (LTV) and evaluate whether the business model is financially viable.

**Exercise 5: Pivot or Persevere Scenario:** A startup experiences high user engagement but low conversion to paid plans. Using the business model testing and iteration framework, recommend whether the startup should pivot or persevere, and justify your decision.

**Exercise 6: Mini Case Analysis:** Choose one of the mini case studies (Airbnb, Netflix, or Dropbox) discussed in the chapter and:

- Identify the core business model type
- Map the company's model onto either the Business Model Canvas or Lean Canvas
- Discuss the key factors contributing to its scalability

# CHAPTER-5

# BUSINESS & STARTUP TERMINOLOGIES

**Abstract**: The chapter *Business & Startup Terminologies*, provides a comprehensive and structured orientation to the language ecosystem that defines contemporary entrepreneurship and startup practice. As startups operate at the intersection of innovation, finance, technology, regulation, and markets, fluency in domain-specific terminology is essential for effective decision-making, stakeholder communication, and strategic execution. This chapter systematically introduces core startup vocabulary and foundational concepts, followed by detailed explanations of funding instruments, valuation methods, and equity structures. It further clarifies product development language, technology frameworks, and growth and performance metrics commonly used in early-stage and scaling ventures. Legal, compliance, and intellectual property terminologies are discussed to ensure regulatory awareness and risk mitigation, while marketing, sales, manufacturing, and operations jargon highlights go-to-market and execution realities. Dedicated sections address digital, SaaS, and platform-based startup terms, along with the nuanced language used by investors, accelerators, and incubators. The chapter also identifies and corrects commonly misused or misunderstood startup terms that often lead to strategic errors. Concluding with a focus on developing startup literacy, this chapter equips students, researchers, and aspiring entrepreneurs with a shared vocabulary, enabling clearer thinking, informed participation in the startup ecosystem, and alignment between innovation, investment, and execution.

**Keywords:** Startup Terminology; Entrepreneurial Ecosystem; Funding and Valuation; Growth Metrics; Intellectual Property; Startup Literacy

## 5.1 CORE STARTUP VOCABULARY AND CONCEPTS

This section introduces only the **most widely used, practically relevant, and foundational startup terminologies** that are essential for understanding entrepreneurial discourse across industries. The focus is on terms that founders, investors, incubators, and policymakers consistently use in decision-making, evaluation, and communication (Fig 5.1).

A **startup** is a newly established venture designed to develop an innovative product or service with the intent of achieving rapid growth and scalability under conditions of uncertainty. **Entrepreneurship** refers to the systematic process of opportunity identification, value creation, and venture execution through innovation and risk-taking.

A **problem statement** clearly defines a customer pain point, while **problem–solution fit** indicates alignment between the identified problem and the proposed solution. **Product–market fit** is achieved when a product demonstrates strong and repeatable demand within a defined market and is considered a critical milestone for sustainable growth.

A **value proposition** describes the unique benefit offered to customers and explains why the solution is preferable to existing alternatives. The **target market** and **customer segment** specify the group of users or buyers the startup intends to serve.

A **business model** explains how the startup creates, delivers, and captures value, including revenue streams and cost structure. The **minimum viable product (MVP)** is a basic functional version of a product developed to test assumptions and gather early customer feedback with minimal resources.

**Bootstrapping** refers to building a startup using personal funds or internal revenues, while a **pivot** denotes a strategic change in product, market, or business model based on validated learning. **Scalability** reflects the ability to grow operations and revenue efficiently without a proportional increase in costs.

Together, these core terms form the foundational vocabulary required for startup literacy and effective participation in the entrepreneurial ecosystem.

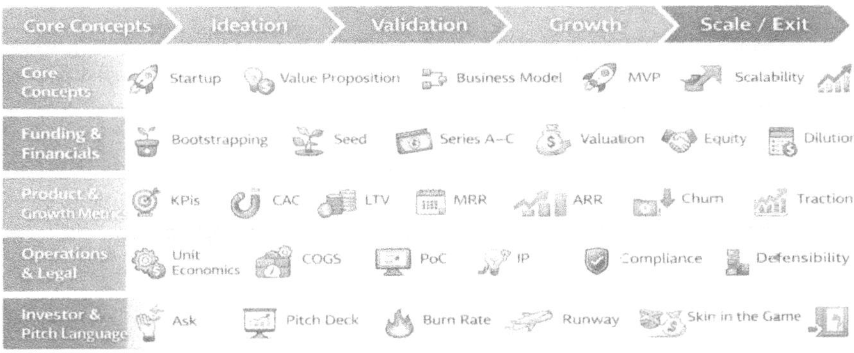


**Figure 5.1: Startup Terminology Landscape Across Venture Lifecycle**. Integrated representation of major startup terminologies mapped across the venture lifecycle and functional domains, illustrating how language usage evolves from ideation to scale and exit.

## 5.2 FUNDING, VALUATION, AND EQUITY TERMINOLOGIES

This section focuses on the **most commonly used and decision-critical financial terminologies** encountered by founders, investors, and startup stakeholders. These terms form the basis of fundraising discussions, ownership structuring, and long-term value creation.

**Startup funding** refers to the capital raised to develop, operate, and scale a venture. Early funding typically progresses through **pre-seed** and **seed**

**funding**, supporting idea validation and early traction. As the startup grows, it may raise **Series A, Series B, and later-stage funding**, primarily aimed at scaling, market expansion, and operational maturity. Common funding sources include **angel investors**, **venture capital (VC) firms**, and **startup accelerators**.

**Valuation** represents the estimated worth of a startup at a given stage. **Pre-money valuation** is the company's value before new investment, while **post-money valuation** includes the invested capital. Valuation is influenced by factors such as market opportunity, traction, revenue potential, team capability, and growth rate.

**Equity** denotes ownership in the startup, usually represented by shares. Founders issue equity to investors in exchange for capital. **Equity dilution** occurs when new shares are created, reducing the percentage ownership of existing shareholders. A **capitalization table (cap table)** records ownership distribution, investor stakes, and dilution over time.

A **term sheet** outlines the key financial and governance terms of an investment deal. **Vesting** defines how founders or employees earn equity over a specified period, promoting long-term commitment. An **exit** refers to a liquidity event such as an acquisition or an initial public offering (IPO), allowing stakeholders to realize returns on their investment.

**Ask** refers to the specific amount of capital a founder seeks from investors in exchange for a defined percentage of equity. The **implied valuation** is derived from this ask and reflects how founders perceive the company's worth. Investors often assess whether the ask is justified based on traction, margins, and scalability.

**Strategic investors** are those who provide not only capital but also industry expertise, market access, or operational support. In some cases, alternative deal structures such as **royalty-based funding** are used, where investors receive a percentage of revenue until a predefined return is achieved, rather than equity ownership.

These terminologies enable transparent fundraising, informed negotiations, and sustainable financial governance in startups.

## 5.3 PRODUCT, TECHNOLOGY, AND GROWTH METRICS

This section presents the **most widely used and practically significant metrics** employed by startups to measure product performance, customer behavior, and business growth. These metrics support data-driven decision-making and are frequently referenced by founders, investors, and accelerators.

A **product roadmap** outlines the planned development of features and improvements over time, aligning product strategy with business objectives. **User experience (UX)** and **user interface (UI)** refer to how users interact with and perceive a product, directly influencing adoption and retention.

**Key Performance Indicators (KPIs)** are measurable values used to track progress toward strategic goals. Among the most critical growth metrics is **customer acquisition cost (CAC)**, which represents the cost of acquiring a new customer. **Lifetime value (LTV)** estimates the total revenue a business can expect from a customer over the entire relationship. A sustainable startup typically aims for an LTV-to-CAC ratio greater than one.

**Monthly recurring revenue (MRR)** and **annual recurring revenue (ARR)** are core metrics for subscription-based and SaaS startups, reflecting predictable revenue streams. **Churn rate** measures the percentage of customers who discontinue using a product within a given period, while **retention rate** indicates the startup's ability to keep customers engaged over time.

**Growth rate** tracks increase in users, revenue, or engagement and is often used as a proxy for market traction. **Traction** itself refers to early evidence of customer adoption or market validation. Collectively, these product, technology, and growth metrics provide a quantitative foundation for evaluating startup performance, scalability, and investment readiness.

**EBITA (Earnings Before Interest, Taxes, and Amortization)** is a profitability metric used to evaluate a startup's core operating performance by excluding financing costs, tax effects, and amortization of intangible assets. EBITA is most relevant for growth-stage startups with stable revenues, particularly those holding intellectual property or acquired intangible assets.

**Margins**, including **gross margin** and **net margin**, are closely monitored indicators of financial health. Gross margin reflects production efficiency, while net margin indicates overall profitability after all expenses. Investors frequently rely on margin analysis to assess sustainability and scalability.

## 5.4 LEGAL, COMPLIANCE, AND IP TERMINOLOGIES

This section introduces the **most essential legal, regulatory, and intellectual property (IP) terms** that startups commonly encounter during formation, operation, and scaling. Familiarity with these terms helps founders manage risk, protect innovation, and ensure regulatory compliance.

**Incorporation** refers to the legal process of registering a business entity, such as a private limited company, limited liability partnership (LLP), or corporation. **Founders' agreements** define roles, responsibilities, equity ownership, and decision-making rights among co-founders, reducing the risk of internal disputes.

**Compliance** involves adhering to applicable laws, regulations, and statutory requirements, including taxation, labor laws, and corporate filings. **Regulatory approvals** may be required depending on the sector, particularly in areas such as healthcare, biotechnology, fintech, and food technology.

**Intellectual property (IP)** protects creations of the mind that provide competitive advantage. **Patents** safeguard novel and useful inventions, while **trademarks** protect brand identifiers such as names, logos, and slogans. **Copyright** applies to original literary, artistic, and software works, and **trade secrets** protect confidential business information and know-how.

A **non-disclosure agreement (NDA)** is a legal contract that restricts the sharing of confidential information with third parties. **Licensing** allows a startup to grant or obtain rights to use IP in exchange for fees or royalties.

Together, these legal, compliance, and IP terminologies form the foundation for responsible governance, innovation protection, and long-term sustainability in startup ventures.

## 5.5 MARKETING AND SALES JARGON

This section covers the **most frequently used and outcome-oriented marketing and sales terminologies** that startups rely on to acquire customers, generate revenue, and scale market presence. These terms are central to go-to-market strategy and performance evaluation.

**Go-to-market (GTM) strategy** defines how a startup introduces its product or service to customers, including pricing, distribution channels, and promotional activities. **Target audience** refers to the specific group of potential customers a startup aims to reach, while a **buyer persona** represents a semi-fictional profile of an ideal customer based on data and insights.

A **lead** is a potential customer who has shown interest in the product. **Lead generation** involves activities that attract and capture such prospects. The **sales funnel** describes the stages a customer moves through, from awareness and interest to purchase and retention. **Conversion rate** measures the percentage of leads that become paying customers.

**Customer acquisition cost (CAC)**, also used in growth analysis, reflects the total cost of marketing and sales efforts required to acquire a customer.

**Revenue model** explains how the startup earns money, such as through subscriptions, licensing, freemium, or direct sales.

**Brand positioning** defines how a startup differentiates itself in the minds of customers relative to competitors. **Customer relationship management (CRM)** systems support the tracking and management of customer interactions and sales pipelines.

These marketing and sales terms enable startups to communicate value effectively, measure performance, and build sustainable customer relationships.

## 5.6 MANUFACTURING AND OPERATIONS TERMINOLOGIES

This section focuses on the **most commonly used manufacturing and operations terms** that startups encounter while converting ideas into deliverable products and services. These terminologies are critical for ensuring efficiency, quality, and scalability, particularly in product-based and hardware-driven ventures.

**Operations** refers to the day-to-day activities involved in producing and delivering a product or service. **Manufacturing** involves the transformation of raw materials or components into finished goods. **Process optimization** is the practice of improving workflows to reduce costs, time, and waste while maintaining quality.

**Supply chain** encompasses the network of suppliers, manufacturers, distributors, and logistics providers involved in product delivery. **Procurement** refers to sourcing and purchasing raw materials, components, or services. **Inventory management** involves controlling stock levels to balance availability with cost efficiency.

**Unit economics** analyzes the direct revenues and costs associated with a single unit of product or service, helping assess profitability at scale. **Cost of goods sold (COGS)** represents the direct costs attributable to production, excluding indirect expenses.

**Quality control (QC)** ensures products meet predefined standards, while **quality assurance (QA)** focuses on preventing defects through process design. **Scalability in operations** refers to the ability to increase production or service delivery without proportionate increases in operational complexity or cost.

**Proof of Concept (PoC)** refers to early evidence demonstrating that a product or technology is feasible and functional. PoC is particularly important in hardware, biotech, and manufacturing startups, where operational validation

precedes large-scale production.
**Defensibility**, often described as a **competitive moat**, reflects a startup's ability to protect its market position through intellectual property, cost advantages, brand strength, or process efficiencies.

Collectively, these manufacturing and operations terminologies support reliable execution, cost discipline, and sustainable growth in startups.

## 5.7 DIGITAL, SAAS, AND PLATFORM STARTUP TERMS

This section introduces the **most widely used and practically relevant terminologies** specific to digital, Software-as-a-Service (SaaS), and platform-based startups. These terms are essential for understanding technology-driven business models and data-centric growth strategies.

**Software as a Service (SaaS)** refers to a cloud-based software delivery model in which users access applications via the internet on a subscription basis. A **platform startup** provides a digital infrastructure that enables interactions between two or more user groups, such as buyers and sellers or service providers and consumers.

**Cloud computing** enables on-demand access to computing resources, reducing infrastructure costs and improving scalability. **Application Programming Interfaces (APIs)** allow different software systems to communicate and integrate with one another, enabling ecosystem expansion.

**User onboarding** describes the process of guiding new users to successfully adopt a product. **Active users**, commonly measured as **Daily Active Users (DAU)** or **Monthly Active Users (MAU)**, indicate user engagement levels. The **DAU/MAU ratio** is often used as a measure of product stickiness.

**Subscription model** is a recurring revenue model typical of SaaS startups, while **freemium** models offer basic services for free with paid premium features. **Churn**, particularly **subscription churn**, measures customer attrition and is a key indicator of long-term sustainability.

**Scalability in digital platforms** refers to the ability to support increasing users and transactions without degrading performance.

These terminologies collectively define how digital and SaaS startups build, deliver, and scale technology-enabled value.

## 5.8 INVESTOR AND INCUBATOR LANGUAGE

This section explains the **most frequently used and practically important terms** employed by investors, incubators, and accelerators when evaluating, mentoring, and funding startups. Familiarity with this language enables founders to communicate effectively with ecosystem stakeholders.

An **investor pitch** is a structured presentation that communicates a startup's problem, solution, market opportunity, traction, and financial outlook. A **pitch deck** is the visual document supporting this presentation. **Due diligence** refers to the detailed evaluation of a startup's business, financials, technology, and legal standing prior to investment.

**Traction** denotes measurable evidence of customer adoption, revenue growth, or market validation and is a primary factor in investment decisions. **Runway** indicates the length of time a startup can operate before exhausting available cash, based on current spending. **Burn rate** measures the rate at which a startup consumes capital.

An **incubator** supports early-stage startups through mentorship, workspace, and resources, while an **accelerator** provides time-bound, cohort-based programs focused on rapid growth and investment readiness. **Mentorship** involves guidance from experienced entrepreneurs or industry experts.

**Valuation expectations**, **follow-on funding**, and **exit potential** are commonly discussed in investor interactions. Understanding this shared language helps founders align expectations, negotiate effectively, and build credible relationships within the startup ecosystem.

**Skin in the game** describes the extent of a founder's personal financial or professional commitment to the startup. Investors often view significant founder commitment as a signal of confidence and accountability.

**Exit readiness** refers to how prepared a startup is for potential acquisition or public listing, based on governance, financial performance, and strategic positioning. Discussions around exit readiness and long-term return potential are common in investor evaluations, including those popularized through platforms such as **Shark Tank**.

## 5.9 COMMONLY MISUSED STARTUP TERMS

This section highlights **frequently misused or misunderstood startup terminologies** that often lead to unrealistic expectations, flawed strategies, or poor communication with stakeholders. Clarifying these terms is essential for developing sound entrepreneurial judgment.

A common misconception exists between **idea** and **startup**. An idea alone does not constitute a startup unless it is supported by execution, validation, and a viable business model. Similarly, **innovation** is often incorrectly equated with novelty; in practice, innovation must create measurable customer or market value.

**Product–market fit** is frequently claimed prematurely. True product–market fit requires consistent customer demand and retention, not isolated sales or user sign-ups. **Revenue** is also confused with **profitability**; generating revenue does not imply financial sustainability if costs exceed income.

The term **scalability** is often misapplied to any growing business. In startup contexts, scalability specifically refers to growth that does not require proportional increases in cost or resources. **Valuation** is another misunderstood term, often mistaken for cash value, whereas it represents an estimated worth based on assumptions and projections.

**EBITA** is often incorrectly used interchangeably with EBITDA. While both exclude interest and taxes, EBITDA also excludes depreciation, making it more common in capital-intensive industries. Misuse of these terms can lead to inaccurate financial interpretation and weakened investor credibility.

Finally, **funding** is sometimes perceived as success rather than a means to achieve growth. Overemphasis on fundraising without execution focus can weaken long-term viability. Addressing these misinterpretations helps founders adopt realistic, disciplined, and evidence-based startup practices.

## 5.10 DEVELOPING STARTUP LITERACY

Startup literacy refers to the **ability to understand, interpret, and apply startup-related terminology and concepts effectively** across business, technology, and investment contexts. It goes beyond memorizing definitions to developing contextual and strategic understanding.

Developing startup literacy enables entrepreneurs to communicate clearly with investors, mentors, customers, and regulators. It supports informed decision-making in areas such as product development, funding negotiations, compliance, and scaling strategies. For students and early-stage founders, literacy reduces cognitive gaps between theory and practice.

Startup literacy is strengthened through exposure to real-world case studies, pitch evaluations, metric analysis, and ecosystem interactions. Understanding when and how specific terms are used—rather than overusing jargon—enhances professional credibility and strategic clarity.

In an increasingly innovation-driven economy, startup literacy has become a core entrepreneurial competency. Mastery of commonly used startup terminology equips individuals to participate meaningfully in venture creation, evaluation, and ecosystem development, forming a strong foundation for sustainable entrepreneurial success.

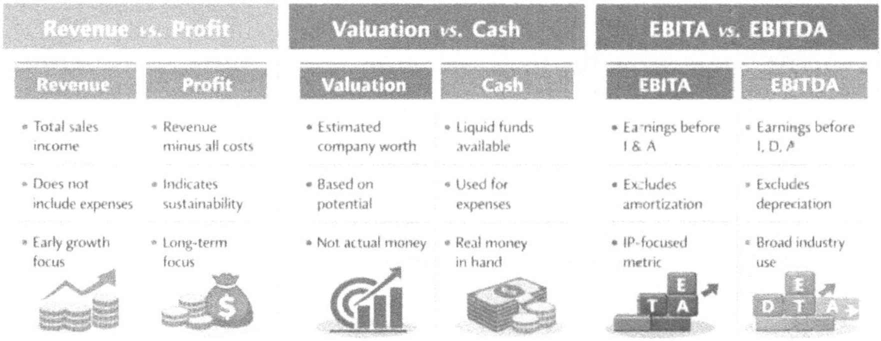


**Figure 5.2: Commonly Confused Startup Metrics (Revenue vs Profit, Valuation vs Cash, EBITA vs EBITDA).** Comparison of commonly confused startup financial metrics—Revenue versus Profit, Valuation versus Cash, and EBITA versus EBITDA—illustrating key distinctions in income measurement, liquidity, and operating profitability used in startup analysis and investor decision-making. In the context of EBITA and EBITDA: **I (Interest)** refers to the cost incurred on borrowed capital such as loans or debt and is excluded to enable comparison of operating performance independent of financing structure; **T (Taxes)** are statutory payments to the government that vary across jurisdictions and are excluded to standardize profitability assessment; **D (Depreciation)** represents the systematic allocation of the cost of tangible assets over their useful life and is a non-cash expense excluded in EBITDA; **A (Amortization)** refers to the gradual expensing of intangible assets such as patents, licenses, software, or goodwill and is excluded in both EBITA and EBITDA. **EBITA (Earnings Before Interest, Taxes, and Amortization)** measures operating profitability excluding financing costs, taxes, and amortization of intangible assets, whereas **EBITDA (Earnings Before Interest, Taxes, Depreciation, and Amortization)** further excludes depreciation and is widely used for capital-intensive and growth-stage businesses.

---

## REVIEW QUESTIONS AND EXERCISES

### A. Short Answer Questions

1. Define a startup and distinguish it from a traditional small business.
2. What is a value proposition, and why is it central to startup success?
3. Explain the difference between problem–solution fit and product–market fit.
4. What is meant by bootstrapping in the startup context?
5. Define valuation and explain the difference between pre-money and post-money valuation.
6. What is equity dilution, and why does it occur?
7. Define Customer Acquisition Cost (CAC) and Lifetime Value (LTV).
8. What is churn, and why is it a critical metric for SaaS startups?
9. Explain the concept of unit economics.

10. What is an exit in a startup lifecycle?

**B. Descriptive Questions**

1. Describe the key components of a startup business model.
2. Discuss the major funding stages in a startup's growth journey.
3. Explain the importance of KPIs in measuring startup performance.
4. Describe the role of intellectual property in creating startup defensibility.
5. Discuss commonly used marketing and sales terminologies in early-stage startups.
6. Explain the relevance of burn rate and runway in investor decision-making.
7. Differentiate between EBITA and EBITDA with suitable examples.
8. Discuss why valuation is often misunderstood by first-time founders.

**C. Analytical and Application-Based Questions**

1. A startup reports high revenue growth but negative profits. Analyze this situation using relevant terminologies from this chapter.
2. Explain how CAC, LTV, and churn together determine the sustainability of a SaaS business.
3. A founder claims product–market fit based on a few early sales. Critically evaluate this claim.
4. Analyze the impact of equity dilution on founders across multiple funding rounds.
5. Using Figure 5.2, explain why valuation should not be equated with cash availability.

## EXERCISES

**1. Terminology Matching Exercise:** Match the following terms with their correct descriptions: Startup, MVP, CAC, Burn Rate, Valuation, Equity, Churn, EBITA, Cap Table, Pivot.

**2. Case-Based Exercise:** You are evaluating a startup pitching for investment with the following details:

- Revenue: ₹50 lakh annually
- Profit: –₹10 lakh
- CAC: ₹2,000
- LTV: ₹12,000
- Monthly Burn Rate: ₹8 lakh

**Tasks:**

- Identify at least five startup terminologies applicable to this case.
- Evaluate whether the startup shows early traction.
- Comment on investment readiness using appropriate terminology.

**3. Figure Interpretation Exercise:** Refer to **Figure 5.2: Commonly Confused Startup Metrics**.
a) Explain one practical consequence of confusing revenue with profit.
b) Explain how misuse of EBITA and EBITDA can mislead investors.

**4. Practical Activity:** Prepare a **one-page glossary** of 15 startup terminologies from this chapter and explain each term in your own words with a real-world or Shark Tank–style example.

**5. Group Discussion / Debate:** "Funding is not success; execution is." Debate this statement using startup terminologies related to funding, traction, scalability, and profitability.

# CHAPTER-6

# TYPES OF E-COMMERCE MODELS

**Abstract**: This chapter examines the structural and technological foundations of modern digital commerce and the diverse business models that enable value creation in online markets. The chapter begins by tracing the evolution of digital business models, highlighting the transition from traditional web-based transactions to platform-driven, data-centric, and ecosystem-oriented commerce. It systematically analyzes core e-commerce formats, including business-to-consumer (B2C), business-to-business (B2B), consumer-to-consumer (C2C), and direct-to-consumer (D2C) models, emphasizing their operational logic, revenue mechanisms, and use cases. The discussion extends to marketplace and aggregator models, subscription and on-demand services, and platform-based ecosystems supported by the API economy. Emerging forms such as social commerce and mobile commerce are explored to illustrate the growing convergence of technology, user behavior, and digital engagement. The chapter also addresses cross-border e-commerce, focusing on global market access, logistics, and regulatory considerations. Critical enabling components such as digital payment systems and supporting infrastructure are examined alongside cybersecurity, data privacy, and compliance requirements. Concluding with an assessment of key challenges and future trends, this chapter equips learners with a comprehensive understanding of contemporary e-commerce models and their strategic implications in a rapidly evolving digital economy.

**Keywords:** E-Commerce Models; Digital Business Platforms; Marketplace and Aggregator Systems; Subscription and On-Demand Commerce; Digital Payments Infrastructure; Cybersecurity and Data Privacy

## 6.1 EVOLUTION OF DIGITAL BUSINESS MODELS

The evolution of digital business models reflects the progressive integration of information technology, the internet, and data-driven innovation into commercial activities. Early digital business models emerged in the 1990s with the commercialization of the internet, primarily focusing on **electronic storefronts** that replicated traditional retail transactions in an online environment (Fig 6.1). These initial models were largely static, transaction-oriented, and limited to basic online catalogues, email-based communication, and simple payment mechanisms.

With the advancement of broadband connectivity, secure payment gateways, and web technologies in the early 2000s, digital businesses began shifting from mere online presence to **process digitization and efficiency-driven models**. E-commerce platforms enabled automated order processing, digital marketing, and supply chain integration, leading to improved scalability and reduced operational costs. During this phase, business models focused on reach expansion, cost optimization, and convenience.

The next stage of evolution was marked by the rise of **platform-based and network-driven models**, fueled by Web 2.0 technologies, social media, and mobile internet. Digital businesses transitioned from selling products alone to facilitating interactions between multiple user groups. Value creation increasingly depended on **network effects**, user-generated content, and data analytics rather than asset ownership. Marketplaces, aggregators, and service platforms became dominant structures in this phase.

In recent years, the evolution has further accelerated with the emergence of **cloud computing, mobile commerce, artificial intelligence, and application programming interfaces (APIs)**. Digital business models are now ecosystem-oriented, enabling seamless integration with third-party services, real-time personalization, and on-demand value delivery. Subscription-based, freemium, and data-driven revenue models have gained prominence, emphasizing recurring income and long-term customer engagement.

Overall, the evolution of digital business models represents a shift from transaction-centric approaches to **platform-enabled, data-intensive, and customer-centric ecosystems**, forming the foundation of contemporary e-commerce and digital entrepreneurship.

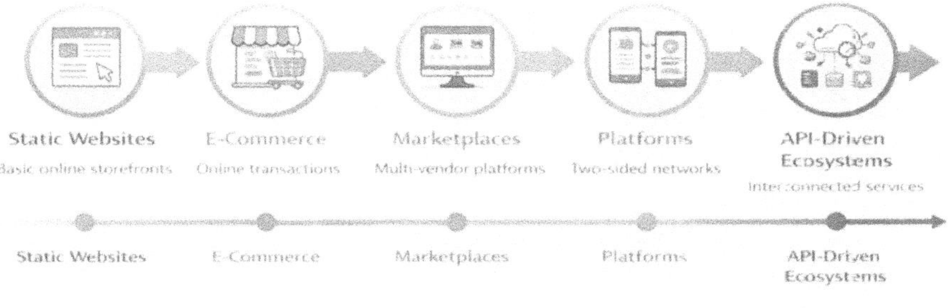


**Figure 6.1: Evolution of Digital Business Models**. Evolution of digital business models illustrating the progression from early web-based online storefronts to integrated e-commerce platforms, marketplace and aggregator structures, and contemporary platform-driven, API-enabled digital ecosystems that emphasize scalability, network effects, and data-centric value creation.

## 6.2 B2C, B2B, C2C, AND D2C MODELS

E-commerce business models are commonly classified based on the nature of participants involved in digital transactions (Fig 6.2). Among these, **Business-to-Consumer (B2C), Business-to-Business (B2B), Consumer-to-Consumer (C2C), and Direct-to-Consumer (D2C)** models represent the most widely adopted and operationally significant structures in the digital economy.

The **Business-to-Consumer (B2C)** model involves online transactions between businesses and individual consumers. This is the most visible and widely recognized form of e-commerce, encompassing online retail, digital services, and content delivery platforms. B2C models focus on high transaction volumes, customer experience, brand engagement, and efficient logistics. Pricing strategies, digital marketing, personalization, and customer service play a critical role in achieving competitive advantage in B2C environments.

The **Business-to-Business (B2B)** model facilitates digital transactions between organizations, such as manufacturers, wholesalers, distributors, and service providers. B2B e-commerce typically involves larger order values, longer sales cycles, negotiated pricing, and repeat contractual relationships. Digital B2B platforms emphasize process automation, supply chain integration, procurement efficiency, and relationship management rather than impulse purchasing.

The **Consumer-to-Consumer (C2C)** model enables individuals to buy and sell goods or services directly with one another through digital platforms that act as intermediaries. These platforms provide listing services, payment facilitation, trust mechanisms, and dispute resolution. Trust, reputation systems, and peer reviews are central to the success of C2C models, which are commonly used for resale, rentals, and peer-based services.

The **Direct-to-Consumer (D2C)** model allows manufacturers or brand owners to sell directly to end consumers without relying on traditional intermediaries such as wholesalers or retailers. D2C models offer greater control over branding, pricing, customer data, and engagement. They are particularly effective in leveraging digital marketing, social media, and personalized communication to build long-term customer relationships.

| Transaction Type of E-commerce | | Consumer of Product/Service | | |
|---|---|---|---|---|
| | | Consumer | Business | Government |
| Provider of Product/Service | Consumer | C2C | C2B | C2G |
| | Businesses | B2C | B2B | B2G |
| | Government | G2C | G2B | G2G |

**Figure 6.2: Classification of E-Commerce Models**. This figure presents a matrix classification of e-commerce transaction types based on the relationship between the provider of a product or service and its end consumer. It illustrates key interaction models including consumer-to-consumer (C2C), business-to-consumer (B2C), business-to-business (B2B), consumer-to-government (C2G), business-to-government (B2G), government-to-citizen (G2C), government-to-business (G2B), and government-to-government (G2G), highlighting the diversity of digital commerce structures.

Collectively, these models illustrate how digital commerce adapts transaction structures to different market needs, value propositions, and strategic objectives, forming the foundational architecture of modern e-commerce ecosystems.

## 6.3 MARKETPLACE AND AGGREGATOR MODELS

Marketplace and aggregator models represent a significant evolution in e-commerce, shifting the focus from direct selling to **facilitating exchanges between multiple stakeholders**. These models derive value primarily from intermediation, coordination, and platform governance rather than ownership of products or services (Fig 6.3).

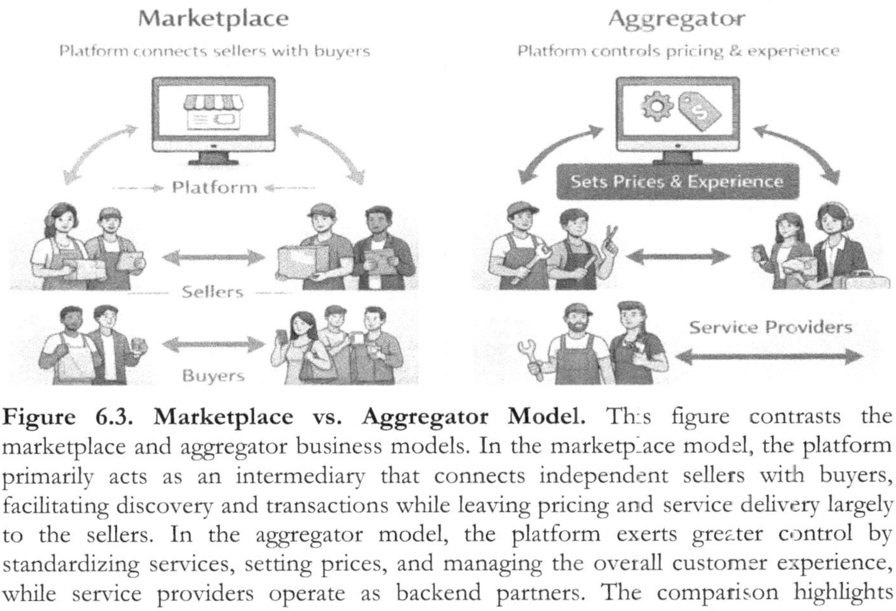


**Figure 6.3. Marketplace vs. Aggregator Model.** This figure contrasts the marketplace and aggregator business models. In the marketplace model, the platform primarily acts as an intermediary that connects independent sellers with buyers, facilitating discovery and transactions while leaving pricing and service delivery largely to the sellers. In the aggregator model, the platform exerts greater control by standardizing services, setting prices, and managing the overall customer experience, while service providers operate as backend partners. The comparison highlights differences in control, value creation, and operational structure between the two models.

A **marketplace model** is a digital platform that connects multiple sellers with multiple buyers, enabling transactions within a unified digital environment. The platform typically does not own inventory but provides infrastructure for product listing, discovery, payment processing, logistics coordination, and dispute resolution. Revenue is generated through commissions, listing fees, transaction fees, or value-added services. Marketplaces benefit from **network effects**, where the value of the platform increases as more buyers and sellers participate. Trust mechanisms such as ratings, reviews, and seller verification play a critical role in sustaining marketplace credibility and user engagement.

An **aggregator model** operates by bringing together multiple service providers under a single brand and standardized user experience. Unlike marketplaces, aggregators often exert greater control over pricing, service quality, and customer interaction. The platform acts as a centralized interface while service delivery is executed by independent providers. Aggregator models are commonly used in sectors such as transportation, food delivery, accommodation, and professional services. Their success depends on demand aggregation, operational efficiency, and consistent service standards.

Both models leverage data analytics to optimize matching, pricing, and customer engagement. However, they differ in governance structure, control mechanisms, and risk distribution. Marketplaces emphasize openness and scalability, while aggregators prioritize uniformity and brand-led trust.

Together, marketplace and aggregator models have reshaped digital commerce by reducing transaction friction, expanding consumer choice, and enabling scalable, asset-light business structures within the e-commerce ecosystem.

## 6.4 SUBSCRIPTION AND ON-DEMAND MODELS

Subscription and on-demand models have emerged as prominent e-commerce structures in response to changing consumer preferences for convenience, flexibility, and continuous value delivery. These models emphasize recurring engagement rather than one-time transactions and are increasingly prevalent across digital products and services.

The **subscription model** is based on customers paying a recurring fee—monthly, quarterly, or annually—to access a product or service. This model provides predictable and stable revenue streams for businesses while offering ongoing value to customers. Subscription-based commerce is widely used in digital content platforms, software services, consumer goods replenishment, and membership-based offerings. Key success factors include customer retention, perceived value, personalization, and low churn rates. Businesses adopting subscription models rely heavily on data analytics to understand usage patterns and optimize pricing and service features.

The **on-demand model** delivers products or services instantly or within a short time frame in response to real-time customer requests. This model is driven by mobile technology, location-based services, and efficient logistics networks. On-demand commerce is commonly applied in food delivery, transportation, home services, and digital labor platforms. Speed, reliability, and user experience are critical determinants of customer satisfaction in on-demand systems.

Both models are supported by digital infrastructure such as cloud computing, mobile applications, and integrated payment systems. While subscription models focus on long-term relationships and recurring value, on-demand models prioritize immediacy and convenience. Together, they represent a shift in e-commerce toward **customer-centric, usage-based, and experience-driven business models**, reshaping consumption patterns and competitive strategies in the digital economy.

## 6.5 PLATFORM-BASED AND API ECONOMY

Platform-based business models represent an advanced stage in the evolution of e-commerce, where value creation occurs through **digital ecosystems rather than linear value chains**. In this model, a platform serves as a technological and organizational foundation that enables interactions among multiple participants such as consumers, producers, service providers, and third-party developers.

A **platform-based model** facilitates exchanges by providing standardized rules, interfaces, and infrastructure rather than directly producing goods or services. The platform's core function is to enable efficient matchmaking, coordination, and value co-creation among ecosystem participants. Revenue generation may occur through transaction fees, subscriptions, advertising, data monetization, or value-added services. Network effects are central to platform success, as increased participation on one side of the platform enhances value for other participants.

Closely associated with platform models is the **API (Application Programming Interface) economy**, which allows external developers and businesses to integrate services, data, and functionalities seamlessly. APIs enable modularity and interoperability, allowing platforms to expand their capabilities without internal development of every feature. Through APIs, businesses can access payment services, logistics solutions, analytics tools, and third-party applications, accelerate innovation and reduce time to market.

The API economy supports the creation of **open and scalable digital ecosystems**, where multiple firms collaborate and compete simultaneously. For startups and digital enterprises, platform-based and API-driven models offer strategic advantages such as rapid scaling, flexibility, and ecosystem leverage.

Overall, platform-based models and the API economy redefine e-commerce by shifting competition from individual firms to interconnected ecosystems, emphasizing collaboration, integration, and continuous innovation.

## 6.6 SOCIAL AND MOBILE COMMERCE

Social and mobile commerce represent the convergence of digital commerce with social networking platforms and mobile technologies, fundamentally transforming how consumers discover, evaluate, and purchase products and services. These models leverage user engagement, peer influence, and ubiquitous mobile access to create seamless and interactive shopping experiences.

**Social commerce** integrates e-commerce functionalities directly within social media platforms, enabling users to browse, review, and purchase products without leaving the social environment. Purchasing decisions in social commerce are strongly influenced by social interactions, user-generated content, reviews, ratings, and influencer endorsements. Trust, community engagement, and authenticity play a critical role, as consumers rely on peer validation rather than traditional advertising alone. Social commerce also enables businesses to engage customers through live selling, interactive content, and personalized recommendations.

**Mobile commerce (m-commerce)** refers to e-commerce transactions conducted via smartphones and other mobile devices. The widespread adoption of mobile internet, digital wallets, and mobile applications has made m-commerce a dominant channel in digital transactions. Mobile commerce emphasizes convenience, speed, and location-based services, allowing consumers to shop anytime and anywhere. Features such as push notifications, app-based loyalty programs, and one-click payments enhance user engagement and repeat purchases.

Both social and mobile commerce models are data-driven and rely heavily on analytics to understand consumer behavior, preferences, and engagement patterns. They reduce friction in the purchasing journey and enable businesses to maintain continuous customer interaction.

Together, social and mobile commerce models reflect a shift toward **experience-driven, community-influenced, and always-connected commerce**, reshaping digital marketing strategies and redefining customer engagement in the e-commerce ecosystem.

## 6.7 CROSS-BORDER E-COMMERCE

Cross-border e-commerce refers to digital commercial transactions in which buyers and sellers are located in different countries. This model enables businesses, particularly small and medium enterprises and startups, to access global markets without establishing a physical presence abroad. Advances in digital platforms, logistics, and payment systems have significantly lowered entry barriers to international trade (Fig 6.4).

In cross-border e-commerce, businesses leverage online marketplaces, direct-to-consumer websites, and platform-based ecosystems to reach international customers. Key drivers include expanding internet penetration, global demand for diverse products, and consumer willingness to purchase from foreign sellers. This model allows firms to diversify revenue sources and reduce dependence on domestic markets.

However, cross-border e-commerce introduces additional complexity compared to domestic transactions. **Logistics and fulfillment** play a critical role, involving international shipping, customs clearance, warehousing, and last-mile delivery. **Customs duties, taxes, and tariffs** directly affect pricing strategies and profit margins. Compliance with international trade regulations, import–export laws, and product standards is essential to avoid legal and operational risks.

**Currency exchange**, **cross-border payments**, and **foreign exchange risk** are also central considerations, requiring reliable payment gateways and transparent pricing mechanisms. Additionally, differences in consumer behavior, language, cultural preferences, and local regulations necessitate localization of content, customer support, and marketing strategies. Overall, cross-border e-commerce expands market reach and growth opportunities but demands strong operational capabilities, regulatory awareness, and digital infrastructure to ensure efficiency, trust, and long-term sustainability in global digital trade.

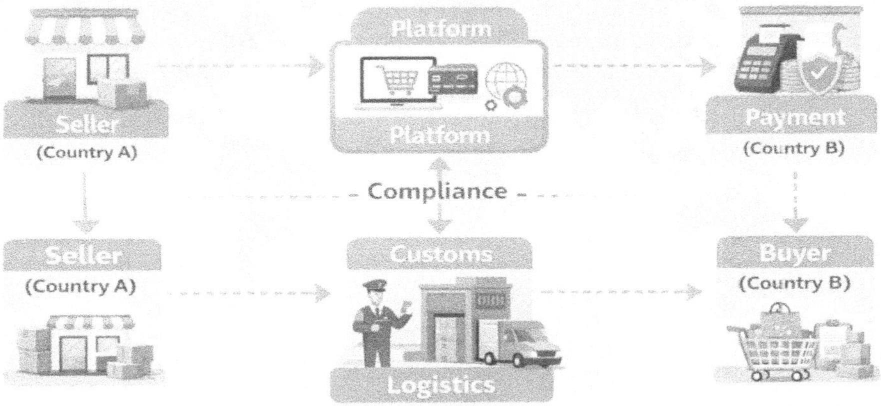


**Figure 6.4: Cross-Border E-Commerce Flow**. Illustration of the cross-border e-commerce transaction process showing the movement of goods, payments, and information between a seller in Country A and a buyer in Country B through a digital platform. The figure highlights key stages including platform intermediation, cross-border payment processing, regulatory compliance, customs clearance, logistics and fulfillment, and final delivery to the international consumer.

## 6.8 PAYMENT SYSTEMS AND DIGITAL INFRASTRUCTURE

Payment systems and digital infrastructure form the backbone of e-commerce operations, enabling secure, efficient, and scalable online transactions. The effectiveness of an e-commerce model is closely linked to the reliability of its payment mechanisms and the robustness of the underlying digital infrastructure (Fig 6.5).

**Digital payment systems** facilitate the transfer of value between buyers and sellers in an online environment. These include credit and debit cards, internet banking, digital wallets, mobile payments, and real-time payment systems. For e-commerce businesses, payment systems must ensure transaction security, speed, convenience, and interoperability across devices and platforms.

Features such as one-click payments, auto-debit, and recurring billing are particularly important for subscription and on-demand models.

Supporting these systems is the broader **digital infrastructure**, which includes cloud computing, data centers, network connectivity, and transaction processing platforms. Cloud-based infrastructure enables scalability, allowing e-commerce platforms to handle fluctuating traffic, seasonal demand, and rapid growth without significant upfront investment. Application programming interfaces (APIs) further enable seamless integration between payment gateways, banks, marketplaces, and third-party services.

Security is a critical component of payment infrastructure. Encryption, authentication mechanisms, and fraud detection systems protect transactions and build user trust. Reliability and uptime are equally important, as payment failures directly affect customer experience and revenue continuity. Overall, efficient payment systems and resilient digital infrastructure are essential enablers of modern e-commerce. They support operational efficiency, enhance customer confidence, and allow digital business models to scale across markets, devices, and geographies.

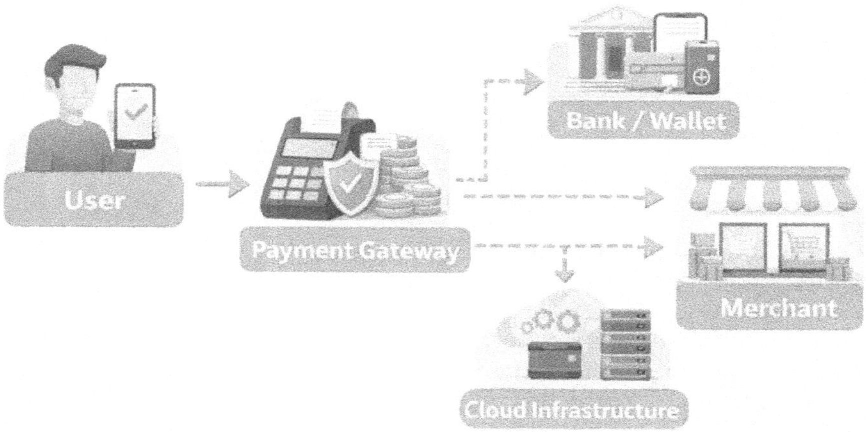


**Figure 6.5: Digital Payment Systems and Infrastructure.** Illustration of the digital payment ecosystem in e-commerce, depicting the flow of transaction data and funds from the user through a secure payment gateway to banks or digital wallets, supported by cloud-based infrastructure, and finally to the merchant. The figure highlights the integration of payment processing, financial institutions, and digital infrastructure that enables secure, scalable, and real-time online transactions.

## 6.9 CYBERSECURITY, DATA PRIVACY, AND COMPLIANCE

As e-commerce platforms increasingly rely on digital transactions, data exchange, and interconnected systems, **cybersecurity, data privacy, and regulatory compliance** have become critical determinants of trust, resilience, and sustainability in digital business models. Any compromise in these areas can lead to financial loss, reputational damage, and legal consequences (Fig 6.6).

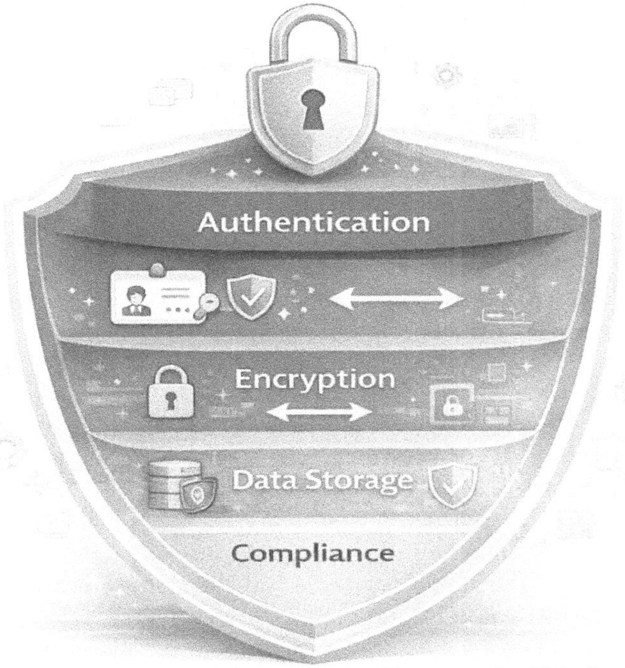


**Figure 6.6: Cybersecurity and Data Privacy Framework.** This figure illustrates a layered cybersecurity and data privacy framework highlighting four critical protection levels: authentication, encryption, secure data storage, and regulatory compliance. The model emphasizes how trust in digital business environments is built through progressive security controls that safeguard user identity, protect information flow, ensure data integrity, and enforce legal and ethical compliance. Together, these layers form a comprehensive foundation for secure, resilient, and trustworthy digital platforms.

**Cybersecurity** refers to the protection of digital systems, networks, and data from unauthorized access, cyberattacks, fraud, and service disruptions. E-commerce platforms are frequent targets of threats such as data breaches, phishing, malware, ransomware, and denial-of-service attacks. Effective cybersecurity strategies include secure system architecture, encryption, authentication protocols, regular security audits, and real-time threat monitoring. Ensuring transaction security is particularly important in payment processing and customer data handling.

**Data privacy** focuses on the responsible collection, storage, processing, and use of personal and transactional data. E-commerce businesses routinely handle sensitive information such as customer identities, payment details, and behavioral data. Compliance with data protection principles—such as consent, purpose limitation, data minimization, and transparency—is essential to maintain user trust. Privacy-by-design approaches and secure data management practices are increasingly integrated into digital business operations.

**Regulatory compliance** involves adherence to applicable laws, standards, and guidelines governing digital commerce. These may include data protection regulations, consumer protection laws, electronic transaction rules, and sector-specific standards. Cross-border e-commerce further increases compliance complexity due to variations in legal frameworks across jurisdictions.

Collectively, cybersecurity, data privacy, and compliance are not merely technical or legal requirements but strategic components of e-commerce governance. Robust practices in these areas enhance platform credibility, reduce risk exposure, and support long-term growth in the digital economy.

## 6.10 CHALLENGES AND FUTURE OF E-COMMERCE

Despite its rapid growth and transformative impact, e-commerce faces several **structural, technological, and regulatory challenges** that influence its sustainability and future trajectory. Understanding these challenges is essential for designing resilient and competitive digital business models.

One of the primary challenges is **intense competition and market saturation**, particularly in B2C and marketplace segments. Low entry barriers have led to price wars, high customer acquisition costs, and declining margins. **Customer trust and retention** also remain persistent issues, driven by concerns related to product authenticity, service quality, data privacy, and cybersecurity threats.

**Logistics and supply chain complexity** present another major challenge, especially in on-demand and cross-border e-commerce. Delays, high fulfillment costs, reverse logistics, and last-mile delivery inefficiencies directly affect customer experience and profitability. Additionally, **regulatory uncertainty and compliance burden**, including taxation, data protection, and consumer rights regulations, create operational challenges, particularly for startups operating across multiple jurisdictions.

Looking ahead, the future of e-commerce is shaped by **technological advancement and evolving consumer behavior**. Artificial intelligence, machine learning, and data analytics are expected to drive hyper-personalization, demand forecasting, and intelligent pricing. The integration of immersive technologies such as augmented reality and virtual reality will enhance product visualization and customer engagement. Platform ecosystems and API-driven integration will continue to expand, enabling collaboration across industries.

Sustainability, ethical commerce, and responsible data use are also emerging as critical priorities. Overall, the future of e-commerce lies in **adaptive, technology-enabled, and trust-centric business models** that balance innovation with regulatory compliance and customer value creation in an increasingly digital global economy.

## KEY CONCEPTS & DEFINITIONS

**E-Commerce**: The buying and selling of goods and services through electronic networks, primarily the internet, including digital payments and online service delivery.
**Digital Business Model**: A framework that explains how a firm creates, delivers, and captures value using digital technologies and online platforms.
**Business-to-Consumer (B2C)**: An e-commerce model in which businesses sell products or services directly to individual consumers through digital channels.
**Business-to-Business (B2B)**: An e-commerce model involving online transactions between businesses, typically characterized by bulk orders, negotiated pricing, and long-term relationships.
**Consumer-to-Consumer (C2C)**: A model that enables individuals to sell goods or services directly to other individuals through digital platforms acting as intermediaries.
**Direct-to-Consumer (D2C)**: An e-commerce model where manufacturers or brand owners sell directly to end customers without intermediaries, gaining control over branding, pricing, and customer data.
**Marketplace Model**: A digital platform that connects multiple sellers with multiple buyers and facilitates transactions without owning inventory.
**Aggregator Model**: A platform-based model that unifies multiple service providers under a single brand, standardized pricing, and controlled customer experience.
**Subscription Model**: A revenue model in which customers pay recurring fees at regular intervals to access products or services.
**On-Demand Model**: A model that delivers goods or services instantly or within a short time frame in response to real-time customer requests.
**Platform-Based Model**: A digital business model that enables interactions and value exchange among multiple user groups through a shared technological infrastructure.
**API Economy**: An ecosystem where businesses expose and consume services through Application Programming Interfaces to enable integration, scalability, and innovation.
**Social Commerce**: E-commerce activities conducted through social media platforms, influenced by social interactions, content sharing, and peer recommendations.
**Mobile Commerce (M-Commerce)**: Online commercial transactions carried out using mobile devices such as smartphones and tablets.
**Cross-Border E-Commerce**: Online trade where buyers and sellers are located in different countries, involving international logistics, payments, and

regulatory compliance.
**Digital Payment Systems**: Electronic mechanisms that enable online monetary transactions, including cards, wallets, mobile payments, and real-time payment platforms.
**Digital Infrastructure**: The technological foundation supporting e-commerce operations, including cloud computing, networks, servers, and transaction-processing systems.
**Cybersecurity**: The protection of digital systems, networks, and data from unauthorized access, cyberattacks, and fraud.
**Data Privacy**: The ethical and legal management of personal and transactional data, ensuring consent, security, and transparency in data usage.
**Regulatory Compliance**: Adherence to laws, standards, and regulations governing digital transactions, consumer protection, data security, and online business operations.
**Network Effects**: A phenomenon where the value of a digital platform increases as more users participate on one or more sides of the platform.
**Scalability**: The ability of an e-commerce model to handle growth in users, transactions, or revenue without a proportional increase in cost or complexity.

---

**Mini Case Study 1: B2C and Marketplace Evolution**

A global e-commerce company began as an online bookstore and gradually expanded into a multi-category digital retail platform. Over time, it transitioned from a pure **B2C model** to a **marketplace-based model**, allowing third-party sellers to list products alongside company-owned inventory. This shift enabled rapid assortment expansion without proportional inventory risk. The platform monetized transactions through commissions, fulfillment services, and advertising. Strong logistics infrastructure, data analytics, and customer-centric policies enhanced trust and repeat purchases.

**Key Learning Points:**

- Transition from inventory-led B2C to asset-light marketplace
- Role of network effects in scaling e-commerce platforms
- Importance of logistics and digital infrastructure in customer experience

---

**Mini Case Study 2: Subscription-Based Digital Commerce**

A digital entertainment company adopted a **subscription-based e-commerce model**, offering unlimited access to content for a recurring monthly fee. Instead of relying on one-time transactions, the firm focused on customer retention, personalization, and content recommendation algorithms. Predictable recurring revenue enabled long-term investment in original content and technology infrastructure. The success of the model depended heavily on low churn, seamless payment systems, and continuous value delivery.

**Key Learning Points:**

- Advantages of subscription models in revenue predictability

- Importance of data analytics and personalization
- Relationship between churn management and long-term sustainability

**Mini Case Study 3: Social and Mobile Commerce Integration**
A direct-to-consumer fashion brand leveraged **social and mobile commerce** to build its customer base without traditional retail presence. The company used social media platforms for product discovery, influencer marketing, and live product launches, while mobile-optimized websites and digital wallets enabled frictionless purchasing. Customer feedback from social channels informed rapid product iterations. This approach reduced marketing costs and strengthened brand–customer relationships.
**Key Learning Points:**

- Integration of social engagement with mobile commerce
- Role of community and influencer trust in purchasing decisions
- Benefits of D2C models in customer data ownership and agility

## REVIEW QUESTIONS AND EXERCISES

## REVIEW QUESTIONS

### A. Short Answer Questions

1. Define digital business models in the context of e-commerce.
2. What factors contributed to the evolution of digital business models?
3. Differentiate between B2C and B2B e-commerce models.
4. What is a D2C model, and how does it differ from traditional retail?
5. Explain the role of network effects in marketplace models.
6. What distinguishes an aggregator model from a marketplace model?
7. Define subscription-based e-commerce.
8. What is on-demand commerce? Provide one example.
9. What is meant by the API economy?
10. Why is digital infrastructure critical for e-commerce operations?

### B. Descriptive Questions

1. Discuss the evolution of digital business models from web-based commerce to platform ecosystems.
2. Explain the operational characteristics of B2C, B2B, C2C, and D2C models.
3. Describe marketplace and aggregator models with their revenue mechanisms.
4. Discuss the advantages and limitations of subscription and on-demand e-commerce models.

5. Explain the significance of platform-based models in modern e-commerce.
6. Discuss the growth of social and mobile commerce and its impact on consumer behavior.
7. Explain the concept of cross-border e-commerce and its operational challenges.
8. Describe the role of payment systems and digital infrastructure in enabling e-commerce.
9. Discuss the importance of cybersecurity and data privacy in digital commerce.

**C. Analytical and Application-Based Questions**

1. Analyze how platform-based models create value compared to traditional linear business models.
2. A manufacturer plans to eliminate intermediaries and sell directly online. Which e-commerce model should be adopted and why?
3. Evaluate the risks and benefits of cross-border e-commerce for startups.
4. Compare subscription and on-demand models in terms of revenue predictability and customer retention.
5. Analyze how cybersecurity failures can impact consumer trust and long-term business sustainability.
6. Assess the future potential of social commerce in emerging markets.

## EXERCISES

**1. Classification Exercise:** Classify the following businesses under appropriate e-commerce models and justify your choice: Online grocery app, SaaS-based accounting software, peer-to-peer resale platform, manufacturer-owned brand website.

**2. Case-Based Exercise:** A startup operates a mobile app that connects independent service providers with customers, controls pricing, and manages customer experience.

**Tasks:**

a) Identify the e-commerce model used.
b) Explain the revenue sources of this model.
c) Discuss two operational challenges associated with it.

**3. Comparative Table Exercise:** Prepare a comparative table highlighting differences among B2C, B2B, C2C, and D2C models with respect to customers, transaction size, pricing, and relationship duration.

**4. Figure Interpretation Exercise:** Using the concepts discussed in this chapter, explain how digital infrastructure and payment systems enable scalability in e-commerce models.

**5. Group Discussion / Debate:** "Platform-based e-commerce models are more sustainable than traditional online retail models." Debate this statement using appropriate concepts from the chapter.

**6. Practical Activity:** Select an existing e-commerce business and:
a) Identify its primary business model.
b) Analyze its payment systems and digital infrastructure.
c) Comment on cybersecurity and data privacy measures likely required for its operations.

# CHAPTER-7

# FUNDING & INVESTMENT STRATEGIES

**Abstract**: This chapter provides a comprehensive and practice-oriented examination of the financial pathways that enable startups to move from ideation to scale and eventual exit. The chapter begins by outlining bootstrapping and early-stage funding approaches, emphasizing founder discipline, resource optimization, and validation-driven capital deployment. It then explores external funding avenues, including angel investors, syndicates, venture capital, private equity, and corporate or strategic investments, highlighting their strategic intent, risk appetite, and value addition beyond capital. With a dedicated focus on India, the chapter reviews key government schemes and grant mechanisms that support innovation, entrepreneurship, and technology commercialization. Core financial concepts such as startup valuation methodologies, term sheets, and deal structures are explained in a structured and accessible manner to equip founders with negotiation and decision-making capabilities. The chapter further addresses financial planning, burn rate management, and investor due diligence as critical components of sustainable growth and investor readiness. It concludes with an analysis of exit strategies and liquidity events, linking funding decisions across the startup lifecycle to long-term value creation and stakeholder outcomes. Collectively, this chapter serves as a strategic guide for students, entrepreneurs, and practitioners to understand, evaluate, and execute effective funding and investment decisions in dynamic entrepreneurial ecosystems.

**Keywords:** Startup funding, Angel investment, Venture capital, Government grants, Startup valuation, Exit strategies

## 7.1 STARTUP BOOTSTRAPPING AND EARLY FUNDING

Startup bootstrapping and early funding represent the foundational phase of venture financing, where entrepreneurs focus on building, validating, and sustaining the business with minimal external capital. This stage is critical because financial decisions made early often shape the startup's culture, ownership structure, risk tolerance, and long-term strategic flexibility (Fig 7.1).

**Bootstrapping** refers to financing a startup using the founders' personal savings, retained earnings, revenues generated from early customers, or informal support from family and friends. The core philosophy of bootstrapping is *capital efficiency*. Founders rely on lean operations, incremental growth, and rapid market feedback rather than aggressive capital infusion. Bootstrapped startups typically prioritize problem–solution fit, customer validation, and early cash flow generation. This approach enables founders to retain full ownership and control, avoid premature dilution, and build resilience through disciplined financial management. However, bootstrapping also imposes constraints, including slower scaling, limited ability to absorb risk, and dependence on early revenue streams.

**Early funding** bridges the gap between pure bootstrapping and institutional investment. It often includes pre-seed and seed capital raised from founders' networks, angel investors, micro-VCs, incubators, and accelerators. Early funding is primarily used to develop a minimum viable product (MVP), validate market demand, acquire initial customers, and build a core team. At this stage, investors typically evaluate the founding team, the problem being addressed, the proposed solution, and early traction indicators rather than formal financial performance.

Common early funding instruments include founder equity contributions, convertible notes, SAFE (Simple Agreement for Future Equity) instruments, and seed equity rounds. These mechanisms are designed to balance investor risk with founder flexibility, often deferring precise valuation until later stages when the business model is clearer. Strategic use of early funding allows startups to achieve key milestones—such as product validation, regulatory approvals, or pilot deployments—that improve credibility and valuation in subsequent funding rounds.

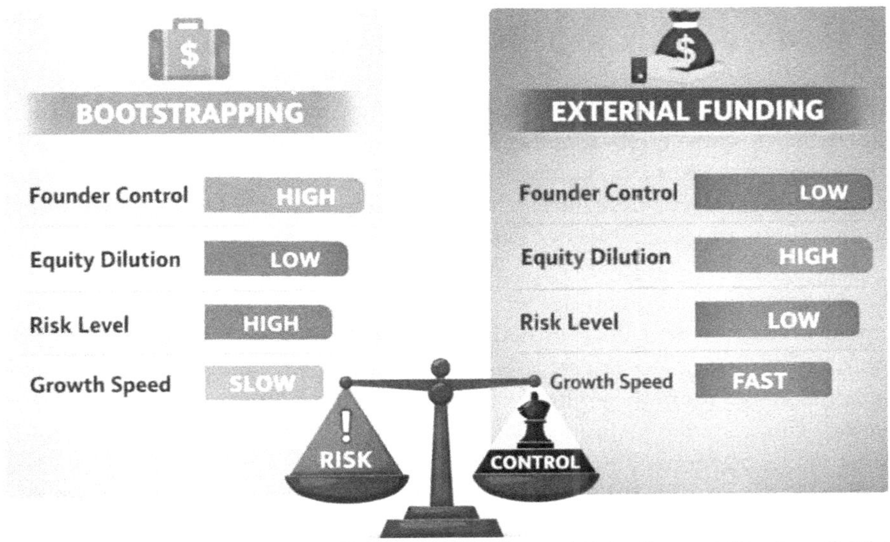


**Figure 7.1: Bootstrapping vs External Funding – Risk–Control Trade-off.** This figure illustrates the strategic trade-offs between bootstrapping and external funding models in startups. Bootstrapping is characterized by high founder control, minimal equity dilution, higher personal and operational risk, and relatively slower growth. In contrast, external funding enables faster scaling and reduced immediate risk through capital infusion, but involves significant equity dilution and reduced founder control. The diagram highlights how funding choice directly influences control, risk exposure, ownership structure, and growth velocity.

In summary, startup bootstrapping and early funding emphasize *financial discipline, validation-first growth, and strategic capital use*. A well-managed early funding phase not only reduces capital risk but also strengthens the startup's negotiating position with future investors, laying a robust foundation for scalable and sustainable growth (Fig 7.2).

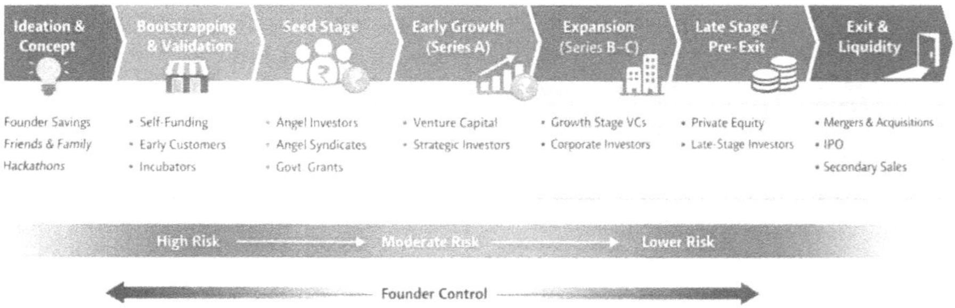


**Figure 7.2: Startup Funding Lifecycle Across Growth Stages**. The figure illustrates the progressive evolution of startup financing aligned with venture maturity, from ideation and bootstrapping through angel and venture capital funding to private equity participation and exit or liquidity events. It highlights the corresponding shift in risk levels and founder control across different stages of the startup lifecycle.

## 7.2 ANGEL INVESTORS AND SYNDICATES

Angel investors and angel syndicates play a pivotal role in bridging the financing gap between early bootstrapping and institutional venture capital. Typically engaging at the pre-seed and seed stages, angels provide not only risk capital but also mentorship, domain expertise, and access to professional networks, making them critical enablers of early-stage startup success.

**Angel investors** are high-net-worth individuals who invest their personal capital in startups with high growth potential. Their investment decisions are often driven by a combination of financial return, strategic interest, and personal motivation to support entrepreneurship or innovation in specific sectors. Compared to institutional investors, angels tend to adopt a longer-term perspective, demonstrate higher risk tolerance, and apply more flexible evaluation criteria. Key factors influencing angel investment include the credibility and commitment of the founding team, clarity of the problem–solution fit, scalability of the business model, and early signs of market traction. In addition to funding, angels frequently act as advisors, board members, or informal mentors, contributing significantly to strategic decision-making during formative stages.

**Angel syndicates** are structured groups of angel investors who collectively invest in startups. Syndication allows individual angels to diversify risk, pool expertise, and participate in larger funding rounds than they could independently. Typically, a *lead angel* conducts initial due diligence, negotiates terms, and represents the syndicate's interests, while other members co-invest under the same terms. For startups, syndicates offer access to a broader base of capital, collective industry knowledge, and extended professional networks, albeit with increased expectations around reporting and governance.

From a founder's perspective, engaging with angels and syndicates requires strategic alignment. Beyond capital, founders must evaluate the investor's experience, sector knowledge, value addition potential, and long-term vision. Misalignment at this stage can lead to governance challenges or strategic conflicts in later funding rounds. Equity dilution, decision rights, and follow-on investment capacity should therefore be carefully assessed before closing angel investments.

In essence, angel investors and syndicates serve as *smart capital providers* at a critical juncture in the startup lifecycle. When effectively leveraged, they accelerate validation, enhance managerial capability, and improve investor readiness, thereby positioning startups for successful engagement with venture capital and other institutional funding sources.

## 7.3 VENTURE CAPITAL AND PRIVATE EQUITY

Venture capital (VC) and private equity (PE) represent institutional forms of startup and growth financing that support enterprises beyond the early validation stage, enabling rapid scaling, market expansion, and long-term value creation. While both involve equity-based investments, they differ significantly in terms of investment stage, risk appetite, operational involvement, and return expectations.

**Venture capital** primarily targets early- to mid-stage startups with high growth potential, scalable business models, and innovative products or services. VC firms typically invest across defined stages—Series A, B, and C—corresponding to product-market fit, growth acceleration, and market leadership, respectively. In addition to capital infusion, venture capitalists provide strategic guidance, governance oversight, access to industry networks, and support in talent acquisition and subsequent fundraising. VC investments are inherently high-risk and high-return, with portfolios designed on the assumption that a small number of successful ventures will compensate for multiple failures. Consequently, venture capitalists focus strongly on scalability, competitive advantage, unit economics, and exit potential through acquisitions or public listings.

**Private equity**, in contrast, generally invests at later stages in more mature companies with established revenues, predictable cash flows, and proven business models. PE firms often pursue larger ownership stakes and emphasize operational efficiency, financial restructuring, and margin optimization to enhance enterprise value. Unlike venture capital, private equity investments are less speculative and more focused on value creation through performance improvement, consolidation, or strategic repositioning. PE investors may adopt active management roles, including board control and executive restructuring, to drive measurable financial outcomes within a defined investment horizon. From an entrepreneurial perspective, the choice between venture capital and private equity depends on the startup's lifecycle stage, growth objectives, and willingness to accommodate external control. Venture capital aligns well with innovation-driven scaling and market capture, whereas private equity is better suited for expansion, consolidation, or pre-exit value enhancement. Both forms of investment require rigorous due diligence, robust governance structures, and clear alignment on growth strategy and exit timelines.

In summary, venture capital and private equity serve as powerful catalysts for scaling and value maximization at different phases of the business lifecycle. A strategic understanding of their objectives, expectations, and engagement models enables founders to select appropriate institutional partners and leverage capital effectively for sustainable growth and successful exits.

## 7.4 GOVERNMENT SCHEMES AND GRANTS (INDIA FOCUS)

Government schemes and grants play a strategic role in strengthening the startup ecosystem in India by addressing early-stage financing gaps, reducing innovation risk, and encouraging entrepreneurship in priority sectors. Unlike private investments, government funding is largely non-dilutive, making it especially valuable for startups engaged in research, technology development, social innovation, and capital-intensive domains.

In India, government support for startups is delivered through a combination of **policy-driven initiatives, direct grants, soft loans, tax incentives, and incubation support** at the central and state levels. These schemes are designed to promote innovation, employment generation, regional development, and commercialization of indigenous technologies. Early-stage startups, particularly those in biotechnology, healthcare, clean energy, agritech, and deep-tech, benefit significantly from such interventions.

Key national-level initiatives include startup recognition and facilitation programs, innovation-linked grant schemes, and sector-specific funding mechanisms administered through ministries and autonomous bodies. These programs typically support activities such as proof-of-concept development, prototype creation, pilot studies, clinical validation, and market entry. Many grants are milestone-based, requiring startups to demonstrate technical progress and prudent financial utilization before subsequent disbursements.

Government-supported **incubators, accelerators, and technology parks** further enhance funding access by combining seed grants with mentorship, infrastructure, regulatory guidance, and industry linkages. For academic spin-offs and research-driven startups, translational funding schemes enable the conversion of laboratory research into commercially viable products. In addition, credit guarantee schemes and subsidized loan programs reduce the financing burden for startups that are not yet attractive to equity investors.

While government funding offers clear advantages—such as reduced dilution, longer gestation support, and credibility enhancement—it also involves procedural complexity. Application processes are often competitive, documentation-intensive, and time-bound. Compliance requirements related to reporting, audits, and outcome measurement demand strong administrative discipline from founders. Therefore, startups must strategically assess scheme suitability, eligibility criteria, and alignment with their development roadmap before applying.

Overall, government schemes and grants in India function as **catalytic capital**, enabling early innovation, de-risking technology development, and improving investor readiness. When effectively leveraged alongside private funding, they significantly enhance a startup's capacity for sustainable growth and long-term value creation within the Indian entrepreneurial ecosystem.

## 7.5 CORPORATE AND STRATEGIC INVESTMENTS

Corporate and strategic investments represent a distinct category of startup financing in which established companies invest in startups to achieve strategic, technological, or market-oriented objectives in addition to financial returns. Unlike purely financial investors, corporate investors seek synergies that align with their long-term business strategy, innovation agenda, or competitive positioning.

**Corporate investments** are commonly executed through corporate venture capital (CVC) arms, strategic partnerships, joint ventures, or direct equity stakes. These investments typically target startups whose technologies, products, or business models complement or extend the corporation's existing capabilities. Common motivations include access to disruptive innovation, entry into new markets, acceleration of digital transformation, supply chain integration, and acquisition of specialized talent or intellectual property.

For startups, strategic investors can provide significant advantages beyond capital. These include access to established distribution channels, manufacturing infrastructure, regulatory expertise, customer bases, and global market reach. Corporate investors may also offer pilot opportunities, co-development arrangements, and long-term commercial contracts, which substantially enhance a startup's credibility and revenue prospects. Such non-financial value often accelerates market adoption and reduces execution risk.

However, corporate and strategic investments also introduce unique considerations and potential challenges. Strategic alignment may constrain the startup's flexibility, particularly if exclusivity clauses, right-of-first-refusal provisions, or restrictive commercial terms are embedded in the investment agreement. Additionally, conflicts may arise if the corporate investor's strategic priorities change or if the startup's growth trajectory begins to compete with the investor's core business. Founders must therefore carefully evaluate governance rights, information-sharing obligations, and long-term implications on future fundraising and exit options.

From an investment structuring perspective, corporate investments may occur at various stages, from early strategic bets to late-stage pre-acquisition positioning. Valuations may reflect strategic premium rather than purely financial metrics, but negotiations often involve complex term sheets balancing strategic control with startup autonomy.

In summary, corporate and strategic investments offer *patient, value-enhancing capital* when there is strong strategic fit and mutual clarity of objectives. When thoughtfully structured, such partnerships can accelerate innovation, scale commercialization, and create win–win outcomes for both startups and corporate investors across the business lifecycle.

**Table 7.1: Comparative Overview of Startup Funding Sources Across Growth Stages**

| Funding Source | Typical Stage | Capital Size | Equity Dilution | Risk Appetite | Value Addition Beyond Capital | Key Considerations |
|---|---|---|---|---|---|---|
| Bootstrapping | Ideation, Validation | Very Low–Low | None | Founder bears all risk | Full control, agility | Limited scale, slow growth |
| Friends & Family | Ideation, Pre-seed | Low | Low | High | Emotional support, trust | Informal terms, relationship risk |
| Angel Investors | Pre-seed, Seed | Low–Medium | Moderate | High | Mentorship, networks | Alignment of vision |
| Angel Syndicates | Seed | Medium | Moderate | High | Collective expertise, credibility | Governance complexity |
| Government Grants | Ideation, Seed | Low–Medium | None | Low | Non-dilutive, credibility | Compliance requirements |
| Venture Capital | Series A–C | Medium–High | High | Moderate–High | Strategic guidance, scaling | Dilution, control rights |
| Corporate / Strategic Investors | Growth, Expansion | Medium–High | Moderate–High | Strategic | Market access, partnerships | Strategic constraints |
| Private Equity | Late-stage, Pre-exit | High | High | Moderate | Operational efficiency | Reduced founder autonomy |
| Exit / Liquidity Events | Maturity | — | — | — | Capital realization | Timing and valuation risk |

## 7.6 STARTUP VALUATION METHODS

Startup valuation is a critical component of fundraising and investment negotiations, as it determines equity ownership, investor returns, and the long-term alignment between founders and investors. Unlike mature firms, startups often lack stable revenues, historical financial data, or predictable cash flows, making valuation more subjective and forward-looking. Consequently, startup valuation relies on a combination of qualitative judgment, market benchmarks, and scenario-based financial projections (Fig 7.3).

At the early stage, **pre-revenue or early-revenue startups** are commonly valued using qualitative and comparative approaches. The *Berkus Method* assigns value across key risk dimensions such as idea quality, founding team, prototype, market opportunity, and strategic relationships. Similarly, the *Scorecard Method* compares the startup against peer companies in the same region and sector, adjusting valuation based on relative strengths and weaknesses. These methods emphasize team capability, innovation potential, and execution readiness rather than financial metrics.

As startups gain traction, **market-based valuation methods** become more relevant. The *Comparable Transactions* or *Market Multiples* approach values startups based on recent funding rounds or acquisitions of similar companies, using metrics such as revenue multiples, user base, or growth rates. This method reflects prevailing investor sentiment and market conditions but may be influenced by short-term trends or speculative pricing.

For later-stage startups with clearer revenue visibility, **income-based approaches** such as the *Discounted Cash Flow (DCF)* method are applied. DCF estimates enterprise value by projecting future cash flows and discounting them to present value using a risk-adjusted discount rate. While theoretically robust, DCF is highly sensitive to assumptions regarding growth, margins, and terminal value, limiting its reliability for early-stage ventures.

Hybrid approaches, including the *Venture Capital Method*, integrate exit value assumptions with target investor returns to derive present valuation. This method is widely used in VC negotiations as it explicitly links valuation to expected exit outcomes. In practice, valuation outcomes are often shaped by negotiation dynamics, investor demand, funding climate, and the strategic value of the startup.

In essence, startup valuation is not a precise calculation but a strategic exercise balancing risk, growth potential, and market expectations. A clear understanding of valuation methodologies enables founders to engage confidently with investors, justify valuation assumptions, and structure funding rounds that support sustainable growth without excessive dilution.

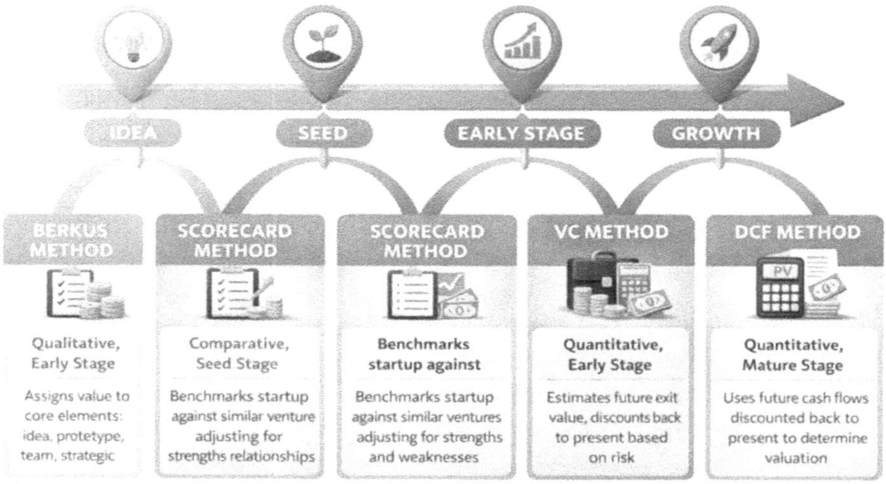


**Figure 7.3: Startup Valuation Methods by Stage of Venture Development**. This figure illustrates how startup valuation approaches evolve with venture maturity. At the idea and pre-revenue stage, qualitative methods such as the Berkus Model are used to assign value based on core business elements. During the seed stage, the Scorecard Method benchmarks the startup against comparable ventures to adjust valuation. As startups enter the early stage, investor-oriented techniques such as the Venture Capital (VC) Method are applied to estimate future exit value and risk-adjusted returns. In the growth stage, when financial performance becomes more predictable, quantitative approaches such as Discounted Cash Flow (DCF) analysis are employed to derive valuation based on projected cash flows and intrinsic value.

## 7.7 TERM SHEETS AND DEAL STRUCTURES

Term sheets and deal structures define the commercial, financial, and governance framework of an investment transaction between startups and investors. While a term sheet is typically a non-binding document, it sets the foundation for legally binding agreements and significantly influences founder control, investor rights, and future fundraising flexibility.

A **term sheet** outlines the key terms of an investment, including valuation, investment amount, equity ownership, and security type (equity, convertible instruments, or preference shares). One of the most critical elements is the distinction between *pre-money* and *post-money valuation*, as this determines the extent of founder dilution. Term sheets also specify liquidation preferences, which define the order and multiple of payouts to investors in the event of an exit or liquidation.

**Control and governance provisions** are central to deal structuring. These include board composition, voting rights, protective provisions, and reserved matters requiring investor consent. While such clauses are intended to safeguard investor interests, overly restrictive governance terms can limit founder autonomy and slow operational decision-making. Balanced governance structures are therefore essential for maintaining alignment and trust between founders and investors.

Another key component is **economic rights**, such as dividend rights, anti-dilution protection, and participation rights. Anti-dilution clauses protect investors against value erosion in down rounds, commonly structured as full ratchet or weighted-average mechanisms. Additionally, vesting schedules for founder shares and employee stock options are often included to ensure long-term commitment and talent retention.

Deal structures may vary depending on the funding stage and investor profile. Early-stage rounds frequently use *convertible notes* or *SAFE instruments* to defer valuation discussions, whereas later-stage investments typically involve priced equity rounds with detailed shareholder agreements. Exit-related provisions, including drag-along, tag-along, and right-of-first-refusal clauses, further shape the startup's strategic flexibility and exit pathways.

In summary, term sheets and deal structures are not merely legal formalities but strategic instruments that govern risk allocation, incentives, and control throughout the investment lifecycle. Founders who understand and negotiate these terms effectively are better positioned to preserve long-term value, maintain operational agility, and build durable investor relationships.

## 7.8 FINANCIAL PLANNING AND BURN RATE MANAGEMENT

Financial planning and burn rate management are essential for ensuring startup survival, capital efficiency, and investor confidence, particularly in the early and growth stages. Effective financial discipline enables startups to allocate resources strategically, extend operational runway, and achieve key milestones without premature or distress-driven fundraising.

**Financial planning** involves forecasting revenues, expenses, cash flows, and capital requirements over defined planning horizons. Startups typically prepare short-term operational budgets and medium-term financial projections aligned with product development, market entry, hiring plans, and regulatory or compliance needs. Unlike mature firms, startup financial planning must accommodate high uncertainty; therefore, scenario-based planning—best case, base case, and worst case—is widely adopted. This approach helps founders anticipate risks, adjust spending priorities, and make informed strategic decisions under changing market conditions.

**Burn rate** refers to the rate at which a startup consumes cash over a given period, usually measured monthly. *Gross burn rate* reflects total monthly expenses, while *net burn rate* accounts for revenues generated during the same period. Closely linked to burn rate is *runway*, which indicates how long the startup can operate before exhausting available cash. Monitoring these metrics is critical, as excessive burn without corresponding value creation can erode investor trust and limit future funding options.

Prudent burn rate management emphasizes aligning expenditure with validated milestones rather than speculative growth. Common cost drivers include personnel, product development, infrastructure, marketing, and compliance. Startups are encouraged to adopt lean operating models, prioritize revenue-generating activities, and defer non-essential expenditures. Regular financial reviews, variance analysis, and cash flow tracking enhance transparency and enable timely corrective action.

From an investor perspective, disciplined financial planning signals managerial competence and capital stewardship. Investors closely evaluate how efficiently capital is deployed and whether spending translates into traction, scalability, or defensible competitive advantage. Startups that demonstrate control over burn rate are better positioned to negotiate favorable funding terms and withstand market volatility.

In essence, financial planning and burn rate management function as strategic control mechanisms rather than mere accounting exercises. When embedded into decision-making processes, they support sustainable growth, extend strategic optionality, and enhance long-term enterprise value.

## 7.9 INVESTOR DUE DILIGENCE

Investor due diligence is a comprehensive evaluation process through which potential investors assess a startup's viability, risk profile, and investment readiness before committing capital. This process serves to validate claims made by founders, identify potential red flags, and determine whether the startup aligns with the investor's strategic, financial, and ethical expectations.

Due diligence typically spans multiple dimensions. **Business and commercial due diligence** examines the startup's value proposition, target market, customer traction, competitive landscape, and scalability of the business model. Investors assess whether the problem being addressed is significant, the solution is differentiated, and the market opportunity is sufficiently large and accessible. Evidence of product–market fit, customer retention, and revenue visibility strengthens investor confidence at this stage.

**Financial due diligence** focuses on historical financial statements, cash flow management, burn rate, unit economics, and funding utilization. Investors analyze revenue quality, cost structures, pricing logic, and financial controls to evaluate sustainability and capital efficiency. Unrealistic projections, weak accounting practices, or unexplained financial inconsistencies often raise concerns.

**Legal and compliance due diligence** involves verification of corporate structure, shareholding patterns, intellectual property ownership, contracts, licenses, and regulatory compliance. Clear title to intellectual property, properly executed shareholder agreements, and adherence to applicable laws are critical, particularly for technology- and IP-driven startups. Any pending litigation or regulatory risk is closely scrutinized.

**Team and governance due diligence** evaluates the founding team's credentials, role clarity, commitment, and governance practices. Investors assess leadership capability, decision-making processes, board composition, and alignment of incentives through equity vesting and employee stock option plans.

For startups, due diligence should be approached as a preparedness exercise rather than a reactive process. Maintaining accurate documentation, transparent reporting, and robust governance significantly improves fundraising outcomes. Ultimately, investor due diligence is not adversarial; it is a risk-mitigation mechanism that fosters trust, clarity, and alignment, laying the groundwork for a stable and productive investor–founder relationship.

## 7.10 EXIT STRATEGIES AND LIQUIDITY EVENTS

Exit strategies and liquidity events represent the culmination of the startup investment lifecycle, enabling founders and investors to realize returns on capital and effort. A well-defined exit strategy provides strategic direction from early stages of venture development and influences funding decisions, growth priorities, and governance structures throughout the startup's journey.

Common **exit routes** include mergers and acquisitions (M&A), initial public offerings (IPOs), secondary share sales, and strategic buyouts. M&A is the most prevalent exit pathway for startups, particularly in technology and innovation-driven sectors. Acquisitions may be driven by strategic fit, market expansion, technology absorption, or talent acquisition, often offering faster and more certain liquidity compared to public listings. IPOs, while less frequent, provide substantial visibility and valuation upside but require strong financial performance, regulatory compliance, and sustained market confidence.

**Secondary liquidity events** allow early investors or founders to partially exit by selling shares to new investors in later funding rounds, without a full company sale. Such transactions improve liquidity while enabling the startup to continue operating independently. Strategic buyouts or management-led exits may also occur, particularly in later stages or private equity-backed ventures.

From an investor perspective, exit potential is a key determinant of investment attractiveness. Venture capital and private equity firms typically operate within defined fund lifecycles and require clear exit pathways to meet return expectations. Consequently, startups must demonstrate scalability, defensible competitive advantage, and strategic relevance to potential acquirers or public markets.

For founders, exit planning involves balancing financial outcomes with long-term vision, stakeholder interests, and organizational legacy. Exit terms, including timing, valuation, and payout structure, are shaped by earlier agreements such as liquidation preferences, vesting schedules, and drag-along rights. Therefore, exit outcomes are often determined well before the exit event itself.

In conclusion, exit strategies and liquidity events are not isolated end-stage considerations but integral components of startup strategy and investment planning. Proactive exit thinking enhances strategic alignment, improves investor confidence, and maximizes value realization for all stakeholders involved.

## KEY CONCEPTS & DEFINITIONS

**Bootstrapping**: Financing a startup using founders' personal resources, internal cash flows, or early revenues, with minimal or no external capital, emphasizing capital efficiency and control.
**Seed Funding**: Early-stage capital used to develop a minimum viable product (MVP), validate market demand, and build an initial team, typically sourced from angels, incubators, or early-stage funds.
**Angel Investor**: A high-net-worth individual who invests personal capital in early-stage startups and often provides mentorship, strategic guidance, and network access.
**Angel Syndicate**: A structured group of angel investors who collectively invest in startups under common terms, usually led by a designated lead investor.
**Venture Capital (VC)**: Institutional equity financing provided to high-growth startups in exchange for ownership, with an expectation of significant returns through scalable growth and exits.
**Private Equity (PE)**: Investment in relatively mature companies with stable revenues, focusing on operational efficiency, value enhancement, and strategic exits.
**Corporate Venture Capital (CVC)**: Equity investments made by corporations in startups to achieve strategic objectives such as innovation access, market expansion, or technology acquisition.
**Non-Dilutive Funding**: Capital, such as government grants or subsidies, that does not require founders to give up equity ownership.
**Startup Valuation**: The process of estimating a startup's economic value based on growth potential, risk profile, market comparables, and expected exit outcomes.
**Pre-Money Valuation**: The value of a startup before receiving new investment.
**Post-Money Valuation**: The value of a startup after new investment capital has been added.
**Term Sheet**: A non-binding document outlining the key financial, control, and governance terms of an investment agreement.
**Liquidation Preference**: A contractual right that determines the order and amount investors receive in the event of a liquidation or exit.
**Burn Rate**: The rate at which a startup consumes cash over a defined period, typically measured monthly.

**Runway**: The amount of time a startup can operate before exhausting available cash, based on its current burn rate.
**Due Diligence**: A comprehensive evaluation conducted by investors to assess a startup's business, financials, legal compliance, and team before investment.
**Exit Strategy**: A planned method through which founders and investors realize returns, such as acquisition, IPO, or secondary share sale.
**Liquidity Event**: An occurrence that enables shareholders to convert equity into cash, partially or fully, through exits or secondary transactions.

---

**Case Study 1: Bootstrapping to Angel Funding – Zoho Corporation (India)**

Zoho Corporation began as a fully bootstrapped software company, relying entirely on founder capital and early customer revenues. The company deliberately avoided external funding during its formative years, focusing on product excellence, customer-centric design, and sustainable revenue generation. This disciplined approach allowed Zoho to retain full ownership and strategic autonomy while building a globally competitive SaaS portfolio.

**Key Insight:** Bootstrapping, when aligned with revenue-driven growth and long-term vision, can eliminate dependence on external investors while still enabling global scale.

**Learning Outcome:**: Early capital efficiency strengthens negotiation power if and when external funding is pursued.

---

**Case Study 2: Angel Syndicates Accelerating Scale – Ola Electric (India)**

In its early stages, Ola attracted capital from angel investors and syndicates who believed in the founders' vision of transforming urban mobility. Beyond funding, these angels provided strategic inputs on market expansion, partnerships, and operational scaling. This early support helped Ola demonstrate traction and credibility, paving the way for large venture capital investments and corporate partnerships.

**Key Insight:** Angel syndicates provide "smart capital" by combining financial resources with collective expertise and networks.

**Learning Outcome:** Strategic angels can significantly reduce execution risk during the transition from early validation to rapid growth.

---

**Case Study 3: Venture Capital, Strategic Investment, and Exit – Flipkart**

Flipkart raised multiple rounds of venture capital to scale operations, strengthen logistics, and dominate India's e-commerce market. Over time, it also attracted strategic investment from global players seeking entry into the Indian market. The company's funding journey culminated in a landmark acquisition by a global retail corporation, delivering substantial liquidity to founders and investors.

**Key Insight:** Sequential funding—from venture capital to strategic investment—can maximize valuation and exit outcomes.

**Learning Outcome:** Exit success is often the result of long-term alignment between funding strategy, market leadership, and strategic relevance.

---

## REVIEW QUESTIONS AND EXERCISES

## REVIEW QUESTIONS

1. Explain the concept of startup bootstrapping. What are its advantages and limitations in the early stages of a venture?
2. Differentiate between angel investors and angel syndicates with respect to risk, value addition, and governance.
3. Compare venture capital and private equity in terms of investment stage, risk appetite, and strategic involvement.
4. Why are government schemes and grants considered non-dilutive funding? Discuss their relevance for startups in India.
5. What motivates corporations to make strategic investments in startups? How do such investments differ from purely financial investments?
6. Describe and compare any three commonly used startup valuation methods.
7. What is a term sheet? Identify the key economic and control-related clauses typically included in it.
8. Explain burn rate and runway. Why are these metrics critical for founders and investors?
9. Outline the major components of investor due diligence. Why is preparedness essential for startups?
10. Discuss different exit strategies available to startups. How do early funding decisions influence exit outcomes?

### Short Answer / Analytical Questions

1. How does early-stage funding impact founder ownership and long-term control?
2. Why do investors emphasize scalability and exit potential while evaluating startups?
3. Explain the role of liquidation preference in protecting investor interests.
4. What challenges do startups face while applying for government grants?
5. How can poor financial planning affect future fundraising rounds?

### Application-Based Exercises

1. **Case Analysis Exercise:** Assume you are the founder of a biotech startup at the prototype stage.
    - Choose between bootstrapping, angel funding, or a government grant.
    - Justify your choice based on risk, capital needs, and control considerations.

2. **Valuation Exercise:** A startup expects an exit valuation of ₹100 crore in 5 years. Using the Venture Capital Method, estimate its present valuation assuming an investor expects a 10× return.

3. **Term Sheet Interpretation:** Review a sample term sheet and identify:
    - Pre-money valuation
    - Investor equity stake
    - Liquidation preference clause
    - Founder vesting conditions

4. **Burn Rate Calculation:** A startup has monthly expenses of ₹12 lakh and monthly revenues of ₹5 lakh.
    - Calculate the net burn rate.
    - If available cash is ₹90 lakh, estimate the runway.
5. **Exit Planning Exercise:** Develop an exit roadmap for a digital startup targeting acquisition within 7 years.
    - Identify potential acquirers
    - Key milestones required
    - Likely funding stages involved

### Reflective Question

- How would you balance growth ambitions with financial discipline while negotiating with investors at different stages of a startup lifecycle?

# CHAPTER-8

# PITCHING & COMMUNICATION SKILLS

**Abstract**: Effective pitching and communication are critical competencies for entrepreneurs, directly shaping venture creation, funding outcomes, stakeholder alignment, and long-term brand credibility. This chapter offers a comprehensive and structured examination of entrepreneurial communication, progressing from core principles to advanced, context-specific applications. It begins by highlighting the strategic role of communication in articulating vision, building trust, and supporting informed decision-making. The chapter categorizes different types of startup pitches, demonstrating how pitch formats vary by audience, purpose, and stage of venture development. It then outlines the essential structure of a winning pitch deck, emphasizing clarity, logical sequencing, and evidence-based messaging. Storytelling is explored as a powerful persuasive tool that transforms complex ideas into compelling value propositions. Special attention is given to scientific and technology pitching, where balancing technical depth with accessibility is essential. The chapter also examines investor psychology and negotiation dynamics to help entrepreneurs navigate expectations and risk perceptions. Guidance on demo days, competitions, media engagement, branding, and crisis communication is provided, along with common pitching mistakes and corrective strategies. Overall, the chapter equips learners with practical communication frameworks essential for entrepreneurial success.

**Keywords:** Entrepreneurial Communication; Startup Pitching; Pitch Deck Design; Storytelling; Investor Psychology; Stakeholder Engagement

## 8.1 IMPORTANCE OF COMMUNICATION IN ENTREPRENEURSHIP

Communication is a foundational pillar of entrepreneurship, shaping how ideas are conceived, articulated, evaluated, and transformed into viable ventures. In entrepreneurial contexts, communication is not limited to information exchange; it is a strategic process through which vision, value, credibility, and trust are constructed among diverse stakeholders such as co-founders, employees, investors, customers, regulators, and the broader public.

At the ideation and early venture stages, effective communication enables entrepreneurs to clearly articulate problems, validate assumptions, and align teams around a shared mission. Internally, transparent and consistent communication facilitates coordination, reduces uncertainty, and strengthens organizational culture. Externally, it allows entrepreneurs to convey the unique value proposition of their products or services, differentiate themselves in competitive markets, and build early customer confidence.

From a funding and growth perspective, communication plays a decisive role in investor engagement and capital acquisition. Investors often evaluate not only the technical or commercial merit of a venture but also the entrepreneur's ability to explain complex ideas succinctly, respond convincingly to questions, and demonstrate strategic clarity. Strong communication skills signal leadership competence, preparedness, and adaptability—qualities that significantly influence investment decisions.

Communication is equally critical in stakeholder management and long-term sustainability. Entrepreneurs must regularly interact with partners, suppliers, policymakers, media, and communities, each requiring tailored messaging and tone. During periods of uncertainty, crisis, or rapid change, effective communication helps manage expectations, mitigate risk, and preserve organizational reputation. Poor or inconsistent communication, by contrast, can lead to mistrust, misalignment, and strategic failure even when the underlying business idea is strong.

In essence, communication functions as both an operational tool and a competitive advantage in entrepreneurship. Mastery of verbal, visual, and written communication enables entrepreneurs to transform innovative ideas into compelling narratives, mobilize resources, influence decision-making, and sustain growth in dynamic and uncertain environments.

## 8.2 TYPES OF STARTUP PITCHES

Startup pitches are structured communication tools designed to convey a venture's value proposition to specific audiences within a limited time frame. The effectiveness of a pitch depends largely on aligning its content, depth, and delivery style with the expectations of the target audience and the stage of the startup. Entrepreneurs must therefore understand the major types of startup pitches and their strategic applications (Fig 8.1).

One of the most common formats is the **elevator pitch**, a concise and compelling summary of a startup idea delivered typically within 30–60 seconds. Its primary purpose is to spark interest rather than provide exhaustive detail. Elevator pitches are particularly useful during networking events, informal investor interactions, and early-stage discussions where attention spans are limited.

The **investor pitch** is a more detailed and structured presentation aimed at securing funding. It focuses on problem–solution fit, market opportunity, business model, traction, competitive advantage, financial projections, and the founding team. Investor pitches vary by funding stage—seed, early-stage, or growth-stage—with increasing emphasis on metrics, scalability, and risk mitigation as the startup matures.

A **demo pitch** or **product pitch** centers on demonstrating the functionality, usability, and value of a product or prototype. Common in technology startups, accelerators, and demo days, this pitch emphasizes user experience, technical feasibility, and real-world application. The objective is to validate claims through live demonstration rather than narrative alone.

The **sales pitch** is directed toward potential customers or clients and focuses on benefits, outcomes, and return on investment rather than internal strategy. Unlike investor pitches, sales pitches emphasize immediate value, customization, and problem-solving from the customer's perspective.

Entrepreneurs also engage in **competition or accelerator pitches**, which are time-bound and evaluated against predefined criteria such as innovation, feasibility, social impact, and scalability. These pitches require strict adherence to format and clarity under pressure. Additionally, **internal pitches** are used to align co-founders, employees, or board members around strategic decisions, new initiatives, or pivots.

Understanding these diverse pitch types allows entrepreneurs to adapt their communication strategically, ensuring relevance, clarity, and persuasion across contexts. The ability to switch seamlessly between pitch formats is a critical entrepreneurial skill that directly influences opportunity recognition and venture advancement.

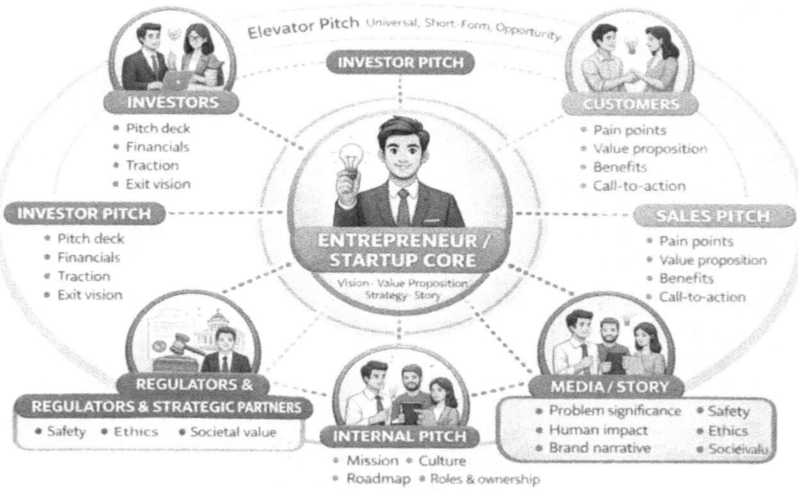


**Figure 8.1: Startup Pitch Communication Framework**. This figure presents a structured framework illustrating how entrepreneurs strategically tailor their startup pitches across different audiences and contexts. The entrepreneur or startup core represents the unified vision, value proposition, strategy, and story from which all communications originate. Surrounding stakeholder groups—investors, customers, team members, media, and regulators or strategic partners—require distinct pitch formats, including investor pitches, sales pitches, internal or vision pitches, media or story pitches, and regulatory or compliance pitches. The outer universal layer highlights the elevator pitch as a concise, adaptable form of communication applicable across all audiences. The framework emphasizes that while the startup's core narrative remains constant, the content, depth, and delivery of messages vary according to the audience and purpose of communication.

## 8.3 STRUCTURE OF A WINNING PITCH DECK

A winning pitch deck is a strategically organized visual narrative that communicates the essence of a startup clearly, convincingly, and efficiently. Rather than overwhelming the audience with excessive detail, an effective pitch deck guides investors and stakeholders through a logical progression of ideas that demonstrate problem relevance, solution strength, and business viability (Fig 8.2).

**Figure 8.2: Structure of a Winning Pitch Deck.** This figure illustrates the recommended sequential structure of a winning startup pitch deck. It begins by clearly defining the problem and presenting the proposed solution, followed by articulation of the value proposition to establish differentiation. The framework then highlights market opportunity and business model to demonstrate commercial potential and sustainability. Traction and validation provide evidence of feasibility and market acceptance, while competitive landscape and technology or product sections explain positioning, innovation, and defensibility. The pitch concludes by introducing the team to emphasize execution capability. Collectively, these components guide entrepreneurs in developing a coherent, persuasive, and investor-ready pitch narrative.

The pitch deck typically begins with a **clear problem statement**, defining the market gap or pain point in a relatable and data-supported manner. This establishes context and urgency, enabling the audience to appreciate why the problem is worth solving. Following this, the **solution** is presented, explaining how the startup addresses the problem in a differentiated and scalable way. Visual clarity and simplicity are critical at this stage to ensure immediate comprehension.

A strong pitch deck then outlines the **market opportunity**, including target customers, market size, and growth potential. This section reassures investors of commercial relevance and scalability. The **business model** follows, detailing how the startup creates, delivers, and captures value, including revenue streams and pricing logic.

Subsequent slides focus on **traction and validation**, such as user growth, partnerships, pilot results, or early revenues. This evidence reduces perceived risk and strengthens credibility. A concise **competitive analysis** highlights alternatives and clearly articulates the startup's unique advantage or defensibility. The **technology or product** slide explains core features or innovations at an appropriate level of technical depth for the audience.

Equally important is the **team slide**, which showcases founders' expertise, roles, and complementary skills, reinforcing execution capability. The deck then presents **financial projections**, funding requirements, and planned use of funds, demonstrating fiscal awareness and strategic foresight. The presentation concludes with a compelling **vision and closing**, reiterating impact, growth trajectory, and the investment opportunity.

Overall, the structure of a winning pitch deck balances storytelling with data, clarity with credibility, and ambition with realism. When designed thoughtfully, it becomes a powerful decision-making tool that supports confident and informed stakeholder engagement.

## 8.4 STORYTELLING FOR STARTUPS

Storytelling is a powerful communication strategy that enables entrepreneurs to transform abstract ideas, complex technologies, and data-driven insights into compelling and memorable narratives. In the startup context, storytelling bridges the gap between innovation and understanding by humanizing the problem, contextualizing the solution, and emotionally engaging diverse audiences such as investors, customers, partners, and the media.

Effective startup storytelling begins with a clearly defined **central narrative**, often structured around a problem–solution–impact framework. The story typically introduces a relatable problem or unmet need, highlights the consequences of inaction, and then presents the startup as a credible and timely solution. By anchoring the narrative in real-world scenarios or user experiences, entrepreneurs make their value proposition more tangible and persuasive.

A strong entrepreneurial story also emphasizes **purpose and vision**. Beyond explaining what the startup does, storytelling communicates why it exists and what change it seeks to create. This sense of purpose resonates strongly with investors and stakeholders who increasingly value mission-driven ventures alongside financial returns. Founders' personal journeys, motivations, and insights can further strengthen authenticity and trust when used appropriately.

Incorporating **data and evidence** within the narrative enhances credibility without disrupting flow. Metrics, market statistics, and validation points should support the story rather than dominate it. Visual storytelling through pitch decks, demos, and prototypes reinforces key messages and improves recall. Consistency across verbal, visual, and written communication ensures that the narrative remains coherent across platforms and touchpoints.

Importantly, storytelling must be **audience-centric**. Technical depth, tone, and emphasis should vary depending on whether the audience consists of investors, customers, regulators, or the general public. When executed effectively, storytelling becomes a strategic asset that differentiates startups, strengthens persuasion, and increases the likelihood of funding, adoption, and long-term engagement.

## 8.5 SCIENTIFIC AND TECHNOLOGY PITCHING

Scientific and technology-based startups operate at the intersection of innovation, research, and commercialization, making communication particularly challenging and critical. Pitching in this domain requires entrepreneurs to translate complex scientific concepts and advanced technologies into clear, credible, and investment-ready narratives without compromising technical integrity.

A central challenge in scientific and technology pitching is balancing **technical rigor with accessibility**. While the underlying science must be robust and defensible, most investors and stakeholders are not domain experts. Effective pitches therefore focus on explaining the problem significance, scientific novelty, and practical application in simple, outcome-oriented language. Technical details should be included selectively, emphasizing proof-of-concept, validation data, patents, and regulatory pathways rather than exhaustive theoretical explanations.

Credibility plays a decisive role in scientific pitching. Entrepreneurs must demonstrate **scientific validity**, reproducibility, and feasibility through experimental results, pilot studies, or peer-reviewed evidence where applicable. At the same time, they must clearly articulate the **commercial relevance** of the technology, including use cases, target industries, scalability, and pathways to market adoption. Failure to link science with business impact often weakens investor confidence.

Technology pitches must also address **risk and uncertainty** transparently. Scientific ventures typically face longer development cycles, regulatory scrutiny, and higher capital requirements. Acknowledging these challenges and presenting clear mitigation strategies—such as staged milestones, partnerships, or phased clinical or technical validation—signals strategic maturity and preparedness.

Finally, scientific and technology pitching benefits from the use of **visual aids**, analogies, and simplified schematics that enhance understanding. Clear communication of intellectual property strategy, regulatory considerations, and competitive differentiation further strengthens the pitch. When executed effectively, scientific and technology pitching builds trust, accelerates translation from lab to market, and attracts stakeholders aligned with long-term innovation and impact.

## 8.6 INVESTOR PSYCHOLOGY AND NEGOTIATION

Understanding investor psychology is essential for effective pitching and successful fundraising. Investors do not evaluate startups solely on financial projections or technological novelty; their decisions are shaped by perceptions of risk, trust, credibility, and potential return. Entrepreneurs who recognize these psychological drivers are better positioned to frame their pitches strategically and engage in constructive negotiations (Fig 8.3).

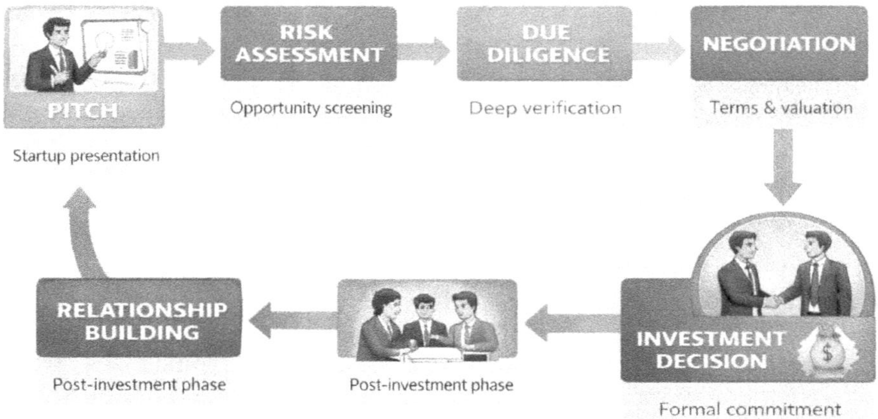


**Figure 8.3: Investor Decision-Making and Negotiation Cycle**. This figure depicts the strictly sequential and cyclical process through which investors evaluate and engage with startup ventures. The cycle begins with the startup pitch, followed by preliminary risk assessment to screen opportunity-level uncertainties. Promising ventures then undergo due diligence, involving in-depth technical, financial, legal, and market validation. Successful evaluations move into negotiation, where valuation, equity structure, and governance terms are finalized, leading to the formal investment decision. The cycle continues into relationship building, representing post-investment collaboration, mentoring, and strategic support, which in turn lays the foundation for future funding rounds and renewed pitching. The framework emphasizes that investor engagement is iterative, relationship-driven, and process-oriented rather than a one-time event.

Investors typically assess opportunities through a **risk–reward lens**, seeking ventures that demonstrate high growth potential with manageable and clearly articulated risks. Communication that highlights traction, validation, and defensibility helps reduce perceived uncertainty. Equally important is the entrepreneur's ability to convey confidence, clarity, and adaptability, as these traits are often interpreted as indicators of leadership and execution capability. Negotiation in entrepreneurial settings extends beyond valuation alone. It involves discussions around equity, control, milestones, governance, and long-term strategic alignment. Effective negotiation is grounded in **preparation and transparency**, where entrepreneurs understand their own priorities, acceptable trade-offs, and non-negotiable elements. Clear communication of assumptions and expectations minimizes misunderstandings and fosters mutual respect.

Psychological factors such as **confirmation bias, herd behavior, and signaling effects** also influence investor decisions. Endorsements, credible advisors, early customers, or co-investors can significantly enhance perceived legitimacy. Entrepreneurs should therefore strategically leverage social proof and third-party validation during pitches and negotiations.

Ultimately, successful investor communication and negotiation are collaborative rather than adversarial processes. By aligning incentives, managing expectations, and maintaining open, ethical dialogue, entrepreneurs can build long-term investor relationships that support sustainable venture growth rather than short-term transactional gains.

## 8.7 DEMO DAY AND COMPETITION READINESS

Demo days and startup competitions are high-stakes platforms where entrepreneurs present their ventures to investors, mentors, industry experts, and the media within strict time constraints. Success in these environments depends not only on the quality of the idea but also on the entrepreneur's preparedness, delivery, and ability to stand out in a crowded and competitive setting.

Preparation begins with **clarity and focus**. Entrepreneurs must refine their core message, ensuring that the problem, solution, value proposition, and impact are communicated succinctly. Given limited presentation time, unnecessary technical detail should be avoided in favor of clear outcomes, traction, and differentiation. Rehearsal is critical to achieve confident delivery, precise timing, and smooth transitions.

An effective demo day pitch integrates **visual storytelling and live demonstration** where appropriate. A well-executed product demo can significantly enhance credibility by validating claims and showcasing usability. However, technical reliability and contingency planning are essential, as failures during live demonstrations can undermine confidence. Visuals should be simple, legible, and aligned with spoken content.

Understanding **evaluation criteria** is equally important. Competitions often assess startups based on innovation, feasibility, scalability, social or economic impact, and team capability. Tailoring the pitch to these criteria increases relevance and scoring potential. Entrepreneurs should also be prepared for rapid questioning, responding concisely and confidently while demonstrating strategic insight. Beyond winning prizes, demo days and competitions offer opportunities for **networking, feedback, and visibility**. Post-pitch engagement with judges, investors, and peers can lead to mentorship, partnerships, and funding opportunities. Readiness, therefore, extends beyond the stage to follow-up communication, reinforcing the venture's professionalism and long-term potential.

## 8.8 MEDIA, BRANDING, AND PUBLIC RELATIONS

Media engagement, branding, and public relations (PR) are critical components of entrepreneurial communication that shape how a startup is perceived by the public, investors, customers, and other stakeholders. Unlike pitching, which is often targeted and time-bound, media and PR communication is continuous and significantly influences long-term reputation and brand equity.

Branding begins with **consistent and coherent messaging** that reflects the startup's mission, values, and value proposition. Entrepreneurs must ensure alignment across all communication channels, including websites, social media, press releases, and public appearances. Clear brand positioning helps differentiate the startup in competitive markets and fosters recognition and trust among audiences.

Effective media communication requires understanding the **logic and expectations of journalists and media platforms**. Media professionals seek stories that are timely, relevant, credible, and impactful. Entrepreneurs should therefore frame their narratives around innovation, problem-solving, societal impact, or industry transformation rather than overt promotion. Accurate, transparent, and jargon-free communication enhances credibility and reduces the risk of misrepresentation.

Public relations also play a strategic role in **reputation management and visibility building**. Proactive PR activities—such as thought leadership articles, expert interviews, and participation in industry forums—can position founders as credible voices in their domains. At the same time, reactive PR capabilities are essential for addressing misinformation, criticism, or negative events promptly and responsibly. In the digital era, entrepreneurs must additionally manage **online presence and social media communication**, where information spreads rapidly and public perception can change quickly. Ethical communication, authenticity, and responsiveness are therefore essential. When managed strategically, media, branding, and public relations strengthen stakeholder trust, amplify startup narratives, and support sustainable growth.

## 8.9 CRISIS AND STAKEHOLDER COMMUNICATION

Crisis situations are inevitable in entrepreneurial ventures, arising from product failures, regulatory issues, financial constraints, data breaches, reputational challenges, or unforeseen external events. In such contexts, effective crisis and stakeholder communication is critical for maintaining trust, minimizing damage, and ensuring organizational continuity.

The primary objective of crisis communication is **timely, transparent, and accurate information sharing**. Delayed or inconsistent messaging can escalate uncertainty, fuel speculation, and erode stakeholder confidence. Entrepreneurs must acknowledge the issue promptly, communicate known facts clearly, and avoid speculation or misleading assurances. Honesty and accountability are central to preserving credibility during periods of disruption.

Stakeholder communication during crises must be **audience-specific**. Employees, investors, customers, regulators, partners, and the media have distinct concerns and information needs. Internal stakeholders require reassurance, clarity on roles, and guidance on next steps, while external stakeholders seek explanations, corrective actions, and implications for their interests. Tailoring messages ensures relevance and reduces misinterpretation. Effective crisis management also involves demonstrating **leadership and empathy**. Entrepreneurs must show concern for affected parties, take responsibility where appropriate, and outline concrete measures to resolve the issue and prevent recurrence. This approach not only mitigates immediate damage but can also strengthen long-term trust if handled professionally.

In the digital and social media landscape, crisis communication must be **continuous and adaptive**, monitoring public response and correcting misinformation swiftly. A well-prepared crisis communication plan, supported by clear governance and spokesperson roles, enables startups to respond decisively. Ultimately, strategic stakeholder communication during crises can transform challenges into opportunities for learning, resilience, and reputational recovery.

## 8.10 COMMON PITCHING MISTAKES

Despite having innovative ideas and strong technical foundations, many startups fail to secure support due to avoidable pitching mistakes. Recognizing and correcting these errors is essential for effective entrepreneurial communication and successful stakeholder engagement.

One of the most frequent mistakes is **lack of clarity**. Overloading pitches with excessive information, jargon, or unfocused narratives can confuse audiences and dilute the core message. Entrepreneurs often underestimate the importance of simplicity, failing to clearly articulate the problem, solution, and value proposition within limited time frames.

Another common error is **poor audience alignment.** Using the same pitch for investors, customers, or technical experts without adapting content and emphasis can reduce relevance and impact. Investors seek scalability and return, while customers prioritize benefits and usability; ignoring these distinctions weakens persuasion.

Startups also frequently make the mistake of **overemphasizing ideas while underemphasizing execution**. Investors are particularly sensitive to evidence of traction, realistic milestones, and team capability. Unrealistic financial projections, unsupported claims, or avoidance of risks can undermine credibility and signal lack of preparedness.

Delivery-related issues, such as **weak presentation skills, lack of confidence, or poor visual design**, further diminish pitch effectiveness. Inadequate rehearsal, reading from slides, or ineffective body language can distract from otherwise strong content. Additionally, failing to anticipate questions or respond defensively to feedback can negatively influence perceptions.

Finally, neglecting follow-up communication is a critical but often overlooked mistake. Pitching should be viewed as the beginning of a relationship rather than a one-time event. Professional, timely, and clear follow-up reinforces interest, demonstrates commitment, and significantly improves the likelihood of long-term engagement and success.

---

## KEY CONCEPTS & DEFINITIONS

**Entrepreneurial Communication**: The strategic process by which entrepreneurs convey vision, value propositions, and operational intent to internal and external stakeholders to mobilize resources, build trust, and drive venture growth.

**Startup Pitch**: A structured and time-bound presentation designed to communicate a startup's idea, business model, and growth potential to a specific audience such as investors, customers, or partners.

**Elevator Pitch**: A concise verbal summary of a startup concept, typically delivered within 30–60 seconds, aimed at generating interest rather than providing comprehensive detail.

**Pitch Deck**: A visual presentation, usually consisting of 10–15 slides, that systematically outlines the problem, solution, market opportunity, business model, traction, team, and funding requirements of a startup.

**Value Proposition**: A clear statement that explains how a product or service solves a customer's problem, delivers specific benefits, and differentiates the startup from competitors.

**Storytelling in Entrepreneurship**: The use of narrative structures to present startup ideas in a compelling, memorable, and emotionally engaging manner, enhancing persuasion and audience recall.

**Scientific Pitching**: A specialized form of pitching that communicates research-driven or technology-intensive innovations by balancing technical credibility with commercial relevance.

**Investor Psychology**: The cognitive and emotional factors influencing investor decision-making, including risk perception, trust, bias, and expectations of return on investment.

**Negotiation**: A structured interaction between entrepreneurs and stakeholders aimed at reaching mutually acceptable agreements on valuation, equity, control, and strategic terms.

**Demo Day**: A formal event where startups present their ventures to investors, mentors, and industry experts, often as part of accelerators, incubators, or competitions.
**Brand Positioning**: The process of defining and communicating a startup's distinct identity, values, and market stance to achieve differentiation and stakeholder recognition.
**Public Relations (PR)**: The planned and sustained effort to manage a startup's public image and media relationships through ethical, accurate, and strategic communication.
**Crisis Communication**: The structured approach to communicating with stakeholders during adverse or unexpected events to protect trust, manage reputational risk, and ensure organizational stability.
**Stakeholder Engagement**: The ongoing process of building, maintaining, and managing relationships with individuals or groups that influence or are affected by the startup's activities.
**Pitching Mistakes**: Common errors in entrepreneurial presentations, including lack of clarity, poor audience alignment, unrealistic claims, weak delivery, and inadequate follow-up, that reduce pitch effectiveness.

---

**Case Study 1: Crafting a Compelling Investor Pitch in an Early-Stage Startup**

A digital health startup developing an AI-enabled patient monitoring platform struggled to secure seed funding despite having a functional prototype and strong technical credentials. Initial investor meetings revealed that the founders' pitch was overly technical and lacked a clear articulation of market need and revenue potential. Feedback indicated that while the technology was impressive, the business case remained unclear.

The founders restructured their pitch by simplifying technical explanations, introducing a patient-centric problem narrative, and clearly defining their target market and pricing model. They incorporated early pilot data and highlighted regulatory preparedness to address investor concerns. Within three months, the startup successfully closed its seed round, demonstrating how clarity, audience alignment, and storytelling significantly influence investor decision-making.

---

**Case Study 2: Scientific Pitching in a Biotechnology Venture**

A university spin-off focused on developing a novel biomarker-based diagnostic assay faced challenges in attracting industry partners. The research team's pitch heavily emphasized experimental methodology and statistical rigor but failed to communicate clinical relevance and commercial scalability.

After mentorship from an incubator program, the team redesigned their pitch to focus on unmet clinical needs, diagnostic accuracy advantages, and integration into existing healthcare workflows. They included a clear intellectual property strategy and a phased commercialization roadmap. This revised scientific pitch led to a strategic partnership with a diagnostics company, illustrating the importance of translating science into value-driven narratives.

---

**Case Study 3: Crisis Communication in a Technology Startup**
A consumer technology startup experienced a data security breach shortly after a major product launch. Initial silence and fragmented communication created confusion among users and negative media coverage. Recognizing the severity of the situation, the founders implemented a structured crisis communication strategy.

They issued a transparent public statement acknowledging the breach, directly informed affected users, and outlined immediate corrective actions and long-term security upgrades. Regular updates were shared through official channels, and customer support was strengthened to address concerns. As a result, the startup retained a significant portion of its user base and restored investor confidence, highlighting the critical role of timely and empathetic stakeholder communication during crises.

---

## REVIEW QUESTIONS AND EXERCISES

### A. Review Questions

1. Explain the role of communication as a strategic resource in entrepreneurship. How does it influence venture success across different stages?
2. Differentiate between an elevator pitch, investor pitch, and sales pitch. Provide suitable contexts for each.
3. Describe the essential components of a winning pitch deck and justify their logical sequence.
4. Discuss the importance of storytelling in startup pitching. How does it enhance persuasion and memorability?
5. What are the unique challenges of scientific and technology pitching compared to conventional startup pitching?
6. Analyze the role of investor psychology in funding decisions. How can entrepreneurs address investor risk perceptions?
7. Explain key negotiation aspects beyond valuation that entrepreneurs must consider during fundraising.
8. What factors determine readiness for demo days and startup competitions?
9. Discuss the significance of media, branding, and public relations for early-stage startups.
10. Why is crisis and stakeholder communication critical for entrepreneurial sustainability?
11. Identify and explain five common pitching mistakes made by startups.
12. How does effective follow-up communication contribute to long-term stakeholder relationships?

**B. Short Answer / Concept-Based Exercises**

1. Define *value proposition* and explain its role in pitching.
2. List any four psychological factors that influence investor decision-making.
3. Identify three elements that make a pitch visually effective.
4. State two differences between scientific pitching and business pitching.
5. Mention four stakeholders that entrepreneurs must communicate with regularly.

**C. Application-Based Exercises**

1. **Pitch Design Exercise:**
   Design a one-minute elevator pitch for a hypothetical startup of your choice. Clearly state the problem, solution, and target customer.
2. **Pitch Deck Structuring Task:**
   Create an outline of a 10-slide pitch deck for a technology-based startup, indicating the objective of each slide.
3. **Storytelling Exercise:**
   Rewrite a technical product description into a short narrative that highlights user pain points and impact.
4. **Investor Role-Play:**
   In groups, simulate an investor–entrepreneur negotiation focusing on valuation, equity, and milestones. Reflect on communication strategies used.
5. **Crisis Communication Scenario:**
   Draft a brief crisis communication message for a startup facing a product recall or data breach, addressing customers and investors.

**D. Reflective and Critical Thinking Questions**

1. Why do strong ideas often fail to receive funding despite technical merit?
2. How can entrepreneurs ethically balance persuasion and transparency in pitching?
3. Reflect on the role of confidence versus competence in entrepreneurial communication.
4. In what ways can poor communication become a strategic risk for startups?

# CHAPTER-9
# SCALING & GROWTH STRATEGIES

**Abstract**: This chapter examines the critical transition from early-stage validation to sustainable, scalable growth. It presents a structured framework for understanding how startups and innovation-driven enterprises can expand operations, markets, and impact without compromising strategic focus, organizational culture, or ethical responsibility. The chapter begins by establishing the importance of a growth mindset and organizational readiness, emphasizing leadership alignment, process maturity, and data-driven decision-making as foundations for scale. It then explores the shift from product–market fit to scale-up execution, detailing how customer acquisition and retention models evolve as firms move from experimentation to repeatable growth. Contemporary growth hacking techniques are discussed as agile, low-cost mechanisms to accelerate traction, alongside a rigorous treatment of partnerships and strategic alliances as levers for market access, technology integration, and competitive positioning. The chapter further addresses the technological and infrastructural demands of scaling, including platform robustness, automation, data systems, and cybersecurity, followed by an analysis of team building and leadership challenges in high-growth environments. Global expansion and localization strategies are presented to guide firms in navigating regulatory diversity, cultural adaptation, and cross-border operations. Finally, the chapter integrates risk management, ethical considerations, and sustainability into growth planning, highlighting how responsible scaling enhances long-term value. It concludes with practical approaches to managing failure, restructuring, and turnaround strategies, reinforcing resilience as a core capability of scalable enterprises. Collectively, this chapter equips readers with strategic, operational, and leadership perspectives required to transform promising ventures into enduring, high-growth organizations.

**Keywords:** Scalable growth, Product–market fit, Customer acquisition and retention, Strategic partnerships, Infrastructure and technology scaling, Sustainable and ethical expansion

## 9.1 GROWTH MINDSET AND ORGANIZATIONAL READINESS

Scaling a startup or innovation-driven enterprise is not merely an outcome of increased demand or capital infusion; it is fundamentally a function of mindset and organizational preparedness. Before pursuing aggressive growth, organizations must cultivate a growth mindset at both leadership and institutional levels and establish internal capabilities that can sustain complexity, speed, and uncertainty (Fig 9.1).

## Growth Mindset as a Strategic Foundation

A growth mindset, originally conceptualized in organizational psychology, refers to the belief that capabilities, performance, and intelligence can be continuously developed through learning, experimentation, and feedback. In the context of startups and scaling enterprises, a growth mindset translates into openness to change and continuous improvement, willingness to experiment, fail fast, and iterate, data-driven decision-making rather than assumption-based execution, and long-term value creation over short-term gains.

Leaders play a pivotal role in embedding this mindset by modeling adaptive behavior, encouraging cross-functional collaboration, and legitimizing calculated risk-taking. Organizations that approach growth as a learning process rather than a linear expansion are better positioned to adapt to market shifts, competitive pressures, and technological disruption.

## Organizational Readiness for Scale

Organizational readiness refers to the degree to which a firm's structures, processes, people, and culture are prepared to support rapid and sustained growth. Premature scaling without readiness often results in operational inefficiencies, customer dissatisfaction, cultural erosion, and financial instability. Key dimensions of organizational readiness include:

1. **Strategic Clarity and Alignment**: The organization must possess a clearly articulated vision, scalable business model, and well-defined growth objectives. All functional units—product, marketing, operations, finance, and technology—should be aligned with common performance indicators and growth priorities.
2. **Process Maturity and Standardization**: Scaling demands a shift from informal, founder-driven execution to documented, repeatable, and optimized processes. Core functions such as customer onboarding, quality assurance, regulatory compliance, and financial management must be systematized to reduce dependency on individuals and ensure consistency at scale.
3. **Capability and Talent Readiness**: Growth requires not only an increase in workforce size but also a transition in talent composition. Organizations must assess leadership depth, technical competencies, and managerial bandwidth. Investing in training, middle management development, and performance systems becomes critical to maintain productivity and accountability.
4. **Cultural Readiness and Change Management**: As organizations grow, cultural dilution is a common risk. A scale-ready organization clearly defines its values, communication norms, and ethical standards, and actively reinforces them through hiring, evaluation, and leadership practices. Change management mechanisms are essential to manage resistance, ambiguity, and role transitions.

5. **Infrastructure and Governance Preparedness**: Robust digital infrastructure, financial controls, legal frameworks, and governance mechanisms are prerequisites for controlled scaling. This includes enterprise systems, cybersecurity protocols, compliance structures, and board-level oversight.

**From Entrepreneurial Intuition to Institutional Capability**

Early-stage ventures often rely heavily on entrepreneurial intuition and informal coordination. Organizational readiness marks the transition toward institutional capability, where performance is driven by systems, talent pipelines, and strategic discipline. This shift does not eliminate innovation; rather, it creates an environment in which innovation can be executed reliably and repeatedly.

**Outcome of Readiness-Driven Growth**

When growth mindset and organizational readiness are jointly developed, scaling becomes a deliberate and resilient process. Such organizations demonstrate higher execution speed, lower operational risk, stronger employee engagement, and superior customer experience. Ultimately, readiness transforms growth from a reactive response to opportunity into a proactive, strategically governed journey.

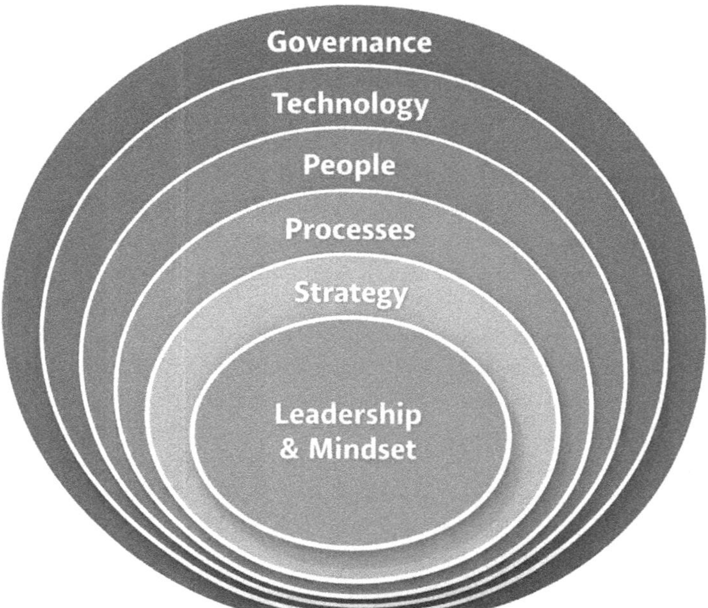


**Figure 9.1: Scaling Readiness Framework**. A multi-layer organizational readiness model illustrating the critical dimensions required for successful and sustainable scaling. The framework progresses from **Leadership & Mindset** at the core, enabling strategic clarity, operational processes, people capability, and technological infrastructure, and culminates in **Governance** to ensure control, compliance, and long-term scalability.

## 9.2 PRODUCT–MARKET FIT TO SCALE-UP TRANSITION

Achieving product–market fit (PMF) is a critical milestone in the startup life cycle, signaling that a product or service effectively solves a real problem for a clearly defined customer segment. However, PMF is not the endpoint of entrepreneurial development; it is the starting point for disciplined scaling. The transition from PMF to scale-up requires a fundamental shift in priorities—from searching and validating to executing, optimizing, and expanding (Fig 9.2).

**Understanding the Shift from Validation to Execution**

During the pre-PMF phase, organizations emphasize experimentation, customer discovery, and rapid iteration. Success is measured through learning velocity, engagement signals, and early traction. Once PMF is established, the organization must pivot toward building repeatable and scalable growth engines. This involves stabilizing the core offering, strengthening value delivery systems, and preparing the enterprise for increased volume, diversity of customers, and operational complexity.

Key indicators that an organization is ready to move from PMF to scale-up include consistent customer demand, strong retention and referral behavior, predictable revenue streams, and validated willingness to pay.

**Key Strategic Transitions in the Scale-Up Phase**

1. **From Product Innovation to Platform Optimization**: The product focus evolves from continuous feature experimentation to performance, reliability, usability, and scalability. Engineering efforts prioritize system architecture, automation, and integration capabilities to support rapid user growth and product extensions.
2. **From Early Adopters to Mainstream Markets**: Scaling requires expanding beyond early adopters to larger, more diverse customer segments. This demands refinement of positioning, clearer value communication, improved onboarding systems, and customer support structures capable of handling volume.
3. **From Ad-hoc Sales to Repeatable Growth Models**: Customer acquisition shifts from founder-led or opportunistic sales to standardized marketing and sales funnels. Conversion optimization, customer segmentation, pricing models, and channel strategies become central to sustaining momentum.
4. **From Learning Metrics to Performance Metrics**: While learning remains important, operational and financial metrics take precedence. Customer lifetime value (LTV), customer acquisition cost (CAC), churn, unit economics, and contribution margins guide strategic and investment decisions.

**Operationalizing Scale-Up Readiness**

The scale-up transition requires codifying what previously worked informally. This includes documenting customer journeys, formalizing go-to-market strategies, building partner ecosystems, and implementing enterprise systems for finance, customer relationship management, and product analytics. Leadership structures must evolve to support delegation, cross-functional coordination, and accountability.

Equally important is risk containment. As volume grows, minor inefficiencies can amplify into systemic failures. Regulatory compliance, data security, quality assurance, and supply-chain resilience must be strengthened before aggressive expansion.

**Avoiding the Pitfalls of Premature Scaling**

One of the most common causes of startup failure is premature scaling—investing heavily in marketing, infrastructure, or hiring before demand and delivery mechanisms are sufficiently validated. The PMF-to-scale transition must therefore be evidence-driven, ensuring that customer satisfaction, economics, and operational capacity are robust enough to absorb growth.

**Strategic Outcome**

A successful transition from product–market fit to scale-up transforms a startup into a growth-oriented enterprise. The organization moves from exploration to execution, from flexibility to disciplined agility, and from isolated success cases to repeatable performance. This stage lays the groundwork upon which customer acquisition systems, partnerships, global expansion, and long-term competitive advantage are built.

In essence, product–market fit answers the question "Should we grow?", while the scale-up transition addresses "How can we grow sustainably, efficiently, and defensibly?"

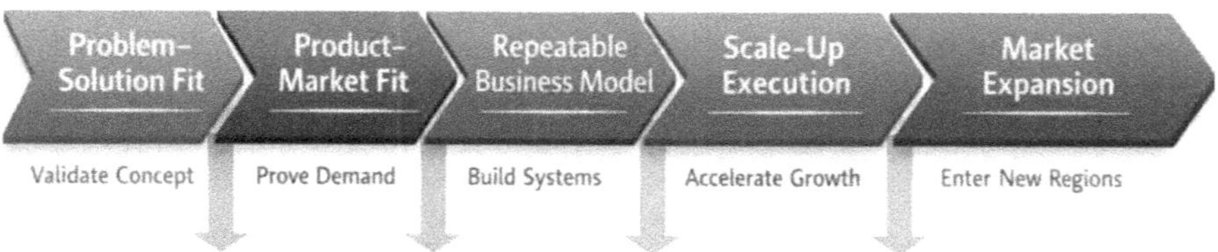


**Figure 9.2: Product–Market Fit to Scale-Up Transition Model.** This figure illustrates the structured progression from early validation to sustained growth. It depicts the stage-gated transition from *Problem–Solution Fit* and *Product–Market Fit,* which emphasize experimentation and demand validation, to *Repeatable Business Model* and *Scale-Up Execution*, where systems, processes, and performance discipline are established. The final stage, *Market Expansion*, represents the shift toward accelerated growth and geographic or segmental scaling. Collectively, the model highlights the strategic shift from exploration to execution that underpins successful scaling.

## 9.3 CUSTOMER ACQUISITION AND RETENTION MODELS

Sustainable scaling is not driven solely by acquiring large volumes of customers; it is determined by the organization's ability to attract the right customers, convert them efficiently, and retain them over time. As ventures move into the growth phase, customer acquisition and retention must transition from opportunistic, founder-led efforts to structured, data-driven, and repeatable models that optimize both growth velocity and unit economics (Fig 9.3).

**From Early Traction to Systematic Growth Engines**
In early stages, customers are often acquired through personal networks, pilot projects, or organic visibility. While valuable for validation, these channels are rarely sufficient for scale. Growth-stage organizations must therefore design formal acquisition engines that integrate marketing, sales, partnerships, and product-led mechanisms into coherent systems.

Common scalable acquisition models include:

- **Marketing-led growth**, driven by brand building, content, performance marketing, and demand generation campaigns.
- **Sales-led growth**, characterized by structured pipelines, lead qualification, enterprise selling, and account management.
- **Product-led growth**, where the product itself functions as the primary acquisition and conversion channel through freemium models, trials, virality, and embedded referrals.
- **Partner-led growth**, leveraging distributors, platforms, institutions, or technology alliances to access new markets.

Selecting and optimizing the appropriate mix depends on customer segment, deal size, buying behavior, regulatory constraints, and competitive intensity.

**Designing Efficient Acquisition Funnels**
At scale, acquisition must be managed as a funnel with clearly defined stages: awareness, interest, evaluation, conversion, onboarding, and activation. Each stage requires targeted strategies, performance metrics, and continuous optimization.

Key acquisition metrics include customer acquisition cost (CAC), conversion rates, sales cycle length, channel efficiency, and payback period. Advanced organizations deploy analytics and automation platforms to track attribution, personalize outreach, and systematically improve funnel performance.

**Retention as a Core Growth Lever**
Retention is often a stronger determinant of long-term growth than acquisition. High churn rates neutralize marketing investments and undermine valuation, whereas strong retention increases lifetime value, enables cross-selling, and

fuels organic growth through referrals.

Retention strategies are centered on creating sustained, long-term value for customers rather than short-term transactional gains. Organizations prioritize the delivery of consistent and measurable customer value to ensure that users clearly perceive the benefits derived from the product or service over time. This is reinforced through structured onboarding and education programs that help customers quickly understand features, optimize usage, and achieve early success. Proactive customer success management further strengthens retention by anticipating customer needs, addressing issues before they escalate, and guiding users toward desired outcomes. In parallel, continuous product improvement is driven by systematic analysis of usage data, enabling organizations to refine functionality, enhance performance, and align offerings with evolving customer expectations. Finally, retention is supported through community building and relationship engagement initiatives that foster trust, encourage peer interaction, and deepen emotional and professional connections between customers and the organization. Organizations that embed retention into product design and service architecture shift from transactional interactions to lifecycle-based customer management.

**Customer Lifetime Value Optimization**

Scalable growth depends on the relationship between lifetime value (LTV) and CAC. Healthy scale-up models typically demonstrate a strong LTV:CAC ratio, indicating that customer relationships generate durable economic returns. This requires coordinated optimization of pricing, packaging, service costs, engagement intensity, and expansion revenue.

Retention models such as subscriptions, usage-based pricing, enterprise contracts, and ecosystem lock-in mechanisms enhance predictability and financial resilience.

**Integration with Organizational Systems**

As scale increases, acquisition and retention functions must integrate closely with product development, data analytics, and finance. Customer insights guide roadmap prioritization, while financial modeling ensures that growth investments reinforce profitability rather than erode it.

**Strategic Outcome**

Robust customer acquisition and retention models transform growth from a campaign-based activity into a systemic capability. They enable organizations to forecast revenue, allocate capital efficiently, and build defensible market positions. Ultimately, scale is not achieved by the number of customers acquired, but by the quality, durability, and economic productivity of customer relationships.

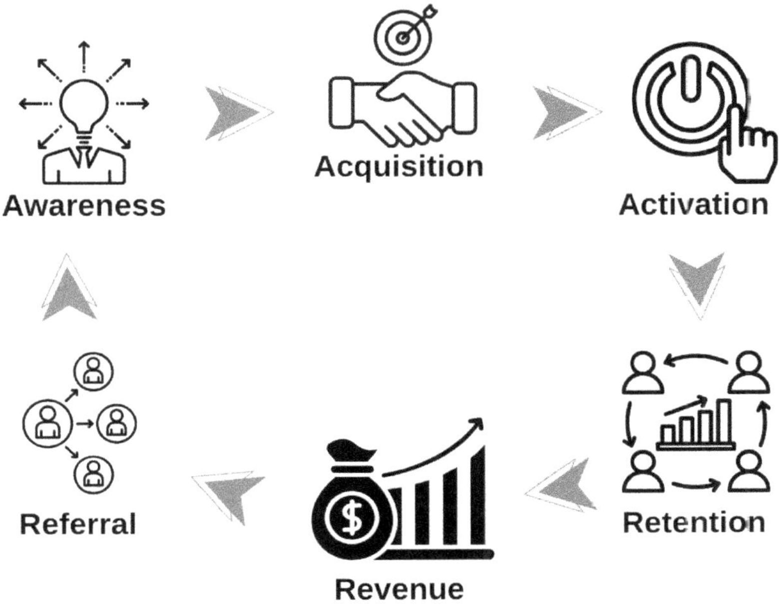


**Figure 9.3: Customer Acquisition and Retention Growth Engine.** This figure illustrates an integrated growth engine in which customer acquisition and retention function as mutually reinforcing processes. Prospective users move through structured stages of awareness, acquisition, activation, and conversion, while post-conversion systems focus on retention, value delivery, and relationship management. Satisfied customers generate recurring revenue, expansion opportunities, and referrals, which feed back into the acquisition funnel. The model emphasizes that sustainable scaling is driven not only by attracting new customers, but by maximizing lifetime value, minimizing churn, and embedding retention as a core growth lever.

## 9.4 GROWTH HACKING TECHNIQUES

Growth hacking represents a systematic, experimentation-driven approach to accelerating user acquisition, engagement, and revenue growth through creative, data-intensive, and low-cost strategies. Unlike traditional marketing, which often relies on large budgets and long planning cycles, growth hacking integrates product development, analytics, marketing, and behavioral science to identify rapid, scalable growth levers (Fig 9.4).

### Concept and Strategic Relevance

Growth hacking emerged from digital startups seeking to achieve rapid market penetration under severe resource constraints. At the scale-up stage, growth hacking evolves from isolated tactics into an institutionalized capability—where cross-functional teams continuously test hypotheses, optimize funnels, and engineer growth loops.

Its core philosophy is to treat growth as a scientific process: define objectives, formulate testable hypotheses, conduct controlled experiments, measure outcomes, and iterate rapidly.

**Core Components of Growth Hacking**

1. **Data-Centric Experimentation**: Growth hacking relies heavily on analytics platforms, cohort analysis, A/B testing, and behavioral tracking. Decisions are evidence-based, focusing on micro-optimizations across acquisition, activation, engagement, retention, and monetization.
2. **Product-Embedded Growth Mechanisms**: Instead of depending solely on external promotion, growth hackers design features that inherently drive expansion—such as referral systems, virality triggers, social sharing tools, in-product incentives, and network effects.
3. **Rapid Prototyping and Iteration**: Short experimentation cycles allow organizations to test landing pages, onboarding flows, pricing tiers, messaging, and feature sets. Low-performing initiatives are terminated quickly, while high-impact interventions are scaled aggressively.
4. **Automation and Scalability**: Marketing automation, CRM systems, AI-driven personalization, and workflow orchestration enable growth initiatives to scale without proportional increases in cost or manpower.

Common growth hacking techniques are designed to accelerate user acquisition, activation, and retention through data-driven and scalable interventions. Viral loops and referral programs leverage existing users as distribution channels, incentivizing sharing behaviors that organically expand the user base. Freemium and trial-based conversion strategies lower adoption barriers by allowing users to experience core value before committing financially, thereby increasing conversion probability. Search engine optimization and app store optimization enhance discoverability by aligning content, keywords, and metadata with user search intent.

Content engineering and community-led growth focus on creating high-value, shareable resources and fostering engaged user communities that drive trust, advocacy, and sustained participation. Behavioral nudging through notifications and personalization techniques subtly influences user actions by delivering timely, relevant prompts based on individual usage patterns and preferences. Funnel compression and friction reduction streamline the user journey by minimizing unnecessary steps, reducing cognitive load, and eliminating conversion barriers. Finally, gamification and engagement triggers—such as rewards, progress indicators, and achievement mechanisms—motivate continued interaction and reinforce desired user behaviors, contributing to rapid and sustainable growth. Each technique is evaluated not by visibility but by its measurable contribution to key performance indicators such as activation rates, retention cohorts, and revenue per user.

## Governance and Ethical Boundaries

While growth hacking emphasizes speed and experimentation, it must be governed by ethical standards and regulatory compliance. Dark patterns, deceptive design, and data misuse may yield short-term gains but erode trust, invite legal risk, and undermine brand equity. Scale-ready organizations therefore integrate growth hacking within formal governance, data privacy, and brand integrity frameworks.

## Strategic Outcome

When institutionalized correctly, growth hacking becomes a high-velocity innovation engine for market expansion. It enables organizations to uncover non-obvious growth levers, improve capital efficiency, and outpace competitors through learning speed rather than spending power. At scale, growth hacking complements traditional marketing and strategic partnerships by continuously optimizing the growth architecture of the enterprise.

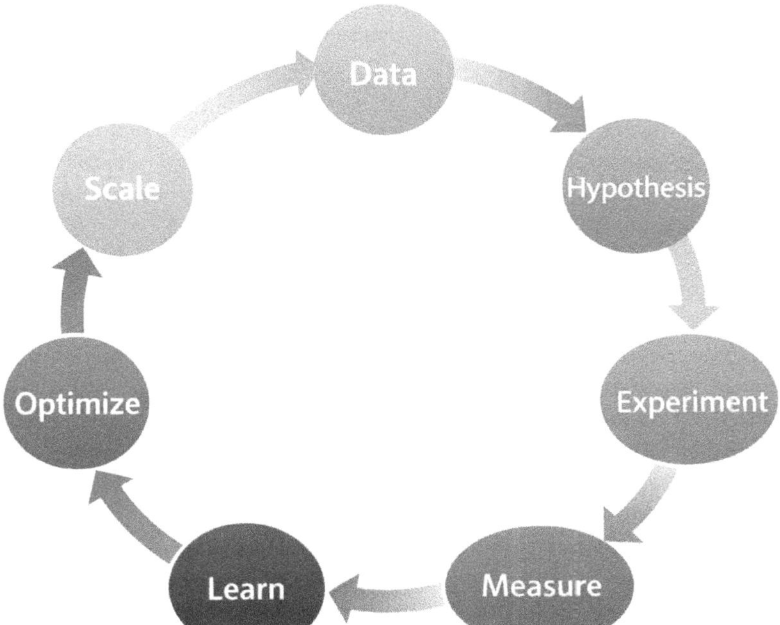


**Figure 9.4: Growth Hacking Experimentation Cycle.** This figure presents growth hacking as a continuous, data-driven experimentation loop. The cycle begins with *Data* analysis, followed by *Hypothesis* formulation and *Experiment* execution. Outcomes are *Measured* and translated into insights through *Learning*, which inform *Optimization* of strategies and product features. Successful interventions are then *Scaled*, feeding new data back into the system. The model emphasizes rapid iteration, evidence-based decision-making, and continuous improvement as core mechanisms for accelerated and sustainable growth.

## 9.5 PARTNERSHIPS AND STRATEGIC ALLIANCES

As organizations move beyond early growth, internal capabilities alone are often insufficient to sustain rapid scaling. Partnerships and strategic alliances become critical instruments for accelerating market access, strengthening technological capabilities, reducing risk, and enhancing competitive positioning. Effective collaborations allow firms to leverage external resources, complementary competencies, and established networks without bearing the full cost and time burden of internal development.

The strategic rationale for partnerships in scaling lies in their ability to accelerate growth while reducing uncertainty and resource constraints. Partnerships enable rapid entry into new markets and geographies by leveraging the local presence, networks, and market knowledge of established partners. They also provide access to existing customer bases and well-developed distribution channels, significantly shortening the time and cost required to achieve market penetration. Through partnerships, organizations can integrate complementary technologies or intellectual property, enhancing product capabilities and differentiation without incurring the full burden of in-house development.

In addition, partnerships facilitate cost sharing and risk mitigation by distributing financial, operational, and strategic risks across multiple stakeholders. They play a critical role in regulatory navigation and in building institutional credibility, particularly in highly regulated industries where compliance, trust, and legitimacy are essential for scale. Finally, partnerships support co-innovation and joint product development, enabling organizations to combine expertise, share insights, and collaboratively create new solutions that are better aligned with market needs and scalable growth objectives.

Unlike transactional vendor relationships, strategic alliances are designed to create long-term, mutual value and to embed growth opportunities into the organization's ecosystem.

### Types of Strategic Partnerships

1. **Technology and Innovation Alliances**: Collaborations with research institutions, biotech or deep-tech firms, platform providers, and infrastructure companies enable access to specialized expertise, accelerate product development, and support modular scalability.
2. **Market and Distribution Partnerships**: Channel partners, resellers, system integrators, and institutional collaborators facilitate customer acquisition, localization, and service delivery, particularly in regulated or fragmented markets.
3. **Corporate and Industry Partnerships**: Engagements with large enterprises provide validation, enterprise-scale contracts, manufacturing capabilities, and global operational reach.

4. **Public Sector and Academic Partnerships**: Alliances with government bodies, universities, and incubators support regulatory alignment, funding access, pilot deployments, and long-term innovation pipelines.

**Designing High-Impact Alliances**

Designing high-impact alliances requires more than opportunistic collaboration; it demands a deliberate focus on strategic fit, governance clarity, and seamless operational integration. Organizations must begin by clearly defining the objectives and value propositions for each partner, ensuring that expectations, contributions, and anticipated outcomes are explicitly aligned. Equally important is the demarcation of roles and responsibilities, along with well-articulated provisions for intellectual property rights and data ownership, to prevent ambiguity and protect strategic assets.

Effective alliances also depend on robust performance management, supported by clearly defined metrics, transparent reporting structures, and predetermined exit mechanisms that allow for orderly disengagement if strategic alignment diminishes. Cultural compatibility and decision-making processes must be carefully assessed and aligned to enable trust, speed, and effective collaboration across organizational boundaries. At scale, partnerships should not be managed as isolated engagements but as a structured portfolio, supported by dedicated alliance management functions that continuously monitor performance, optimize value creation, and ensure long-term strategic coherence.

**Managing Risks and Power Asymmetries:** Strategic alliances introduce dependencies and coordination complexity. Risks include misaligned incentives, intellectual property leakage, reputational exposure, and strategic drift. These risks are amplified when partnering with significantly larger or more established entities. Robust legal frameworks, transparent communication, and phased collaboration models are essential to preserve strategic autonomy while enabling value creation.

**Ecosystem Thinking and Platform Strategy:** At scale, partnerships evolve into ecosystems. Organizations position themselves as platform orchestrators or critical nodes within industry networks, enabling third parties to build complementary offerings. Such ecosystem strategies enhance switching costs, stimulate innovation, and reinforce competitive moats.

**Strategic Outcome:** When aligned with growth strategy, partnerships and alliances act as force multipliers. They compress time-to-market, amplify innovation capacity, and extend organizational reach beyond internal constraints. For scaling enterprises, the ability to systematically identify, structure, and govern partnerships becomes a core strategic competence, shaping not only how fast the organization grows, but also how defensibly and sustainably it competes.

## 9.6 TECHNOLOGY AND INFRASTRUCTURE SCALING

Technology and infrastructure form the operational backbone of any scaling enterprise. As customer volumes, data flows, product complexity, and geographic reach expand, systems that were sufficient at the startup stage often become performance bottlenecks and risk multipliers. Effective scaling therefore requires a deliberate transition from lightweight, flexible architectures to robust, secure, and extensible infrastructures capable of supporting sustained growth.

### From Prototype Systems to Enterprise-Grade Platforms

Early-stage ventures typically emphasize speed and experimentation over stability, relying on minimal technical architectures, manual interventions, and loosely integrated tools to validate assumptions and achieve early traction. While these arrangements are appropriate during the validation phase, they become increasingly fragile and prone to failure as user volumes, transaction complexity, and operational demands increase. As organizations transition into the growth stage, there is a clear imperative to invest in enterprise-grade platforms that provide reliability, security, interoperability, and regulatory compliance.

This transformation requires the deliberate adoption of modular, microservices-based system architectures that support flexibility and independent scaling of components. Cloud-native infrastructure plays a central role by enabling elastic scaling, high availability, and cost-efficient resource utilization. Standardized APIs and integration frameworks are essential to ensure seamless interoperability across internal systems and external partners. In parallel, automated deployment, testing, and monitoring systems must be implemented to reduce operational risk, improve release velocity, and maintain system performance and resilience at scale.

The objective is to decouple growth from linear increases in operational effort.

### Core Dimensions of Technology Scaling

1. **Product and Platform Scalability**: Systems must handle increasing user loads, transaction volumes, and functional complexity without performance degradation. This includes database optimization, load balancing, redundancy planning, and disaster recovery mechanisms.
2. **Data and Analytics Infrastructure**: At scale, data becomes a strategic asset. Organizations require integrated data warehouses, real-time analytics, AI-enabled decision systems, and governance protocols to convert raw data into actionable intelligence.

3. **Process Automation and Digital Operations**: Manual workflows must be replaced with automated pipelines across customer support, finance, HR, compliance, and supply chains. Robotic process automation and enterprise software suites reduce error rates, improve cycle times, and free human capital for higher-value activities.
4. **Cybersecurity and Regulatory Compliance**: Scaling increases exposure to cyber threats, privacy risks, and regulatory scrutiny. Investment in identity management, encryption, access controls, audit systems, and compliance frameworks is non-negotiable, particularly in health, finance, and data-intensive sectors.
5. **Technology Governance and Architecture Management**: Formal governance structures ensure that technology investments remain aligned with strategic objectives, avoid fragmentation, and support long-term maintainability.

**Build, Buy, and Partner Decisions:** Technology scaling requires careful evaluation of whether to build proprietary systems, procure commercial solutions, or integrate partner platforms. These decisions must consider cost, speed, strategic differentiation, data ownership, and long-term flexibility.

**Infrastructure as a Strategic Enabler:** Rather than viewing infrastructure as a cost center, scale-ready organizations treat it as a strategic growth enabler. Well-designed systems support rapid experimentation, seamless global deployment, personalized customer experiences, and real-time performance management.

**Strategic Outcome:** When technology and infrastructure scaling are proactively managed, organizations gain operational resilience, execution speed, and analytical depth. This foundation not only supports current expansion but also positions the enterprise to integrate future innovations, regulatory changes, and market opportunities without destabilization. In high-growth contexts, technology maturity becomes a decisive factor separating scalable enterprises from those constrained by their own systems.

## 9.7 TEAM BUILDING AND LEADERSHIP AT SCALE

As organizations scale, growth is no longer constrained primarily by ideas or capital, but by people and leadership systems. What begins as a small, founder-centric team must evolve into a multi-layered organization with specialized roles, formal management structures, and a shared leadership culture. Team building and leadership development therefore become central to sustaining performance, preserving culture, and executing strategy at scale.

**From Founding Team to Organizational Capability**

In early stages, founders and core team members operate as generalists, relying on informal coordination, personal commitment, and rapid decision-making. Scaling demands a shift toward role clarity, professional management, and institutionalized accountability. This transition often represents one of the most challenging phases of growth, as it requires founders to delegate authority, redesign workflows, and redefine their own leadership identities.

**Strategic Workforce Planning**

Scale-up organizations must adopt forward-looking workforce strategies that align talent acquisition with long-term growth objectives. This includes:

- Identifying critical capability gaps in technology, operations, regulatory affairs, marketing, and finance
- Developing hiring roadmaps linked to expansion milestones
- Building employer branding to attract high-quality, mission-aligned talent
- Structuring compensation, performance incentives, and career progression frameworks

Hiring errors at scale are costly; therefore, recruitment must be competency-based, culturally aligned, and strategically sequenced.

**Leadership Development and Management Systems**

Rapid growth often outpaces managerial maturity. High-performing individual contributors are promoted into leadership roles without adequate preparation, creating execution and morale risks. Scalable organizations proactively invest in leadership development through training programs, mentoring structures, and performance coaching.

Key leadership priorities at scale extend beyond operational oversight to the orchestration of complex organizational systems. Leaders must effectively translate vision into clear strategic intent and communicate it consistently across teams, ensuring alignment as the organization grows. Strong cross-functional coordination and disciplined conflict management are essential to break down silos, balance competing priorities, and maintain execution velocity. At the same time, leaders are expected to rely on data-informed decision-making, using reliable metrics and evidence to guide strategy, allocate resources, and manage risk.

As scale increases, ethical governance and stakeholder accountability become central leadership responsibilities, particularly in relation to compliance, transparency, and long-term trust. Talent development and succession planning also emerge as critical priorities, ensuring leadership continuity and organizational resilience. Fundamentally, leadership at scale shifts from direct control to system design, with leaders focusing on creating structures, processes, and cultures that enable others to perform consistently at high levels.

**Culture Preservation and Organizational Cohesion:** As headcount increases and teams become geographically distributed, informal cultural transmission weakens. Organizations must therefore articulate and operationalize their values, behaviors, and norms through onboarding programs, evaluation systems, and leadership modeling. Culture becomes a managed asset rather than an emergent byproduct.
Transparent communication channels, psychological safety, and diversity-oriented practices are essential to sustaining engagement and innovation in large, complex organizations.

**Structures, Teams, and Execution Models:** Scaling enterprises must design organizational structures that balance speed with control. Functional, divisional, matrix, or product-based models may be adopted depending on strategy and industry context. High-performing scale-ups increasingly rely on agile, cross-functional teams supported by clear governance frameworks.

**Strategic Outcome:** Effective team building and leadership at scale transform growth from a founder-dependent process into an institutional capability. Organizations that invest systematically in people, culture, and leadership infrastructure achieve higher execution reliability, lower attrition, and greater strategic coherence. Ultimately, sustainable scale is not built by strategy alone, but by the collective capacity of the organization to learn, adapt, and lead in complexity.

## 9.8 GLOBAL EXPANSION AND LOCALIZATION

Global expansion represents a major inflection point in the scaling journey, transforming an organization from a domestic or regional player into an international enterprise. While cross-border growth offers access to larger markets, diversified revenue streams, and global talent pools, it also introduces significant complexity in regulation, culture, operations, and risk. Successful global scaling therefore requires a structured strategy that balances standardization with localization.

### Strategic Rationale for Global Expansion

Organizations pursue international growth to achieve market diversification, leverage core technologies across borders, follow existing customers into new geographies, and strengthen competitive positioning. However, global expansion should be driven by strategic fit and readiness rather than opportunity alone. Market selection must consider demand intensity, regulatory feasibility, infrastructure maturity, competitive dynamics, and alignment with long-term corporate vision.

**Modes of International Scaling**

Scale-ready organizations select expansion pathways by carefully balancing resource availability, risk tolerance, and desired levels of operational control. Rather than adopting a one-size-fits-all approach, firms align their mode of expansion with strategic objectives and contextual constraints. Export-based models and cross-border digital delivery offer relatively fast and capital-efficient access to international markets, making them attractive for organizations seeking speed with limited exposure. Licensing and franchising enable rapid geographic reach while transferring a portion of operational responsibility to local partners, thereby reducing capital requirements but also limiting direct control.

Strategic alliances and joint ventures provide a collaborative route to expansion, allowing organizations to share risks, access local expertise, and navigate complex regulatory environments. In contrast, foreign direct investment through wholly owned subsidiaries represents a more capital-intensive approach that offers maximum control over operations, brand, and intellectual property, but also entails higher regulatory and execution risk. Increasingly, platform-based and ecosystem-driven internationalization models are enabling organizations to scale globally by orchestrating networks of partners, developers, and users across borders. Each expansion mode reflects deliberate trade-offs among speed, capital intensity, regulatory exposure, and operational control, underscoring the importance of strategic fit in scaling decisions.

**Localization as a Competitive Necessity**

Global success is rarely achieved through uniform replication. Localization is essential across multiple dimensions:

- **Product and service adaptation:** tailoring features, language, usability, and compliance to local needs.
- **Market communication:** aligning branding, messaging, and engagement strategies with cultural norms and consumption behaviors.
- **Operations and supply chains:** adjusting logistics, sourcing, and service delivery to local infrastructures.
- **Regulatory alignment:** complying with country-specific legal, data protection, taxation, and sectoral requirements.

Organizations that fail to localize risk weak adoption, reputational damage, and regulatory setbacks.

**Organizational and Leadership Implications:** International scaling requires globally competent leadership, decentralized decision-making, and strong coordination mechanisms. Cross-cultural management skills, global governance frameworks, and international compliance functions become essential. Firms must invest in local leadership development while maintaining strategic coherence across regions.

Digital collaboration platforms, global performance metrics, and standardized operational playbooks help balance autonomy and alignment.

**Risk Management in Global Growth:** Global expansion exposes organizations to geopolitical uncertainty, currency fluctuations, regulatory volatility, and cross-border operational disruptions. Structured risk assessment, diversified market portfolios, and scenario planning are critical to sustaining international growth.

**Strategic Outcome:** When executed with strategic discipline, global expansion multiplies the scalability of business models and strengthens long-term resilience. Localization transforms international presence from a symbolic footprint into a source of sustainable competitive advantage. Ultimately, global scaling is not the replication of domestic success abroad, but the construction of a globally integrated yet locally responsive enterprise.

## 9.9 RISK, ETHICS, AND SUSTAINABLE SCALING

As organizations scale, the magnitude of their impact—economic, social, technological, and environmental—expands significantly. Growth amplifies not only opportunity, but also risk exposure, ethical responsibility, and stakeholder scrutiny. Sustainable scaling therefore requires integrating risk management, ethical governance, and long-term value creation into the core growth strategy, rather than treating them as compliance afterthoughts.

**Risk Amplification in High-Growth Contexts**

Scaling intensifies multiple categories of risk, including operational failures, financial instability, regulatory non-compliance, cybersecurity breaches, reputational damage, and strategic misalignment. Minor inefficiencies or ethical lapses that are manageable at small scale can rapidly evolve into systemic crises. Scale-ready organizations adopt enterprise risk management frameworks to systematically anticipate, assess, and mitigate uncertainties that accompany growth. These frameworks enable the identification and categorization of strategic, operational, financial, and technological risks, ensuring that potential threats are comprehensively understood rather than addressed in isolation. Early-warning indicators and continuous monitoring systems are established to detect emerging risks in a timely manner, allowing management to intervene before issues escalate into material disruptions.

Effective risk management further depends on clearly defined escalation protocols and crisis response structures that specify decision rights, communication flows, and accountability during high-impact events. Importantly, risk evaluation is integrated into strategic planning and investment decision-making, aligning growth initiatives with the organization's risk appetite and governance standards. Through proactive risk governance, organizations strengthen operational resilience, reduce downside exposure, and build sustained confidence among investors and other key stakeholders.

### Ethics as a Strategic Asset

High-growth organizations increasingly operate under intense public, regulatory, and investor scrutiny. Data practices, labor policies, environmental impact, algorithmic accountability, and customer transparency are no longer peripheral issues. Ethical failures erode trust, invite regulatory intervention, and undermine long-term competitiveness.

Ethical scaling requires organizations to deliberately integrate ethical considerations into their growth strategies rather than treating them as secondary compliance obligations. This begins with clearly articulated codes of conduct and governance policies that define acceptable behavior, decision-making standards, and accountability across all levels of the organization. Responsible innovation frameworks are particularly critical in domains such as artificial intelligence, biotechnology, and health technologies, where societal impact, safety, and long-term consequences must be carefully evaluated alongside commercial objectives.

Robust data privacy, informed consent, and security practices form another cornerstone of ethical scaling, especially as organizations collect, process, and monetize increasing volumes of sensitive data. Ethical growth also depends on fair labor systems, genuine commitments to diversity and inclusion, and meaningful stakeholder participation in organizational processes. Transparent and consistent communication with customers, partners, and regulators further reinforces trust and legitimacy. By embedding ethics into product design, operational processes, and leadership incentives, organizations ensure that scale is achieved without compromising integrity, public trust, or long-term sustainability.

### Sustainability and Long-Term Value Creation

Sustainable scaling extends beyond financial performance to encompass environmental stewardship, social responsibility, and institutional durability. Organizations must assess resource consumption, carbon footprints, supply chain ethics, and community impact as part of growth planning.

Adopting environmental, social, and governance (ESG) frameworks enables organizations to scale responsibly while strengthening long-term strategic positioning. ESG integration enhances regulatory preparedness and risk mitigation by ensuring that environmental compliance, social responsibility, and governance standards are proactively addressed rather than reactively enforced. It also supports brand differentiation and the development of customer trust, as increasingly informed stakeholders favor organizations that demonstrate measurable commitments to sustainability and ethical conduct.

From a financial perspective, strong ESG performance improves access to impact-oriented capital and strategic partnerships, particularly with investors and institutions that prioritize responsible growth. In addition, ESG-driven practices contribute to long-term operational efficiency and organizational resilience by promoting resource optimization, workforce stability, and robust governance structures. Sustainability-oriented enterprises therefore align profitability with societal contribution, reinforcing the premise that responsible conduct and commercial success are mutually reinforcing rather than competing objectives.

**Balancing Speed with Responsibility**

The central tension in scaling is between rapid execution and responsible governance. High-performing scale-ups resolve this tension not by slowing innovation, but by systematizing responsibility through automation, policy frameworks, and leadership accountability.

**Strategic Outcome**

Organizations that integrate risk management, ethics, and sustainability into their growth architecture achieve more durable scale. They are better positioned to navigate regulatory complexity, withstand market volatility, and maintain stakeholder trust. Ultimately, sustainable scaling transforms growth from a short-term performance objective into a long-term institutional legacy.

## 9.10 MANAGING FAILURE AND TURNAROUND STRATEGIES

Failure is an inherent component of entrepreneurial and scaling journeys. As organizations grow, the stakes of failure increase, affecting capital structures, workforce stability, brand reputation, and stakeholder confidence. However, failure at scale does not necessarily signify organizational decline; when managed strategically, it can become a catalyst for renewal, restructuring, and long-term resilience. This section examines how scaling enterprises can systematically diagnose underperformance, contain damage, and execute effective turnaround strategies.

**Nature of Failure in Scaling Organizations**

Failure in growth-stage enterprises rarely occurs as a single event. It typically emerges through cumulative misalignments between strategy, execution, market realities, and organizational capacity. Common drivers include premature scaling, flawed business models, leadership breakdowns, unsustainable cost structures, technological fragility, regulatory non-compliance, and erosion of customer trust.

At scale, failures manifest as revenue stagnation, cash flow crises, declining retention, operational breakdowns, cultural fragmentation, or loss of strategic relevance.

### Early Warning Systems and Failure Detection

Effective turnaround begins with early recognition. Scale-ready organizations establish performance dashboards, financial stress indicators, customer health metrics, and operational audits to detect deviations before they become existential threats. Leadership must foster a culture where negative data is surfaced, not suppressed, and where corrective action is rewarded rather than politicized.

### Strategic Diagnosis and Stabilization

Turnaround processes typically proceed through three sequential priorities:

1. **Stabilization** – securing liquidity, restoring operational continuity, protecting core customers, and managing stakeholder communication.
2. **Diagnosis** – identifying root causes across strategy, market fit, cost structures, leadership systems, and technology platforms.
3. **Restructuring** – realigning business models, divesting non-core assets, redesigning organizations, and recalibrating growth assumptions.

Decisive leadership, credible communication, and disciplined execution are essential during this phase.

### Turnaround Levers

Common turnaround strategies are deployed to restore organizational viability while laying the foundation for sustainable recovery. These efforts often begin with business model reinvention and value proposition redesign, enabling the organization to realign offerings with market demand and competitive realities. Cost rationalization and operational streamlining are typically pursued in parallel to stabilize cash flows, eliminate inefficiencies, and improve short-term financial performance. Organizations may also undertake portfolio refocusing by exiting unviable markets or discontinuing underperforming products in order to concentrate resources on core strengths.

Leadership reconfiguration and governance strengthening play a critical role in turnarounds, as renewed strategic direction and accountability are often required to regain stakeholder confidence. Technology modernization and process reengineering further support recovery by enhancing productivity, transparency, and scalability. In some cases, strategic partnerships, mergers, or acquisitions are leveraged to access new capabilities, markets, or capital. Successful turnarounds therefore balance immediate survival-oriented actions with deliberate long-term capability rebuilding, ensuring that recovery is both rapid and durable.

### Learning-Oriented Recovery

Beyond financial and operational recovery, organizations must institutionalize learning from failure. Post-crisis reviews, governance reforms, leadership development, and cultural realignment ensure that past breakdowns strengthen future performance. This learning orientation converts failure into organizational intelligence.

**Strategic Outcome**

Managing failure and executing turnarounds are not peripheral skills; they are core leadership competencies in high-growth environments. Organizations that develop structured crisis response and renewal capabilities demonstrate superior longevity, investor confidence, and adaptive strength. In the scaling context, resilience—the ability to absorb shock, restructure, and re-emerge stronger—becomes a defining feature of enduring enterprises.

---

## KEY CONCEPTS & DEFINITIONS

**Scaling**: The process of increasing an organization's capacity, market reach, and operational scope while maintaining or improving efficiency, quality, and unit economics. Unlike simple growth, scaling emphasizes non-linear expansion of impact and revenue relative to resources consumed.

**Growth Mindset**: An organizational and leadership orientation characterized by continuous learning, experimentation, adaptability, and resilience, enabling enterprises to evolve capabilities and strategies in response to dynamic environments.

**Organizational Readiness**: The extent to which a firm's structures, processes, culture, talent, governance, and infrastructure are prepared to support sustained and complex growth without performance degradation.

**Product–Market Fit (PMF)**: A condition in which a product or service demonstrably satisfies a strong, identifiable market demand, reflected through consistent customer adoption, retention, and willingness to pay.

**Scale-Up Transition**: The strategic shift from validation and experimentation to execution and expansion, where focus moves toward repeatable growth systems, operational maturity, and performance optimization.

**Customer Acquisition Model**: A structured framework defining how an organization attracts, converts, and onboards customers through coordinated marketing, sales, product, and partnership channels.

**Customer Retention Model**: A system of practices and mechanisms designed to sustain long-term customer engagement, minimize churn, and maximize lifetime value through service quality, product evolution, and relationship management.

**Growth Hacking**: A data-driven, experimentation-based approach to accelerating growth by rapidly testing and optimizing product features, marketing tactics, and user engagement mechanisms.

**Strategic Partnership**: A long-term, value-driven collaboration between organizations to access complementary capabilities, markets, technologies, or resources in support of shared growth objectives.

**Ecosystem Strategy**: A growth approach in which an organization positions itself as a central platform or integrator, enabling multiple partners to co-create value and reinforcing network-based competitive advantage.

**Technology Scaling**: The systematic enhancement of digital platforms, infrastructure, and systems to support increased user volumes, data complexity, automation, security, and regulatory compliance.

**Organizational Infrastructure**: The integrated set of technological, operational, financial, and governance systems that enable consistent execution, coordination, and control at scale.

**Leadership at Scale**: The evolution of leadership roles and competencies from direct operational control to strategic orchestration, talent development, and institutional capability building.

**Global Expansion**: The strategic extension of operations, products, and markets across national boundaries to access new customers, diversify revenue, and strengthen competitive positioning.

**Localization**: The adaptation of products, services, processes, and communication strategies to align with local cultural, regulatory, linguistic, and market conditions.

**Enterprise Risk Management (ERM)**: A structured framework for identifying, assessing, monitoring, and mitigating strategic, operational, financial, technological, and compliance risks in high-growth organizations.

**Ethical Scaling**: The integration of responsible innovation, transparency, stakeholder protection, and regulatory compliance into growth strategies.

**Sustainable Scaling**: A growth approach that balances financial performance with environmental stewardship, social responsibility, and long-term organizational resilience.

**Turnaround Strategy**: A structured set of actions aimed at stabilizing an underperforming organization, diagnosing root causes, restructuring operations, and restoring growth and competitiveness.

**Organizational Resilience**: The capacity of an enterprise to anticipate disruption, absorb shocks, adapt to changing conditions, and emerge stronger from failure or crisis.

---

### Mini Case Study 1: From Laboratory Innovation to Scalable Health-Tech Enterprise

A university-incubated health-technology startup developed an AI-enabled diagnostic support platform for early detection of neurological disorders. Initial pilots with two hospitals confirmed strong clinical relevance and physician acceptance, demonstrating clear product–market fit. However, when demand increased, the organization struggled with slow deployments, inconsistent service quality, and regulatory documentation gaps.

Recognizing the risk of premature scaling, the leadership initiated an organizational readiness assessment. They invested in cloud-based infrastructure, standardized deployment protocols, implemented quality and compliance systems aligned with healthcare regulations, and recruited experienced operations and regulatory professionals. Simultaneously, they shifted from opportunistic hospital outreach to structured institutional partnerships and subscription-based enterprise contracts.

Within eighteen months, the company expanded into multiple regions, reduced deployment time by over 60%, and built a sustainable acquisition and retention model anchored in long-term hospital collaborations. The case illustrates how growth mindset combined with operational maturity enables scientific innovations to transform into scalable, credible healthcare enterprises.

**Key learning:** Product–market fit must be reinforced by regulatory readiness, infrastructure scaling, and leadership evolution before aggressive expansion.

---

**Mini Case Study 2: Growth Hacking and Platform Scaling in an EdTech Venture**

An early-stage edtech company offering virtual biotechnology training programs experienced rapid user sign-ups through academic referrals and webinars. However, revenue growth lagged and user drop-off after registration was high. Rather than increasing marketing expenditure, the company adopted a growth hacking framework.

Cross-functional teams ran continuous experiments on onboarding flows, course packaging, freemium access, and referral incentives. Data analysis revealed that users who completed a structured first-week learning pathway were three times more likely to convert into paid subscribers. The company redesigned its product to embed guided learning journeys, automated progress nudges, peer communities, and certificate-linked referrals.

At the same time, the technology team migrated the platform to a scalable cloud infrastructure and introduced analytics-driven personalization. Conversion rates doubled, customer acquisition costs declined significantly, and organic referrals became the dominant growth channel.

**Key learning:** When growth hacking is product-integrated and supported by scalable infrastructure, it can transform marketing from an expense center into a self-reinforcing growth engine.

---

**Mini Case Study 3: Strategic Alliance and Turnaround in a Biotech Manufacturing Startup**

A biotech manufacturing startup specializing in enzyme-based industrial solutions expanded aggressively after securing venture funding. It invested heavily in facilities and hiring before stabilizing long-term customer contracts. Within two years, operational costs outpaced revenues, quality deviations increased, and investor confidence declined.

The board initiated a structured turnaround. Non-core projects were discontinued, and the firm entered a strategic manufacturing and distribution alliance with an established industrial partner. This partnership provided validated market access, regulatory support, and shared infrastructure, significantly reducing financial pressure.

Internally, leadership was reorganized, quality systems were rebuilt, and the growth strategy shifted from rapid expansion to focused, partnership-led scaling. Within a year, the company restored financial stability and repositioned itself as a specialized innovation partner rather than a standalone large-scale manufacturer.

**Key learning:** Strategic partnerships can serve not only as growth accelerators, but also as powerful turnaround instruments when aligned with core capabilities and disciplined restructuring.

## REVIEW QUESTIONS AND EXERCISES

### A. Review Questions

1. Differentiate between *growth* and *scaling*. Why is this distinction critical for startup leaders and investors?
2. Explain the role of a growth mindset in preparing organizations for scale. How does it influence leadership behavior and organizational culture?
3. What is meant by organizational readiness? Discuss the key dimensions that determine whether a venture is prepared to scale.
4. Describe the strategic transition from product–market fit to scale-up execution. What operational and managerial changes are required at this stage?
5. Compare and contrast marketing-led, sales-led, product-led, and partner-led customer acquisition models. Under what conditions is each most appropriate?
6. Why is customer retention often more important than customer acquisition during the scaling phase? Support your answer with strategic reasoning.
7. Define growth hacking. How does it differ from traditional marketing approaches in high-growth organizations?
8. Discuss the strategic importance of partnerships and alliances in scaling. What risks do they introduce, and how can these be managed?
9. Explain how technology and infrastructure limitations can constrain organizational growth. What are the key components of scale-ready digital infrastructure?
10. Analyze the leadership challenges that emerge as organizations move from startup to scale-up. How should leadership roles evolve?
11. What strategic considerations guide global expansion decisions? Why is localization essential for international scaling?
12. Examine the role of risk management and ethics in sustainable scaling. Why must they be integrated into growth strategy rather than treated as compliance functions?

13. Identify common causes of failure during scaling. How can early-warning systems reduce the probability of collapse?
14. Outline the stages of a structured turnaround strategy in a scaling enterprise.
15. How does organizational resilience contribute to long-term competitive advantage?

**B. Short Answer / Concept-Based Questions**

1. Define organizational readiness and list any four of its components.
2. What is product–market fit, and how is it validated?
3. State two examples of growth hacking techniques.
4. What is a strategic alliance?
5. Explain the concept of localization with one example.
6. What is enterprise risk management (ERM)?
7. Differentiate between customer acquisition cost (CAC) and customer lifetime value (LTV).
8. What is premature scaling?
9. What is a turnaround strategy?
10. Define sustainable scaling.

**C. Analytical and Applied Exercises**

1. **Scale-Readiness Audit Exercise**: Select a startup or early-stage company. Design a scale-readiness assessment covering leadership, technology, finance, culture, and market systems. Present your findings and recommend whether the company should scale now or delay expansion.
2. **Product–Market Fit to Scale Plan**: Develop a transition roadmap for a hypothetical venture that has just achieved product–market fit. Outline changes required in operations, marketing, staffing, and infrastructure.
3. **Customer Growth Model Design**: Create a customer acquisition and retention model for a biotech, health-tech, or edtech startup. Identify channels, metrics, and retention mechanisms.
4. **Growth Hacking Experiment Framework**: Propose three growth experiments for a digital startup. Define objectives, hypotheses, metrics, and decision rules for scaling or terminating each experiment.
5. **Partnership Strategy Simulation**: Assume your startup is entering a new market. Identify two potential strategic partners and design a partnership structure including goals, value exchange, and risk controls.
6. **Technology Scaling Blueprint**: Prepare a high-level technology and infrastructure scaling plan for a data-intensive startup, including cybersecurity and compliance elements.

7. **Leadership at Scale Case Analysis**: Analyze a real or hypothetical organization that struggled during rapid growth. Identify leadership and team-building gaps and propose corrective strategies.
8. **Global Expansion Planning Exercise**: Select a country for international expansion. Conduct a brief market, regulatory, and cultural analysis and propose an entry and localization strategy.
9. **Ethics and Risk Scenario Analysis**: Develop a risk and ethics scenario (e.g., data misuse, product failure, regulatory breach) and design a response and prevention framework.
10. **Turnaround Strategy Workshop**: Given a failing scale-up with declining revenues and high burn rate, design a 12-month turnaround plan covering stabilization, restructuring, and renewed growth.

### D. Reflective Questions (For Discussion)

- What personal leadership shifts are required when moving from startup founder to scale-up leader?
- How can rapid growth threaten organizational values, and how can this be prevented?
- Is it better to scale fast and correct later, or scale cautiously and risk being outpaced? Justify your position.

# CHAPTER-10

# MANUFACTURING & INVESTMENT READINESS LEVELS (MRL & IRL)

**Abstract**: This chapter provides a structured and practice-oriented framework to guide innovators, entrepreneurs, and technology managers from laboratory-scale innovation to scalable, investable products. The chapter begins by situating technology commercialization within established pathways, integrating Technology Readiness Levels (TRL) with Manufacturing Readiness Levels (MRL) and Investment Readiness Levels (IRL) to present a unified readiness continuum. It systematically examines the critical transition from prototype to market-ready product, emphasizing design for manufacturability, quality systems, regulatory compliance, and certification requirements essential for industrial deployment. Further, the chapter explores supply chain configuration, vendor development, and sourcing strategies as determinants of scalability and resilience. Financial readiness is addressed through detailed discussion on costing models, pricing strategies, and unit economics, linking technical feasibility with commercial viability. Investment readiness is treated holistically, covering investor expectations, documentation, data rooms, and risk mitigation narratives. The integration of regulatory, legal, and intellectual property considerations ensures alignment between technical development, market entry, and long-term value creation. To reinforce applied learning, the chapter includes a readiness assessment tool, an illustrative case study, review questions, and an industry mapping activity. Collectively, this chapter equips readers with actionable insights and diagnostic frameworks to identify gaps, avoid common commercialization pitfalls, and strategically advance innovations toward sustainable manufacturing and successful investment outcomes.

**Keywords:** Manufacturing Readiness Level (MRL); Investment Readiness Level (IRL); Technology Commercialization; Design for Manufacturability; Unit Economics; Regulatory and Quality Compliance

## 10.1 TECHNOLOGY COMMERCIALIZATION PATHWAYS

Technology commercialization pathways describe the structured routes through which an innovation transitions from research and development to market adoption and value creation. These pathways integrate technical maturity, manufacturing feasibility, regulatory alignment, and business viability to ensure that innovations do not stall at the prototype stage but progress toward scalable and sustainable deployment (Fig 10.1).

At an early stage, commercialization typically begins with **research translation**, where fundamental discoveries are validated through proof-of-concept and feasibility studies. This phase focuses on technical risk reduction, intellectual property identification, and alignment with unmet market needs. Successful translation establishes the foundation for downstream development by demonstrating that the technology can solve a real-world problem under controlled conditions.

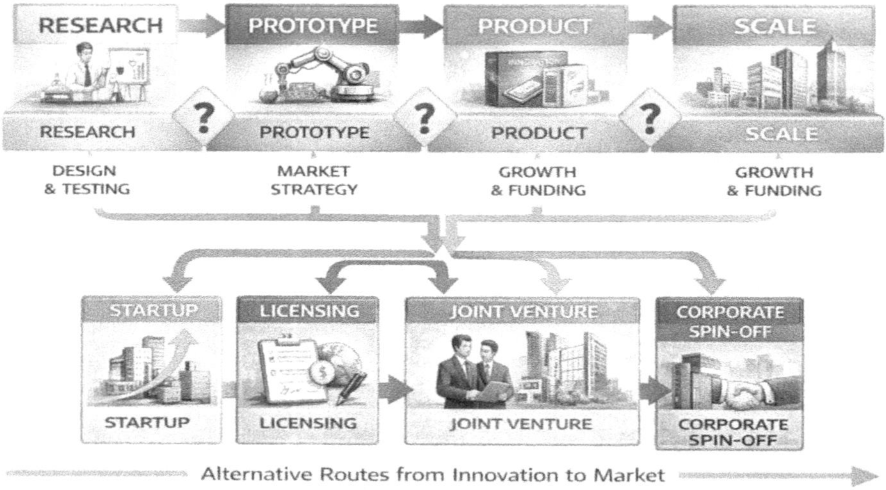


**Figure 10.1: Technology Commercialization Pathways.** This figure illustrates the progressive journey of an innovation from research to large-scale market deployment, highlighting the core stages of research, prototype development, product realization, and scale-up. At each transition point, key strategic decisions determine the most appropriate commercialization pathway. The framework presents alternative routes to market, including startup formation, technology licensing, joint ventures, and corporate spin-offs. It emphasizes that technology commercialization is not a single linear process but a flexible, decision-driven pathway where innovators and organizations select models based on market readiness, risk, resources, and strategic objectives.

The next pathway phase involves **technology development and validation**, where prototypes are iteratively refined to meet functional, performance, and reliability benchmarks. Here, market feedback, customer discovery, and use-case validation play a critical role. Decisions regarding build-versus-license, spin-off creation, or strategic partnerships are often initiated at this stage, as organizations assess whether internal capabilities or external collaborations are better suited for commercialization.

As technologies mature, the pathway shifts toward **manufacturing and scale-up planning**. This includes process stabilization, design optimization, pilot manufacturing, and early supply chain engagement. Commercialization risk now extends beyond technical uncertainty to encompass production yield, quality consistency, cost control, and regulatory compliance. Alignment with manufacturing readiness becomes essential to avoid delays and cost overruns during scale-up.

The final pathway emphasizes **market entry and growth**, where distribution channels, pricing strategies, customer acquisition, and post-market surveillance are integrated into the commercialization strategy. At this stage, investor confidence, regulatory approvals, and operational scalability determine the speed and extent of market penetration. Feedback loops from the market inform continuous improvement, product line extensions, or strategic pivots.

Overall, technology commercialization pathways are not strictly linear but iterative and decision-driven. They require coordinated progression across technical readiness, manufacturing capability, and investment preparedness. Understanding these pathways enables innovators to select appropriate commercialization models, allocate resources efficiently, and synchronize innovation milestones with market and investor expectations.

## 10.2 OVERVIEW OF TRL, MRL, AND IRL

The successful commercialization of technology requires more than scientific novelty; it demands coordinated progress across technical maturity, manufacturability, and investment preparedness. Technology Readiness Levels (TRL), Manufacturing Readiness Levels (MRL), and Investment Readiness Levels (IRL) together provide a comprehensive, stage-gated framework to assess and manage this multidimensional progression. When applied in an integrated manner, these readiness levels reduce uncertainty, align stakeholder expectations, and support informed go/no-go decisions.

**Technology Readiness Level (TRL)** focuses on the maturity of the core technology itself. Originating from aerospace and defense sectors, TRL frameworks evaluate progression from basic principles observed (TRL 1) to fully validated systems proven in operational environments (TRL 9). TRL assessment helps determine whether a technology performs reliably and consistently under intended use conditions, but it does not address whether the technology can be manufactured at scale or attract investment. Technology Readiness Levels (TRL) provide a standardized framework—originally developed by the National Aeronautics and Space Administration (NASA)—to assess the maturity of a technology from fundamental research to operational deployment. The TRL framework consists of **nine levels**, progressing from basic scientific discovery to proven real-world application.

**TRL 1 – Basic Principles Observed:** Fundamental scientific principles relevant to the technology are observed and reported. Research is primarily theoretical or experimental, with no specific application defined.

**TRL 2 – Technology Concept Formulated:** Potential applications of the technology are identified. Conceptual designs and hypotheses are proposed, but experimental validation has not yet occurred.

**TRL 3 – Experimental Proof of Concept:** Analytical and experimental studies demonstrate proof of concept. Key functions or characteristics are validated under controlled laboratory conditions.

**TRL 4 – Technology Validated in Laboratory Environment:** Technology components are integrated and validated in a laboratory setting. Performance is demonstrated using laboratory-scale prototypes or simulations.

**TRL 5 – Technology Validated in Relevant Environment:** The technology is tested in an environment that approximates real-world conditions. Performance, reliability, and integration are evaluated using representative components.

**TRL 6 – Technology Demonstrated in Relevant Environment:** A system or subsystem model is demonstrated in a relevant operational environment. The technology shows consistent performance beyond laboratory conditions.

**TRL 7 – System Prototype Demonstrated in Operational Environment:** A near-final prototype is demonstrated in an actual operational environment. Integration, reliability, and usability are evaluated under real-use conditions.

**TRL 8 – Actual System Completed and Qualified:** The technology is fully developed and qualified through testing and demonstration. Regulatory, safety, and performance requirements are met.

**TRL 9 – Actual System Proven in Operational Use:** The technology is successfully deployed and proven in routine operational use. Performance is validated through sustained, real-world application.

---

**Manufacturing Readiness Level (MRL)** complements TRL by assessing the maturity of manufacturing processes, infrastructure, and supply chains. MRL evaluates factors such as process capability, production yield, quality control, tooling, workforce skills, and supplier readiness. A technology may reach a high TRL yet fail commercially if manufacturing risks—such as high defect rates, unstable processes, or excessive costs—are not resolved. MRL provides visibility into these risks and supports planning for pilot production and scale-up. Manufacturing Readiness Levels (MRL) provide a structured framework—originally formalized by the U.S. Department of Defense—to assess the maturity of manufacturing processes, capabilities, and risks across the product lifecycle. The standard MRL framework consists of 10 levels, progressing from basic manufacturing concepts to full-rate, stable production.

**MRL 1 – Basic Manufacturing Implications Identified:** Manufacturing feasibility is considered at a conceptual level. Basic manufacturing implications of the technology are recognized, but no formal assessment or process definition exists.

**MRL 2 – Manufacturing Concepts Identified:** Potential manufacturing approaches are identified. Preliminary considerations include materials, fabrication methods, and high-level process concepts, without experimental validation.

**MRL 3 – Manufacturing Proof of Concept Developed:** Early manufacturing proof-of-concept is demonstrated. Laboratory-scale processes are explored, and initial producibility risks are identified.

**MRL 4 – Capability to Produce the Technology in a Laboratory Environment:** Manufacturing processes are validated in a laboratory setting. Key process parameters are identified, and basic tooling and equipment requirements are understood.

**MRL 5 – Capability to Produce Prototype Components in a Production-Relevant Environment:** Manufacturing processes are demonstrated in a relevant (but not full production) environment. Prototype components are produced using production-representative materials and methods.

**MRL 6 – Capability to Produce a Prototype System or Subsystem in a Production-Relevant Environment:** Pilot-scale manufacturing is established. Processes, tooling, and workforce skills are sufficiently mature to support limited production runs with acceptable quality.

**MRL 7 – Capability to Produce Systems, Subsystems, or Components in a Production-Representative Environment:** Manufacturing processes are stable and controlled. Supply chains are identified, quality systems are operational, and low-rate initial production is feasible.

**MRL 8 – Capability to Achieve Low-Rate Initial Production (LRIP):** Manufacturing processes are proven, repeatable, and compliant. Production yields, costs, and quality metrics meet defined targets under low-rate production conditions.

**MRL 9 – Capability to Achieve Full-Rate Production (FRP):** Manufacturing systems support sustained, high-volume production. Processes are optimized, supply chains are robust, and quality performance is consistent and predictable.

**MRL 10 – Lean, Efficient, and Continuous Full-Rate Production**: Manufacturing operations demonstrate continuous improvement, cost optimization, and high operational efficiency. Lean manufacturing principles, advanced quality analytics, and resilient supply chains are fully implemented.

---

**Investment Readiness Level (IRL)** addresses the commercial and financial dimensions required to secure funding and partnerships. IRL assesses the preparedness of a venture or technology to engage investors by examining market validation, business models, revenue logic, regulatory pathways, intellectual property protection, and governance structures. High IRL indicates that technical and manufacturing risks are sufficiently mitigated and clearly communicated in a manner aligned with investor expectations. Investment Readiness Levels (IRL) describe the progressive maturity of a venture or technology in terms of its preparedness to attract funding, form strategic partnerships, and scale commercially. Unlike TRL and MRL, IRL is **not governed by a single global standard**; however, a **nine-level framework** is widely used across entrepreneurial, startup, and technology-transfer ecosystems. The structure below is **academically sound, industry-aligned, and suitable for textbook use**, provided the scale is clearly defined.

**IRL 1 – Idea and Opportunity Identification:** A problem or opportunity is identified, and a preliminary solution concept is articulated. No formal market, financial, or technical validation has been conducted.

**IRL 2 – Value Proposition Defined:** The target customer, unmet need, and proposed value proposition are clearly defined. Initial assumptions about market relevance are articulated, but evidence remains limited.

**IRL 3 – Market and Customer Validation Initiated:** Early customer discovery, stakeholder interviews, or pilot use cases provide preliminary evidence of demand. Competitive landscape and differentiation begin to emerge.

**IRL 4 – Business Model Conceptualized:** A viable business model is outlined, including revenue logic, cost structure, and pricing approach. Go-to-market assumptions are defined but not yet proven.

**IRL 5 – Commercial Feasibility Demonstrated:** Market demand, pricing logic, and unit economics show early feasibility. Key risks are identified, and mitigation strategies are proposed. Intellectual property positioning is clarified.

**IRL 6 – Investor-Ready Documentation Prepared:** Core investment documents are developed, including a pitch deck, financial projections, regulatory roadmap, and commercialization plan. Governance and team roles are defined.

**IRL 7 – Due Diligence Readiness Achieved:** The venture is prepared for investor due diligence. Data rooms are organized, legal and IP documentation is in place, and risks are transparently articulated.

**IRL 8 – Capital Engagement and Validation:** Active engagement with investors occurs. Term sheets, strategic partnerships, or conditional funding commitments are negotiated based on validated readiness.

**IRL 9 – Scale-Ready and Growth-Oriented Venture:** The venture demonstrates the ability to deploy capital effectively, scale operations, and execute growth strategies. Revenue traction or strong commercialization momentum is evident.

**Table 10.1: Comparative Overview of Technology, Manufacturing, and Investment Readiness Levels (TRL, MRL, and IRL)**

| Aspect | Technology Readiness Level (TRL) | Manufacturing Readiness Level (MRL) | Investment Readiness Level (IRL) |
|---|---|---|---|
| **Primary Focus** | Technology maturity and functional performance | Manufacturing maturity and production capability | Business and investment maturity |
| **Conceptual Origin** | National Aeronautics and Space Administration (NASA) | U.S. Department of Defense (DoD) | Entrepreneurial and investment ecosystems |
| **Typical Scale** | Levels 1–9 | Levels 1–10 | Commonly expressed as Levels 1–9 or stage-based maturity* |
| **Core Assessment Question** | Does the technology work as intended? | Can the technology be manufactured reliably and at scale? | Is the opportunity credible, scalable, and investable? |
| **Key Output** | Proven science and validated technology | Reliable, repeatable, and scalable production | Sustainable and fundable business |
| **Primary Risks Addressed** | Technical feasibility and performance risk | Process variability, yield loss, quality, and supply chain risk | Market, financial, regulatory, and execution risk |
| **Evidence and** | Experimental data, | Pilot manufacturing | Pitch deck, |

| Artifacts Required | lab validation, prototypes, field-test results | data, process capability studies, quality documentation, supplier audits | financial models, market validation data, legal and IP documentation |
|---|---|---|---|
| **Relation to Scale-Up** | Confirms readiness to exit laboratory development | Determines feasibility, cost, and stability of production scale-up | Determines timing and likelihood of securing growth capital |
| **Role in Commercialization** | Establishes scientific and engineering credibility | Enables compliant and cost-effective manufacturing | Enables fundraising, partnerships, and market expansion |
| **Failure Risk if Ignored** | Technology does not function or cannot be validated | Cannot build reliably or production becomes prohibitively costly | Unable to raise funds or scale operations |
| **Decision Support Use** | Go / No-Go decisions for technical advancement | Decisions on pilot plants, tooling, capacity, and supplier investments | Decisions on fundraising strategy, valuation, and growth trajectory |
| **Outcome of High Readiness** | Proven and reliable technology | Efficient, compliant, and scalable manufacturing system | Investor-ready and growth-capable enterprise |

Individually, TRL, MRL, and IRL offer valuable but partial perspectives. Collectively, they form an integrated readiness framework that aligns innovation development with manufacturing feasibility and capital deployment. Effective commercialization requires synchronized advancement across all three dimensions, ensuring that technical success translates into scalable production and investable opportunities.

## 10.3 PROTOTYPE TO PRODUCT TRANSITION

The transition from prototype to product represents one of the most critical and failure-prone phases of technology commercialization. While prototypes primarily demonstrate technical feasibility and functional performance, products must satisfy additional requirements related to reliability, manufacturability, compliance, cost, and user experience. This stage demands a fundamental shift in mindset—from experimental validation to industrial execution.

Prototypes are often developed using laboratory-scale processes, custom components, and manual assembly methods that are unsuitable for large-scale production. During the product transition phase, these elements must be re-engineered into standardized, repeatable, and cost-effective processes. Design decisions are revisited to ensure consistency, durability, and ease of assembly, while maintaining core performance specifications. This process frequently reveals hidden dependencies and constraints that were not apparent during prototyping.

Another essential aspect of the transition is **risk migration**. Technical risks decline as functionality stabilizes, but manufacturing, supply chain, and regulatory risks increase. Material selection, tolerance definition, process variability, and quality assurance mechanisms become central concerns. Early pilot builds and pre-production runs are therefore critical to identify failure modes, validate production workflows, and establish baseline performance metrics.

User requirements and market expectations also intensify during this stage. Products must deliver predictable performance across diverse operating conditions and comply with safety, regulatory, and certification standards. Feedback from beta users, early adopters, and field trials informs refinements in design, packaging, documentation, and after-sales support. These refinements are essential to avoid costly redesigns after-market launch.

Ultimately, the prototype-to-product transition serves as the bridge between innovation and commercialization. Organizations that invest in structured transition planning—integrating engineering, manufacturing, quality, and business teams—are significantly more likely to achieve scalable production, regulatory approval, and investor confidence. This phase lays the foundation for manufacturing readiness and long-term commercial sustainability.

## 10.4 DESIGN FOR MANUFACTURABILITY (DFM)

Design for Manufacturability (DFM) is a systematic engineering approach that ensures products are designed in a manner that enables efficient, reliable, and cost-effective manufacturing at scale. While prototypes prioritize performance and proof of concept, DFM shifts the focus toward simplifying production, reducing variability, and minimizing total lifecycle costs without compromising functional requirements (Fig 10.2).

A core principle of DFM is **design simplification**. This involves reducing part counts, standardizing components, and avoiding unnecessary complexity in geometry and assembly. Fewer parts and simpler assemblies lead to lower material costs, reduced assembly time, improved yield, and easier quality control. Early engagement between design engineers and manufacturing teams is essential to identify features that may be difficult, expensive, or inconsistent to produce at scale.

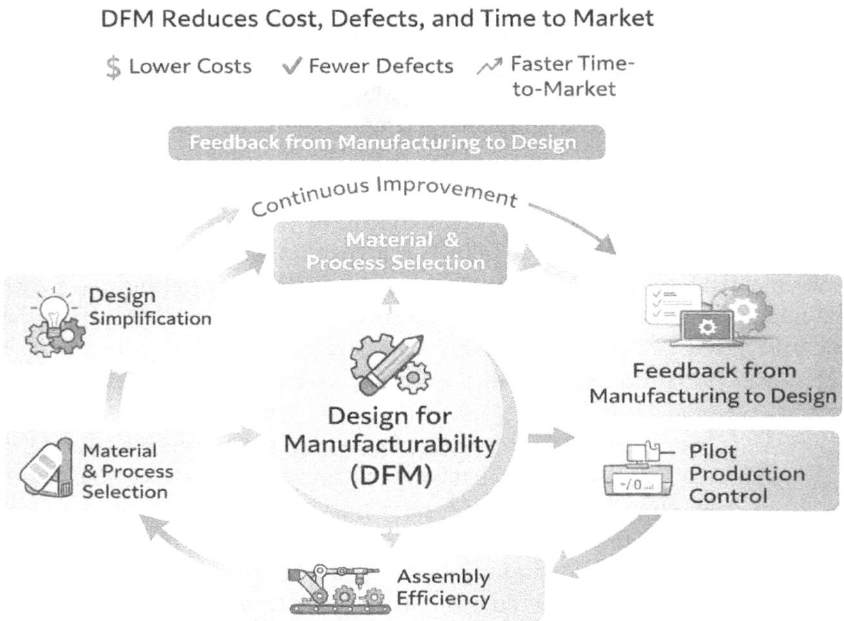


**Figure 10.2: Design for Manufacturability (DFM) Impact Loop.** This figure illustrates the continuous feedback-driven impact of Design for Manufacturability (DFM) on product development. By integrating design simplification, material and process selection, tolerance control, and assembly efficiency with systematic feedback from manufacturing to design, the DFM loop reduces production costs, minimizes defects, and accelerates time-to-market while supporting scalable and reliable manufacturing.

Material and process selection are equally critical within DFM. Designers must consider material availability, supplier capability, process maturity, and regulatory constraints. Selecting materials that are readily available and compatible with established manufacturing processes reduces supply risk and accelerates scale-up. Process-aware design—such as designing for injection molding, machining, additive manufacturing, or bioprocess scale-up—ensures that production methods are aligned with design intent.

Tolerance management and variability control form another key pillar of DFM. Overly tight tolerances increase production costs and defect rates, while poorly defined tolerances compromise product performance. DFM promotes robust design practices that accommodate natural process variation through appropriate tolerances, statistical process control, and design margins. Finally, DFM extends beyond initial production to encompass maintenance, repair, and lifecycle considerations. Products designed with manufacturability in mind are easier to assemble, test, service, and upgrade, resulting in lower warranty costs and higher customer satisfaction. By embedding DFM principles early in development, organizations enhance manufacturing readiness, reduce time to market, and improve the overall commercial viability of their innovations.

## 10.5 QUALITY, COMPLIANCE, AND CERTIFICATION

Quality, compliance, and certification form the backbone of credible and sustainable commercialization, particularly in regulated and high-risk industries such as biotechnology, healthcare, pharmaceuticals, food, and advanced manufacturing. As technologies transition from development to production, informal laboratory controls must evolve into formalized quality systems that ensure consistency, safety, and regulatory acceptance.

**Quality management systems (QMS)** provide the structural foundation for controlled manufacturing. These systems define standard operating procedures, documentation practices, change control mechanisms, and corrective and preventive actions (CAPA). Implementation of recognized quality standards ensures that products are manufactured reproducibly and that deviations are identified and addressed systematically. A mature QMS not only supports compliance but also builds customer and investor confidence.

**Regulatory compliance** requires alignment with applicable national and international regulations governing product safety, performance, labeling, and post-market surveillance. Regulatory requirements influence design decisions, material selection, testing protocols, and manufacturing processes. Early integration of regulatory strategy reduces the risk of costly redesigns, delayed approvals, or market withdrawal. Regulatory readiness is therefore an integral component of both manufacturing and investment readiness.

**Certification and conformity assessment** serve as external validation of quality and compliance. Certifications demonstrate that products and processes meet established standards and are fit for intended use. Depending on the industry, certification may involve product testing, facility audits, process validation, or third-party inspections. Achieving certification often represents a critical commercialization milestone, enabling market entry, procurement eligibility, and strategic partnerships.

Beyond compliance, a strong quality culture drives operational excellence. Continuous improvement, risk-based thinking, and data-driven decision-making help organizations reduce defects, improve yield, and manage scale-up challenges effectively. In commercialization contexts, quality, compliance, and certification are not merely regulatory obligations but strategic assets that protect brand reputation, reduce liability, and support long-term market success.

## 10.6 SUPPLY CHAIN AND VENDOR DEVELOPMENT

An effective supply chain is a critical enabler of manufacturing scalability and commercial sustainability. As technologies move toward market deployment, organizations must transition from ad hoc sourcing used during prototyping to structured, resilient, and cost-efficient supply networks. Supply chain and vendor development directly influence production continuity, quality consistency, and the ability to respond to market demand.

The first step in supply chain development is **supplier identification and qualification**. Vendors must be evaluated not only on cost, but also on technical capability, capacity, quality systems, regulatory compliance, and long-term reliability. Single-source dependencies, while convenient in early stages, pose significant risks during scale-up. Diversification strategies and secondary sourcing plans are therefore essential to mitigate disruptions.

**Vendor development** extends beyond supplier selection to include relationship building, performance monitoring, and capability enhancement. Early engagement with suppliers allows alignment on specifications, tolerances, delivery schedules, and quality expectations. In some cases, organizations may need to support vendors through process optimization, tooling investments, or technology transfer to ensure consistent output at scale.

Logistics, inventory management, and lead-time optimization are additional dimensions of supply chain readiness. Poorly managed inventory can tie up working capital or lead to stockouts that delay production. Strategic decisions regarding make-versus-buy, local versus global sourcing, and just-in-time versus buffer inventory models must be aligned with production volume, regulatory requirements, and risk tolerance.

A mature supply chain also supports transparency and traceability, which are increasingly important for quality assurance and regulatory compliance. Digital supply chain tools, supplier audits, and performance metrics enable real-time monitoring and continuous improvement. Robust supply chain and vendor development practices strengthen manufacturing readiness, reduce operational risk, and enhance investor confidence in the scalability of the business model.

## 10.7 COSTING, PRICING, AND UNIT ECONOMICS

Costing, pricing, and unit economics translate technical and manufacturing feasibility into financial viability. Even highly functional and manufacturable products can fail commercially if cost structures are poorly understood or pricing strategies are misaligned with market expectations. This section focuses on building financial clarity that supports both operational decision-making and investment readiness.

**Costing analysis** begins with a comprehensive understanding of all direct and indirect costs associated with production. Direct costs include raw materials, components, labor, and packaging, while indirect costs encompass overheads such as utilities, quality assurance, depreciation, logistics, and regulatory compliance. As production scales, cost structures evolve, making it essential to model costs across different volume scenarios to identify economies of scale and cost inflection points.

**Pricing strategy** must balance customer value perception, competitive dynamics, and cost recovery. Pricing decisions are influenced by market positioning, willingness to pay, regulatory constraints, reimbursement mechanisms, and distribution channels. Cost-plus pricing may be appropriate in early stages, but value-based and market-driven pricing models often provide better long-term competitiveness and margin sustainability.

**Unit economics** integrate costing and pricing to evaluate profitability at the level of a single unit sold. Key metrics such as gross margin, contribution margin, customer acquisition cost, and lifetime value provide insight into whether the business can scale profitably. Strong unit economics demonstrate that each incremental sale contributes positively to covering fixed costs and generating returns.

From an investor perspective, transparent and defensible unit economics signal managerial discipline and commercial realism. Sensitivity analyses, break-even calculations, and scenario modeling help anticipate risks related to cost fluctuations, pricing pressure, or demand variability. By aligning costing, pricing, and unit economics with manufacturing and market realities, organizations strengthen their commercial foundations and enhance overall investment readiness.

## 10.8 INVESTMENT READINESS AND DOCUMENTATION

Investment readiness reflects the extent to which a venture or technology is prepared to engage potential investors with clarity, credibility, and reduced perceived risk. While technical validation and manufacturing preparedness are necessary conditions, they are insufficient on their own to attract capital. Investors require structured evidence that risks are understood, mitigated, and translated into a coherent commercial opportunity.

A central component of investment readiness is **strategic documentation**. This includes a well-articulated business plan, pitch deck, financial projections, and go-to-market strategy that clearly link the problem, solution, market opportunity, and competitive advantage. These documents must be internally consistent and supported by data derived from TRL, MRL, and early market validation activities. Overly optimistic assumptions or poorly substantiated claims often undermine investor confidence.

Equally important is the preparation of an **investment data room**. A data room consolidates technical reports, intellectual property filings, regulatory pathways, quality certifications, pilot results, customer feedback, and legal agreements into a structured repository. This level of transparency facilitates due diligence and signals organizational maturity. For later-stage investments, audited financial statements, contracts, and governance records become essential components of this repository.

**Risk communication** is a defining feature of high IRL. Rather than obscuring challenges, investment-ready organizations clearly identify technical, manufacturing, regulatory, and market risks, along with mitigation strategies and timelines. This approach enables investors to assess risk-adjusted returns and aligns expectations regarding milestones, capital deployment, and exit horizons.

Finally, investment readiness encompasses **team and governance readiness**. Investors evaluate not only the technology, but also the capability of the leadership team to execute at scale. Clearly defined roles, advisory boards, decision-making structures, and ethical governance frameworks enhance credibility. Collectively, robust documentation, transparent risk narratives, and strong governance elevate IRL and position the venture for successful capital engagement and strategic partnerships.

## 10.9 REGULATORY, LEGAL, AND IPR INTEGRATION

Regulatory, legal, and intellectual property rights (IPR) integration is essential for protecting innovation, enabling market access, and safeguarding long-term commercial value. These dimensions must be addressed proactively and in parallel with technology and manufacturing development, rather than treated as post hoc compliance activities. Effective integration reduces uncertainty, accelerates approvals, and strengthens both manufacturing and investment readiness (Fig 10.3).

**Regulatory strategy integration** ensures that product development aligns with applicable laws, standards, and approval pathways. Regulatory requirements influence design controls, material selection, testing protocols, labeling, and post-market obligations. Early engagement with regulatory experts and authorities helps clarify classification, approval routes, and data expectations, minimizing the risk of redesigns or delayed market entry. Regulatory alignment also directly affects investor perception of time-to-market and capital efficiency.

**Legal readiness** encompasses corporate structure, contracts, liability management, and compliance with labor, environmental, and commercial laws. Clear ownership of assets, well-defined shareholder agreements, and enforceable contracts with suppliers, partners, and customers reduce legal ambiguity. From an investor perspective, unresolved legal risks represent potential liabilities that can significantly devalue an otherwise promising opportunity.

**Intellectual property integration** protects the competitive advantage derived from innovation. This includes identifying patentable elements, securing appropriate filings, managing trade secrets, and ensuring freedom-to-operate. IPR strategy must be aligned with commercialization pathways—whether through product sales, licensing, joint ventures, or technology transfer. Weak or misaligned IP protection can deter investment, even when technical and market potential are strong.

The integration of regulatory, legal, and IPR considerations creates a coherent commercialization architecture. It ensures that innovation is not only technically viable and manufacturable, but also legally defensible and regulatorily compliant. Such integration reduces downstream risk, enhances valuation, and supports sustainable market participation and strategic growth.

**Figure 10.3: Regulatory, Legal, and IPR Integration Across the Commercialization Lifecycle.** This figure illustrates how regulatory strategy alignment, legal structuring, intellectual property (IP) creation and protection, and freedom-to-operate checkpoints must evolve in parallel with technical development from early feasibility through market launch and growth. Integrating these non-technical dimensions throughout the lifecycle reduces compliance and legal risks, protects competitive advantage, and supports sustainable commercialization and investment readiness.

## 10.10 COMMON COMMERCIALIZATION PITFALLS

Despite strong technical innovation, many commercialization efforts fail due to predictable and avoidable pitfalls. These failures often arise not from lack of scientific merit, but from misalignment across technology readiness, manufacturing capability, regulatory preparedness, and business strategy. Understanding common pitfalls enables organizations to anticipate risks and implement corrective actions early in the commercialization journey.

One of the most frequent pitfalls is **overreliance on technical readiness**. Innovators often assume that a high Technology Readiness Level automatically implies market success. In reality, insufficient attention to manufacturing scalability, quality systems, and cost structures can derail commercialization even when technical performance is proven. Neglecting

Manufacturing Readiness Level considerations leads to production delays, yield losses, and unexpected capital requirements.

Another critical pitfall is **late-stage regulatory and compliance planning**. Treating regulatory requirements as an afterthought frequently results in redesigns, revalidation, or market entry delays. Early regulatory missteps can also erode investor confidence, as approval timelines and compliance costs become uncertain. Proactive regulatory integration is therefore essential to avoid downstream disruptions.

**Weak market and customer validation** represents a further risk. Technologies developed in isolation from end users may fail to address real market needs or fit existing workflows. Inadequate customer discovery and pricing validation lead to poor adoption, even when the product is technically sound. This disconnect is often compounded by unrealistic revenue projections and flawed unit economics.

From an investment perspective, **poor documentation and risk communication** are common failure points. Inconsistent data, unsupported claims, and opaque risk narratives undermine credibility during due diligence. Similarly, weak intellectual property protection or unresolved legal issues can significantly reduce valuation or halt investment discussions altogether.

Finally, **organizational and execution gaps**—such as inexperienced leadership, fragmented decision-making, or misaligned incentives—can impede scale-up and partnership formation. Avoiding these pitfalls requires a holistic commercialization mindset that synchronizes technical development, manufacturing planning, regulatory compliance, and investment strategy. By systematically identifying and addressing these challenges, organizations increase the probability of successful market entry and long-term value creation.

## 10.11 READINESS ASSESSMENT TOOL

The Readiness Assessment Tool is designed as a practical diagnostic framework to evaluate the preparedness of a technology or venture across **technology, manufacturing, and investment dimensions**. Its primary objective is to identify gaps early, prioritize actions, and support evidence-based decision-making before major commercialization or funding milestones.

The tool integrates **TRL, MRL, and IRL indicators** into a single assessment matrix. Each dimension is evaluated against clearly defined criteria such as technical performance stability, process repeatability, quality system maturity, regulatory clarity, cost visibility, market validation, and investor documentation readiness. Scores or qualitative ratings (e.g., low, medium, high readiness) can be assigned to each criterion to generate an overall readiness profile.

From an operational perspective, the tool supports **stage-gate decisions**. For example, a technology with high TRL but low MRL may proceed with pilot manufacturing rather than full-scale launch. Similarly, a venture with strong technical and manufacturing readiness but low IRL may prioritize customer validation, financial modeling, or governance strengthening before approaching investors.

The assessment tool is also valuable for **cross-functional alignment**. By involving R&D, manufacturing, quality, regulatory, and business teams in the evaluation process, organizations develop a shared understanding of risks, assumptions, and priorities. This reduces internal silos and ensures that readiness gaps are addressed collaboratively rather than reactively.

When used iteratively, the Readiness Assessment Tool becomes a **living management instrument** rather than a one-time checklist. Periodic reassessment allows organizations to track progress, validate risk mitigation efforts, and demonstrate maturity to external stakeholders such as investors, partners, and regulators. As such, it serves as a critical enabler of disciplined commercialization and informed capital deployment.

---

## KEY CONCEPTS & DEFINITIONS

**Technology Readiness Level (TRL)**: A systematic scale used to assess the maturity of a technology, ranging from basic scientific principles (TRL 1) to fully validated and operational systems in real-world environments (TRL 9). TRL focuses on technical feasibility and performance reliability.

**Manufacturing Readiness Level (MRL)**: A structured framework that evaluates the maturity and robustness of manufacturing processes, infrastructure, supply chains, and quality systems required for scalable production. MRL identifies production-related risks that may not be captured by technical readiness alone.

**Investment Readiness Level (IRL)**: A measure of how prepared a technology or venture is to engage investors, based on market validation, financial modeling, regulatory clarity, intellectual property protection, governance, and risk communication.

**Technology Commercialization**: The process of transforming research outputs and innovations into marketable products or services that generate economic and societal value through licensing, startups, or industrial deployment.

**Prototype**: An early-stage physical or functional model developed to demonstrate feasibility, performance, or proof of concept, often using non-scalable materials or processes.

**Productization**: The structured transition of a prototype into a market-ready product by incorporating manufacturability, reliability, compliance, usability, and cost optimization.

**Design for Manufacturability (DFM)**: An engineering approach that integrates manufacturing considerations into product design to simplify production, reduce costs, improve yield, and ensure consistent quality at scale.

**Pilot Manufacturing**: A limited-scale production phase used to validate manufacturing processes, equipment, workflows, and quality controls before full-scale commercial production.
**Quality Management System (QMS)**: A formalized system of policies, procedures, and records that ensures products are consistently manufactured and controlled in accordance with defined quality and regulatory standards.
**Regulatory Compliance**: Adherence to applicable laws, standards, and guidelines governing product safety, performance, manufacturing, labeling, and post-market responsibilities.
**Certification**: Third-party verification that a product, process, or organization conforms to recognized standards or regulatory requirements, enabling market access and stakeholder trust.
**Supply Chain Readiness**: The capability of sourcing networks, logistics, and vendor relationships to reliably support planned production volumes while maintaining quality, cost, and delivery performance.
**Unit Economics**: Financial metrics that evaluate profitability on a per-unit basis, including cost per unit, selling price, gross margin, and contribution margin.
**Cost Structure**: The composition of fixed and variable costs associated with product development, manufacturing, distribution, compliance, and operations.
**Investment Data Room**: A structured repository of technical, financial, legal, regulatory, and operational documents prepared to support investor due diligence.
**Risk Mitigation Strategy**: A planned set of actions designed to identify, reduce, or manage technical, manufacturing, regulatory, financial, and market risks during commercialization.
**Intellectual Property Rights (IPR)**: Legal protections, including patents, trademarks, copyrights, and trade secrets, that safeguard innovation and provide competitive advantage.
**Freedom to Operate (FTO)**: An assessment determining whether a product or technology can be commercially deployed without infringing existing intellectual property rights.
**Stage-Gate Decision Making**: A structured management approach in which commercialization progress is evaluated at predefined milestones to decide whether to proceed, pivot, or halt development.
**Commercialization Pitfall**: A recurrent failure point—technical, manufacturing, regulatory, financial, or organizational—that impedes successful market entry despite innovation potential.

## REVIEW QUESTIONS AND EXERCISES

### A. Review Questions

1. Explain the purpose of integrating Technology Readiness Levels (TRL), Manufacturing Readiness Levels (MRL), and Investment Readiness Levels (IRL) in the commercialization process.
2. Why can a technology with a high TRL still fail during commercialization? Illustrate with manufacturing-related examples.
3. Differentiate between a prototype and a market-ready product in terms of design, quality, and compliance requirements.
4. Discuss the role of Design for Manufacturability (DFM) in reducing commercialization risk and time to market.
5. How do quality management systems and certification contribute to investor confidence and market access?
6. Analyze the importance of supply chain and vendor development during scale-up.
7. What is unit economics, and why is it critical for evaluating commercial scalability?
8. Identify key components of an investment data room and explain their relevance during due diligence.
9. Discuss how regulatory, legal, and intellectual property considerations influence valuation and investment decisions.
10. List and explain any four common commercialization pitfalls and propose strategies to avoid them.

### B. Short Answer / Application-Based Exercises

1. A startup has achieved TRL 7 but MRL 3. Identify three major risks the startup may face and suggest corrective actions.
2. Given a hypothetical product, map its transition from prototype to product by identifying design, manufacturing, and quality changes required.
3. Prepare a brief checklist for assessing investment readiness before pitching to venture capital investors.
4. Calculate a simple unit economics scenario using assumed values for cost per unit, selling price, and monthly fixed costs. Interpret the result.

### C. Case-Based Exercises

1. Analyze a real or hypothetical case where delayed regulatory planning led to commercialization failure. Identify lessons learned.
2. Evaluate a technology commercialization effort where strong IP protection increased investor interest. Discuss why this occurred.

## D. Practical / Activity-Based Exercises

1. **Readiness Mapping Activity**: Select a technology of your choice and map its current TRL, MRL, and IRL. Identify gaps and recommend priority actions for the next six months.
2. **DFM Critique Exercise**: Review an existing product or prototype design and identify at least five design elements that could be simplified to improve manufacturability.
3. **Investment Documentation Exercise**: Draft an outline for a pitch deck that aligns technical readiness, manufacturing scalability, and commercial viability.

## E. Reflective Questions

1. At which stage of commercialization do you believe most innovations fail, and why?
2. How can early integration of manufacturing and investment considerations improve long-term innovation success?

# CHAPTER-11

# INCUBATORS, ACCELERATORS & BIO-INCUBATORS IN INDIA

**Abstract**: This chapter examines the strategic role of incubators, accelerators, and bio-incubators in shaping India's startup and deep-tech innovation ecosystem. It begins by highlighting the importance of structured incubation in improving startup survival, scalability, and commercialization outcomes, followed by a clear differentiation between incubators, accelerators, and innovation hubs based on their objectives, operating models, and value propositions. Special emphasis is placed on bio-incubation and deep-technology support systems, addressing the specialized infrastructure, regulatory guidance, and translational pathways required for biotechnology, biomedical, pharmaceutical, and agri-biotech ventures. The chapter analyzes the evolution and functioning of government-supported and university-anchored incubators, with reference to national initiatives such as Startup India, Atal Innovation Mission, and BIRAC. It further explores funding, mentorship, and shared infrastructure models that collectively reduce early-stage risk through access to capital, expertise, and prototyping facilities. Industry–academia partnerships and Technology Transfer Offices are discussed as critical interfaces for intellectual property management, licensing, spin-off creation, and laboratory-to-market transition. Operational aspects including admission criteria, evaluation mechanisms, and performance metrics are examined, along with national and global incubation networks. The chapter concludes with an ecosystem mapping of Indian incubators and a forward-looking perspective on the future of incubation in India.

**Keywords:** Incubation ecosystem, bio-incubators, deep-tech startups, technology transfer, industry–academia partnerships, Startup India

## 11.1 ROLE OF INCUBATION IN STARTUP SUCCESS

The journey from an idea to a sustainable, scalable enterprise is marked by high uncertainty, constrained resources, and significant technical and market risks. A large proportion of startups fail not because of the absence of innovation, but due to weaknesses in execution, poor market alignment, regulatory unpreparedness, and inadequate access to capital and networks. Incubation addresses these gaps by providing a structured, resource-rich, and mentor-driven environment in which early-stage ventures can systematically transform concepts into viable businesses. In this sense, incubation functions as a critical institutional mechanism that converts entrepreneurial intent into entrepreneurial capability.

At its core, incubation reduces the "liability of newness" that characterizes young firms. Startups typically lack credibility, operating experience, established networks, and validated business models. Incubators mitigate these disadvantages by offering shared infrastructure, business development support, and access to expert guidance. Physical incubation facilities provide affordable workspaces, laboratories, fabrication units, and digital resources that substantially lower the cost of experimentation and prototyping. Equally important is the intellectual infrastructure—regular mentoring, structured training programs, and peer learning communities—which strengthens entrepreneurial competencies in strategy, finance, regulatory affairs, marketing, and team management.

One of the most decisive contributions of incubation lies in early risk reduction. Through continuous mentoring and milestone-based monitoring, incubators encourage evidence-based decision-making and rapid iteration. Startups are guided to validate problems, test product–market fit, and refine value propositions before committing substantial capital. This disciplined approach limits premature scaling, a common cause of startup failure. In technology-intensive and life-science ventures, incubation further supports technical validation, regulatory planning, and intellectual property strategy, ensuring that scientific innovation is aligned with commercial feasibility from the outset.

Incubators also play a pivotal role in capability building. Founders are often domain experts but first-time entrepreneurs. Incubation programs therefore focus on developing entrepreneurial skills alongside technological progress. Structured workshops, founder clinics, and investor readiness programs equip startups with competencies in financial modeling, compliance, negotiation, customer discovery, and go-to-market execution. Over time, this systematic exposure converts fragmented efforts into coherent organizational processes, enabling startups to move from experimentation to disciplined venture building.

Another critical dimension is network integration. Incubators act as nodes within broader innovation ecosystems, connecting startups to investors, corporate partners, research institutions, government agencies, and professional service providers. These linkages expand market access, facilitate pilot deployments, and open pathways to follow-on funding. The credibility conferred by a reputed incubator significantly improves a startup's ability to attract partners and capital, particularly in high-risk sectors such as biotechnology, medical devices, and deep technology.

From a strategic perspective, incubation enhances startup survival and growth by synchronizing four essential pillars: infrastructure, knowledge, capital access, and ecosystem connectivity. Startups emerging from effective incubation environments typically demonstrate stronger business model clarity, improved regulatory and operational preparedness, and greater resilience to early-stage shocks. Empirical studies consistently show higher survival rates, faster revenue generation, and improved investment outcomes among incubated firms compared to non-incubated counterparts.

In the Indian context, the role of incubation has become even more pronounced. Diverse founder backgrounds, limited early-stage risk capital, and complex regulatory landscapes make structured support indispensable. Incubators embedded within universities, research institutes, and government programs have emerged as catalytic platforms that democratize entrepreneurship, translate academic research into enterprises, and enable regionally distributed innovation. They are not merely service providers, but institutional enablers that shape entrepreneurial behavior, standardize venture development practices, and align innovation with national socio-economic priorities (Fig 11.1).

In summary, incubation is not an auxiliary component of the startup ecosystem; it is a foundational driver of startup success. By systematically reducing uncertainty, strengthening entrepreneurial capability, and embedding startups within supportive networks, incubation transforms fragile early-stage ventures into investment-ready, market-oriented, and growth-capable enterprises.

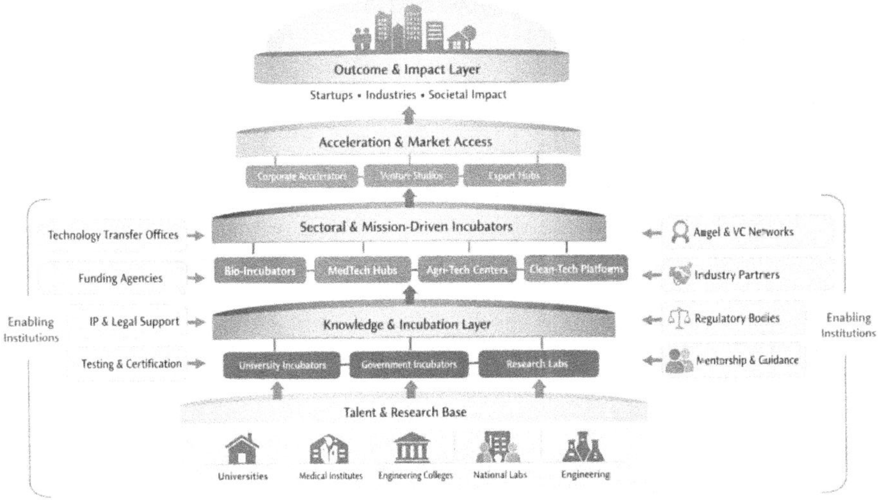


**Figure 11.1: Indian Startup Incubation Ecosystem Map**. This figure presents a layered representation of the Indian startup incubation ecosystem, illustrating the progression from the talent and research base to incubation, sectoral specialization, acceleration, and eventual market and societal impact. It highlights the central role of university and government incubators, the emergence of mission-driven and bio-incubation platforms, and the function of accelerators in enabling scale-up and market access. Cross-cutting enabling institutions—including technology transfer offices, funding agencies, regulatory bodies, industry partners, and investor networks—are shown as integrative forces that support startups across all stages, emphasizing incubation as a coordinated national innovation system rather than a standalone activity.

## 11.2 INCUBATORS VS ACCELERATORS VS INNOVATION HUBS

As startup ecosystems mature, multiple institutional support structures emerge to address different stages of the entrepreneurial journey. Among these, incubators, accelerators, and innovation hubs are often used interchangeably, despite serving distinct strategic purposes. Understanding their differences is essential for founders, policymakers, and academic institutions to effectively design, select, and engage with appropriate support mechanisms. Each model varies in its objectives, duration of engagement, intensity of intervention, and expected outcomes (Fig 11.2).

**Incubators** primarily focus on the earliest stages of venture creation, where ideas are still being validated and business foundations are under development. Their core mandate is nurturing—providing a protected environment in which startups can experiment, prototype, and iteratively refine both technology and business models. Incubation programs are typically long-term, ranging from 12 months to several years, and emphasize infrastructure access, technical mentoring, regulatory guidance, and entrepreneurial capacity building. In sectors such as biotechnology, healthcare, and deep technology, incubators often include laboratories, pilot-scale facilities, and compliance support, recognizing that product development cycles are longer and capital-intensive. Success in incubation is measured not by rapid scaling, but by technological validation, intellectual property creation, and the establishment of a credible, investment-ready enterprise.

**Accelerators**, in contrast, are designed for startups that have already moved beyond ideation and early validation. Their primary objective is rapid growth, market traction, and investment readiness. Accelerator programs are short, intensive, and cohort-based, usually lasting three to six months. They operate on a highly structured model that includes weekly milestones, demo days, and close engagement with mentors, investors, and corporate partners. While accelerators may offer limited infrastructure, their strongest value lies in market access, fundraising preparation, customer acquisition strategies, and strategic partnerships. Equity participation is common, aligning the accelerator's success with the startup's scaling outcomes. Accelerators are execution-oriented platforms that compress learning cycles and push startups toward commercial expansion.

**Innovation hubs** represent a broader and more ecosystem-centric construct. Rather than focusing exclusively on startup development, innovation hubs are designed to catalyze collaboration among universities, industries, government bodies, investors, and entrepreneurs. They function as convergence spaces that promote ideation, applied research, proof-of-concept development, and open innovation. Innovation hubs may host incubators and accelerators within their physical or institutional framework, but their scope extends to hackathons, corporate innovation programs, skilling initiatives, and translational research platforms. The emphasis is not only on venture creation, but on building innovation capacity across a region or sector. Their success is reflected in knowledge exchange, technology pipelines, startup density, and industry engagement rather than immediate financial returns.

From a lifecycle perspective, these three models are complementary rather than competitive. Incubators support the transition from idea to viable startup, accelerators drive the shift from validated startup to scalable enterprise, and innovation hubs cultivate the surrounding ecosystem that sustains long-term innovation. In advanced ecosystems, startups often move sequentially across these platforms—originating in innovation hubs, maturing within incubators, and scaling through accelerators.

In the Indian context, this differentiation is particularly significant. University and government incubators play a foundational role in capacity building and regional inclusion, accelerators bridge startups to national and global markets, and innovation hubs—often linked to smart cities, research parks, and industrial corridors—integrate entrepreneurship with policy objectives and industrial development. Recognizing and aligning these distinct but interlinked functions enables a more coherent, efficient, and impact-oriented startup support architecture.

| | Incubators | Accelerators | Innovation Hubs |
|---|---|---|---|
| Stage of Startup | Early-stage or Idea-stage | Growth-stage or Scale-stage | Any stage of startups |
| Duration of Support | 6–24 months | 3–6 months | Ongoing/co-working |
| Type of Infrastructure | Office space + mentorship | Intensive program & network | Co-working, labs, resources |
| Funding Orientation | Not-for-profit / for-profit | Equity-based investments | Varied / partnership-driven |
| Key Outcomes | Viable product, early growth | Rapid scaling, fundraising | Innovation, collaboration |

**Figure 11.2: Incubators vs Accelerators vs Innovation Hubs – Functional Comparison Model.** A structured comparative framework highlighting the functional distinctions among **incubators**, **accelerators**, and **innovation hubs** across key dimensions, including stage of startup engagement, duration of support, infrastructure provision, funding orientation, and expected outcomes. The model clarifies the unique roles each support mechanism plays within the startup and innovation ecosystem, reducing conceptual ambiguity and aiding informed selection by entrepreneurs, policymakers, and academic stakeholders.

## 11.3 BIO-INCUBATION AND DEEP-TECH SUPPORT SYSTEMS

Bio-incubation and deep-tech incubation represent specialized extensions of the conventional incubation model, designed to support ventures whose innovations are rooted in advanced science, complex engineering, and long development cycles. Unlike digital or service-based startups, biotechnology, biomedical, pharmaceutical, agri-biotech, and other deep-tech enterprises operate under conditions of high technical uncertainty, heavy capital requirements, and stringent regulatory oversight. Consequently, their success depends not only on entrepreneurial capability, but on sustained access to sophisticated infrastructure, translational expertise, and long-term institutional support.

Bio-incubators are purpose-built environments that integrate wet laboratories, controlled instrumentation facilities, pilot-scale production units, biorepositories, and compliance-ready workspaces. These facilities enable startups to conduct molecular biology, microbiology, cell culture, bioinformatics, biomaterials, and bioprocess experiments that would otherwise be financially and logistically inaccessible. By offering shared, pay-per-use access to high-cost equipment, bio-incubators dramatically reduce entry barriers, democratize scientific entrepreneurship, and accelerate the conversion of academic research into commercial assets (Fig 11.3).

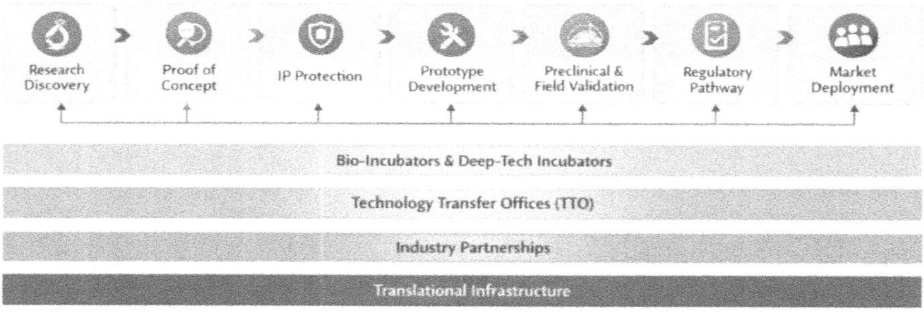


**Figure 11.3: Bio-Incubation and Deep-Tech Translation Pipeline**. This figure illustrates the structured pathway through which scientific and engineering discoveries are transformed into commercial bio-based and deep-technology products. It maps the progression from research discovery and proof of concept to intellectual property protection, prototype development, preclinical or field validation, regulatory alignment, and market deployment, in parallel with increasing Technology Readiness Levels (TRLs). The layered bands emphasize the continuous support roles of bio-incubators, technology transfer offices, industry partnerships, and translational infrastructure, highlighting incubation as a coordinated, end-to-end system for de-risking innovation and enabling successful commercialization.

Beyond physical infrastructure, bio-incubation emphasizes translational mentoring. Startups are supported by domain experts in drug discovery, diagnostics, medical devices, agricultural biotechnology, and industrial biotechnology, alongside specialists in regulatory affairs, clinical validation, biosafety, and quality systems. This multidisciplinary guidance ensures that product development is aligned from the outset with regulatory pathways, reimbursement logic, and real-world deployment requirements. In life-science ventures, where technical success alone does not guarantee market adoption, such early alignment is a decisive determinant of survival.

Deep-tech support systems extend this framework to include advanced engineering, artificial intelligence, robotics, advanced materials, and climate technologies. These systems focus on long-horizon innovation, where commercialization may take five to ten years or more. Deep-tech incubators and centers of excellence therefore adopt milestone-based funding, extended residency periods, and strong research linkages with universities, national laboratories, and corporate R&D units. Their mandate is not rapid exit, but sustained de-risking of frontier technologies through proof-of-concept development, prototype validation, field trials, and early industrial integration.

A defining characteristic of bio-incubation and deep-tech support is their tight coupling with intellectual property generation and technology readiness advancement. Startups are guided to build defensible patent portfolios, conduct freedom-to-operate analyses, and structure licensing or co-development arrangements. Simultaneously, structured progression along Technology Readiness Levels (TRLs) and Manufacturing Readiness Levels (MRLs) ensures that scientific outputs evolve into scalable, compliant, and investable products.

In India, bio-incubation has acquired strategic importance due to national priorities in healthcare, pharmaceuticals, agriculture, sustainability, and bio-manufacturing. Institutions supported by bodies such as BIRAC, DBT, DST, ICMR, CSIR, and AICTE have created a distributed network of bio-incubators embedded in universities, medical institutes, and research centers. These platforms not only nurture startups, but also build indigenous innovation capacity, reduce dependence on imported technologies, and foster region-specific solutions.

In essence, bio-incubation and deep-tech support systems redefine incubation from a business facilitation model into a translational innovation infrastructure. They serve as bridges between laboratories and markets, scientists and entrepreneurs, and public research and private enterprise—making them indispensable to the development of a knowledge-driven and technology-sovereign economy.

## 11.4 GOVERNMENT AND UNIVERSITY INCUBATORS

Government and university incubators constitute the institutional backbone of the Indian startup and innovation ecosystem. Unlike purely private incubation initiatives, these platforms are designed not only to generate commercial success, but also to advance national development objectives such as employment creation, technology self-reliance, regional innovation, and translation of publicly funded research into societal and economic value. Their strategic positioning within public institutions and higher education campuses enables them to integrate policy support, academic knowledge, and entrepreneurial practice within a single operational framework.

Government-supported incubators are typically established under national and state-level innovation missions and sector-focused programs. Their primary role is ecosystem building—expanding access to entrepreneurship beyond metropolitan clusters and lowering entry barriers for students, researchers, and first-generation entrepreneurs. Through grant funding, subsidized infrastructure, and structured startup schemes, these incubators provide early-stage ventures with non-dilutive capital, prototyping support, market linkage programs, and regulatory facilitation. They often act as implementing agencies for flagship initiatives in areas such as healthcare, biotechnology, electronics, clean energy, and agritech, aligning startup development with strategic national priorities.

University incubators occupy a uniquely influential position in this landscape. Embedded within academic institutions, they operate at the interface of education, research, and enterprise. Their most distinctive contribution lies in enabling research-to-startup translation. Faculty members, doctoral scholars, and postgraduate students are supported in converting laboratory discoveries into intellectual property, prototypes, and spin-off companies. University incubators leverage campus resources—laboratories, instrumentation centers, clinical and pilot facilities, and interdisciplinary expertise—to support technology maturation at significantly lower cost and risk than external environments.

Equally important is the human capital function of university incubators. They institutionalize entrepreneurship education through experiential learning, student startup programs, innovation fellowships, and industry-linked projects. By embedding venture creation within academic ecosystems, they cultivate entrepreneurial mindsets, normalize interdisciplinary collaboration, and create a continuous pipeline of innovation-driven enterprises. Over time, successful alumni startups reinforce this cycle through mentorship, investment, and collaborative research, strengthening the university's innovation culture.

From a governance perspective, government and university incubators typically adopt hybrid operational models. While anchored within public institutions, they increasingly function through professionally managed special purpose vehicles, foundations, or Section 8 companies. This structure allows operational flexibility, industry engagement, and investment facilitation while preserving public-interest objectives. Advisory boards comprising policymakers, academics, investors, clinicians, technologists, and corporate leaders ensure strategic alignment and performance accountability.

In the Indian context, these incubators have been instrumental in geographically decentralizing innovation. By establishing incubation centers in tier-2 and tier-3 cities, agricultural universities, medical institutes, and technical campuses, they have broadened participation in entrepreneurship and localized technology solutions. This distributed model has enabled startups to address region-specific challenges in healthcare delivery, agricultural productivity, environmental management, and manufacturing. Overall, government and university incubators function as catalytic institutions rather than mere service providers. They mobilize public infrastructure for private innovation, convert academic outputs into economic assets, and create structured pathways through which talent, technology, and policy converge to produce sustainable startup ecosystems (Fig 11.4).

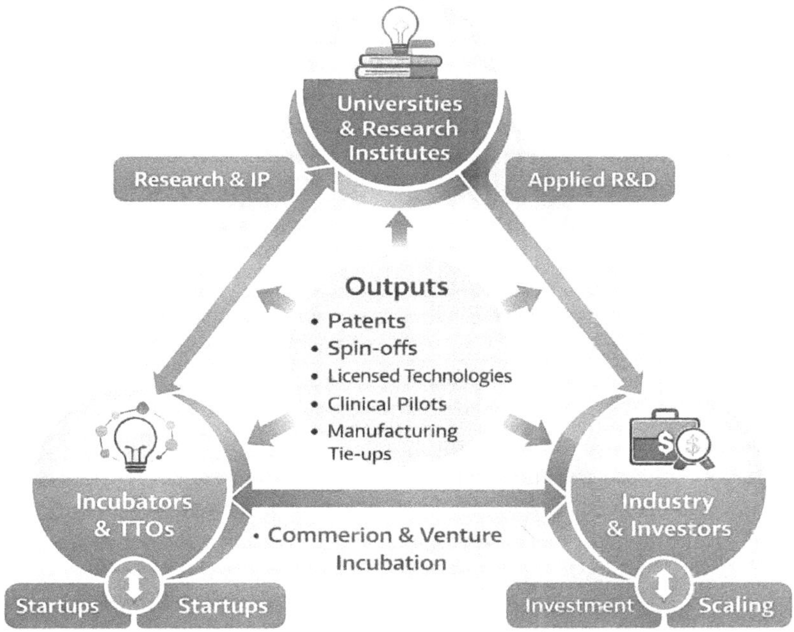


**Figure 11.4: University–Industry–Incubator Convergence Model**. A tri-nodal convergence framework illustrating the collaborative dynamics among **universities and research institutes**, **incubators and technology transfer offices (TTOs)**, and **industry and investors**. The model highlights how academic research and intellectual property flow through incubation and commercialization mechanisms into industry-led validation, investment, and scaling, resulting in tangible outputs such as patents, spin-offs, licensed technologies, clinical pilots, and manufacturing tie-ups.

## 11.5 FUNDING, MENTORSHIP, AND INFRASTRUCTURE MODELS

The effectiveness of any incubation system is fundamentally determined by how well it integrates three core pillars: access to funding, quality of mentorship, and availability of appropriate infrastructure. These elements collectively shape a startup's capacity to innovate, survive early-stage uncertainty, and progress toward commercialization. Successful incubators do not treat these as isolated services, but as an interdependent support architecture aligned to the venture's stage, sector, and strategic trajectory.

**Funding models** within incubators are increasingly diversified to address the heterogeneous needs of startups. At the earliest stages, non-dilutive funding—such as ideation grants, proof-of-concept support, and prototype development funds—plays a critical role in enabling experimentation without immediate pressure of equity dilution. Government and university incubators frequently deploy challenge grants, milestone-based disbursements, and seed support to catalyze innovation, particularly in high-risk domains such as biotechnology and deep tech. As ventures mature, incubators facilitate access to angel investors, venture capital firms, corporate venture arms, and impact funds. Many incubators operate seed funds or co-investment vehicles, while others focus on investor readiness programs, demo days, and curated pitching forums to bridge startups with external capital markets.

**Mentorship models** constitute the intellectual core of incubation. High-performing incubators curate structured mentor networks comprising entrepreneurs-in-residence, domain scientists, clinicians, engineers, regulatory experts, IP attorneys, and investment professionals. Mentorship is typically delivered through a layered approach: continuous operational mentoring for day-to-day execution, specialized clinics for functional problem-solving, and strategic advisory support for long-term positioning. Increasingly, incubators employ milestone-linked mentorship, where expert engagement is synchronized with product development stages—problem validation, prototyping, regulatory planning, pilot deployment, and scale-up. This targeted intervention ensures relevance, accountability, and measurable progress.

Equally critical is the shift from informal guidance to institutionalized capability-building programs. Workshops on financial modeling, regulatory strategy, quality systems, manufacturing scale-up, and enterprise sales are embedded within incubation curricula. In science- and engineering-driven ventures, mentorship also extends to experimental design, translational research planning, and industry-standard documentation practices. Such depth of engagement transforms incubators into learning organizations that systematically build entrepreneurial competence.

**Infrastructure models** differentiate general incubation from technology-intensive incubation. Conventional incubators focus on co-working spaces, digital resources, and business support services. In contrast, sectoral incubators—particularly bio-incubators and deep-tech centers—develop shared laboratories, clean rooms, pilot plants, testing facilities, and fabrication units. These infrastructures are increasingly organized as modular, pay-per-use platforms, enabling startups to scale resource consumption in alignment with technical maturity. Advanced incubators further integrate common services such as regulatory documentation support, quality management systems, biorepositories, cloud computing clusters, and product testing labs.

A notable evolution in incubation infrastructure is the emergence of distributed and virtual models. Cloud laboratories, remote mentoring, digital incubation platforms, and satellite centers allow incubators to reach geographically dispersed innovators while centralizing high-end facilities. This hybrid architecture enhances inclusivity, resilience, and national integration of innovation capacity.

Strategically aligned funding, mentorship, and infrastructure models transform incubators from real-estate-driven entities into venture-building systems. They enable startups to transition from concept to validated technology, from isolated teams to networked enterprises, and from grant dependence to sustainable revenue and investment pathways. In doing so, they operationalize incubation as a structured process of de-risking, capability creation, and ecosystem integration.

## 11.6 INDUSTRY–ACADEMIA PARTNERSHIPS

Industry–academia partnerships represent one of the most powerful levers within modern incubation ecosystems. They connect the exploratory strength of academic research with the market orientation, scale capabilities, and deployment pathways of industry. Within incubators, these partnerships are not peripheral relationships, but structured collaboration mechanisms that accelerate technology translation, validate market relevance, and de-risk commercialization.

From the academic perspective, industry engagement ensures that research and innovation activities are aligned with real-world needs. Faculty-driven discoveries and student innovations gain exposure to practical constraints such as manufacturability, regulatory compliance, cost structures, and user adoption. Through joint problem statements, sponsored research, and co-creation programs, incubators channel industrial challenges into university laboratories and startup pipelines. This demand-driven orientation significantly improves the probability that incubated technologies will evolve into deployable solutions rather than remaining confined to publications or prototypes.

For industry, incubator-linked partnerships function as strategic innovation gateways. Corporations increasingly leverage academic incubators to access frontier research, emerging talent, and high-risk innovation without internalizing full development costs. Startups emerging from incubators offer industry partners opportunities for early-stage technology scouting, pilot projects, licensing, acquisitions, and corporate venture investments. In regulated sectors such as healthcare, biotechnology, and medical devices, these partnerships also enable clinical validation, field testing, and compliance alignment through shared expertise and infrastructure.

Operationally, industry–academia partnerships within incubators take multiple forms. These include corporate-sponsored incubation cohorts, joint accelerator programs, shared laboratories, endowed chairs linked to translational outcomes, and industry-mentored startup studios. Many incubators establish formal collaboration frameworks covering intellectual property ownership, revenue sharing, data governance, and confidentiality to ensure clarity and long-term sustainability. Such institutionalization reduces transaction costs and fosters trust, enabling continuous rather than episodic engagement.

A critical outcome of these partnerships is enhanced startup readiness. Industry-embedded startups gain early customer access, product feedback, and procurement pathways—factors that dramatically shorten the time from prototype to revenue. Simultaneously, academic founders benefit from exposure to professional product management, quality systems, and enterprise integration processes, strengthening their capacity to build scalable organizations.

In the Indian innovation context, industry–academia partnerships are particularly significant due to historical gaps between research institutions and manufacturing or service sectors. Incubators now serve as structured interfaces that reconcile academic incentives with commercial imperatives. By convening corporations, public research bodies, hospitals, and startups within shared innovation platforms, they enable co-development of indigenous technologies, localization of global solutions, and rapid response to national challenges in healthcare, agriculture, sustainability, and advanced manufacturing.

Ultimately, industry–academia partnerships within incubators convert isolated strengths into systemic capability. They transform incubators from startup shelters into translational engines—where knowledge flows bi-directionally, risks are collectively managed, and innovation outcomes are aligned with both economic value creation and societal impact.

## 11.7 TECHNOLOGY TRANSFER OFFICES

Technology Transfer Offices (TTOs) serve as the institutional bridge between knowledge creation and market realization. Within incubation ecosystems, they perform the critical function of transforming academic and public-sector research outputs into protected, investable, and commercially deployable assets. While incubators focus on venture development, TTOs concentrate on intellectual property stewardship, licensing strategy, and translational governance—together forming the backbone of sustainable research-driven entrepreneurship.

The primary mandate of a TTO is to identify, protect, and manage intellectual property emerging from universities, hospitals, and research institutions. This begins with systematic invention disclosure processes through which faculty members, researchers, and students report potentially commercializable discoveries. TTOs then conduct novelty assessments, patentability analyses, and market scoping to determine the most appropriate protection and commercialization pathways. By financing and coordinating patent filings, freedom-to-operate studies, and prior-art searches, TTOs reduce the legal and financial barriers that often prevent researchers from pursuing commercialization.

Beyond protection, TTOs design commercialization strategies aligned with both institutional objectives and startup trajectories. These may include licensing technologies to existing firms, creating spin-off companies, or establishing co-development partnerships with industry. In incubation contexts, spin-off formation is increasingly prioritized, as it enables closer founder involvement, deeper technology maturation, and higher long-term value capture. TTOs work closely with incubators to structure equity distribution, define IP assignment terms, and embed startups within incubation programs at early stages.

A defining contribution of TTOs is risk translation. Scientific discoveries are rarely immediately investable; they must be reframed into product concepts, development roadmaps, and regulatory narratives. TTOs support this translation by facilitating proof-of-concept funding, connecting inventors with entrepreneurial teams, and coordinating validation studies. In life sciences and deep tech, this includes managing material transfer agreements, clinical research linkages, and sponsored research contracts, ensuring continuity between academic inquiry and product development.

TTOs also play a governance role. They establish institutional policies on IP ownership, revenue sharing, conflict of interest, and founder participation, creating transparent frameworks that build confidence among researchers, investors, and industry partners. In incubation environments, such clarity is indispensable; uncertainty over IP rights is one of the most common barriers to early-stage investment and corporate collaboration.

In India, the expansion of TTOs across universities and national laboratories has been a transformative development. Supported by policy reforms and innovation missions, these offices are professionalizing technology commercialization, standardizing processes, and embedding entrepreneurial thinking within research cultures. When effectively integrated with incubators, TTOs ensure that scientific creativity is not lost at the laboratory boundary, but systematically channelled into startups, licenses, and scalable solutions.

In essence, Technology Transfer Offices institutionalize the pathway from discovery to deployment. They convert knowledge into property, property into enterprise, and enterprise into impact—making them indispensable to research-led incubation ecosystems.

## 11.8 ADMISSION AND EVALUATION CRITERIA

Admission and evaluation frameworks define the strategic orientation and performance standards of an incubator. They determine not only which startups gain access to scarce resources, but also how progress, accountability, and impact are measured over time. Well-designed criteria ensure alignment between an incubator's mission and its portfolio, while structured evaluation mechanisms enable evidence-based decision-making, continuous improvement, and responsible allocation of public and private support.

**Admission criteria** in effective incubators extend far beyond the novelty of an idea. While innovation potential remains central, selection processes increasingly emphasize founder capability, problem relevance, and feasibility of translation. Typical screening parameters include the clarity and significance of the problem being addressed, differentiation and defensibility of the proposed solution, and the maturity of the underlying technology. In science- and deep-tech-focused incubators, technical credibility, preliminary data, and alignment with institutional research strengths carry particular weight. Equally critical is assessment of the founding team. Incubators evaluate domain expertise, execution capability, commitment level, and openness to mentoring. Since early-stage ventures often pivot significantly, founder adaptability, ethical orientation, and collaborative capacity are treated as strategic assets. Market awareness, regulatory consciousness, and preliminary customer validation further inform admission decisions, especially in healthcare, biotechnology, and industrial innovation.

Most incubators adopt multi-stage selection processes combining written applications, expert reviews, pitch presentations, and technical due diligence. University and government incubators frequently include sectoral panels comprising scientists, clinicians, investors, and industry professionals to ensure balanced evaluation. This layered approach reduces bias, improves portfolio quality, and aligns startup intake with ecosystem needs.

**Evaluation criteria** shift focus from selection to structured venture development. Rather than emphasizing short-term revenue alone, incubators employ milestone-based assessment systems aligned to startup stage and sector. Typical indicators include technology validation progress, intellectual property generation, prototype development, regulatory preparedness, customer discovery outcomes, team expansion, and capital mobilization. These metrics are often mapped to Technology Readiness Levels (TRLs), business maturity frameworks, and investment readiness benchmarks.

Periodic reviews—quarterly or biannual—serve as decision points for continuation, graduation, intensification of support, or redirection. Through formal review committees, incubators assess whether startups are effectively utilizing resources, responding to mentoring inputs, and achieving defined development goals. This performance-based approach promotes discipline, reduces stagnation, and reinforces a culture of accountability.

At the institutional level, incubators also evaluate portfolio-level impact. Metrics such as startup survival rates, follow-on funding, patents filed and granted, products commercialized, jobs created, and industry partnerships formed inform strategic planning and funding justification. In public-sector incubators, additional indicators—regional inclusion, student entrepreneurship, social impact, and sectoral alignment—reflect broader policy objectives.

In sum, admission and evaluation criteria operationalize incubation strategy. They convert abstract goals into actionable standards, balance inclusivity with excellence, and ensure that incubation remains a results-driven, learning-oriented, and impact-focused enterprise rather than a passive hosting function.

## 11.9 NATIONAL AND GLOBAL NETWORKS

National and global networks extend the influence of incubators beyond their physical boundaries, embedding startups within interconnected innovation systems that span regions, sectors, and markets. These networks function as strategic multipliers: they expand access to knowledge, capital, infrastructure, and customers, while simultaneously positioning incubators as active nodes within larger entrepreneurial and technological ecosystems.

At the national level, incubator networks facilitate coordination, specialization, and resource sharing. Linkages among university incubators, government-supported centers, sectoral hubs, and corporate accelerators enable startups to access complementary capabilities—ranging from advanced laboratories and testing facilities to clinical sites and manufacturing partners. Through national platforms, incubators align their activities with priority sectors, standardize best practices, and co-develop programs for mentoring, funding access, and capacity building. Such integration reduces duplication of effort and promotes efficient utilization of public and private innovation infrastructure.

For startups, national networks create mobility and scalability. Ventures may begin in a university incubator, progress to a sector-specific bio-incubator, and later engage with a corporate accelerator or manufacturing cluster. This staged mobility allows startups to match evolving needs with specialized support environments. National demo platforms, investor summits, startup exchanges, and technology showcase further connect incubated ventures to capital providers, procurement agencies, and industry consortia.

Global networks elevate incubation from local venture support to international market integration. Partnerships with foreign incubators, research parks, venture funds, and multinational corporations open pathways for cross-border mentoring, technology validation, and market entry. These networks enable startups to access international regulatory insights, participate in global pilot programs, and position their technologies for worldwide deployment. For science-driven ventures, global research collaborations and co-development agreements significantly enhance credibility and innovation velocity.

From an institutional perspective, global engagement strengthens incubator capability. Exposure to international best practices informs program design, governance models, and performance frameworks. Faculty exchanges, joint incubation programs, and international startup cohorts enrich local ecosystems with diverse perspectives, advanced methodologies, and global benchmarks. Over time, these interactions support the evolution of incubators into internationally competitive innovation platforms.

In the Indian context, the strategic integration of national and global networks has become central to innovation policy. Distributed domestic incubator systems now interface with international accelerators, diaspora entrepreneurship platforms, and multinational innovation programs. This connectivity not only enhances startup success probabilities but also positions India as a contributor to, rather than merely a consumer of, global technological advancement.

Ultimately, national and global networks transform incubators from isolated facilities into ecosystem orchestrators. They enable continuous circulation of talent, capital, and ideas—creating dynamic innovation environments in which startups can emerge locally, mature nationally, and compete globally.

## 11.10 FUTURE OF INCUBATION IN INDIA

The future of incubation in India is poised to move beyond foundational ecosystem building toward a more sophisticated, impact-driven, and globally integrated innovation architecture. As the startup landscape matures, incubators are transitioning from generalized support centers into specialized venture-building institutions that combine advanced infrastructure, translational expertise, and strategic capital orchestration. This evolution reflects both the growing complexity of emerging technologies and India's ambition to position itself as a global hub for deep-tech, biotechnology, and sustainability-led innovation.

One of the defining trends will be **sectoral and mission-driven incubation**. Rather than broad-based models, incubators are increasingly aligning around priority domains such as precision healthcare, biopharmaceuticals, medical devices, climate technologies, agri-biotech, advanced materials, and artificial intelligence. These mission-oriented platforms will integrate domain-specific laboratories, regulatory support units, clinical or field validation networks, and industry consortia. Such specialization enables higher-quality venture development, accelerates technology readiness progression, and strengthens India's capacity for indigenous product creation.

**Digital and distributed incubation models** will further reshape the landscape. Virtual incubation platforms, cloud laboratories, remote mentoring systems, and national startup management portals will enable incubators to serve innovators regardless of geography. This hybrid model will be particularly significant for tier-2 and tier-3 regions, medical and agricultural universities, and grassroots innovation clusters. Digital integration will also allow performance monitoring, investor engagement, and knowledge sharing at a national scale, transforming incubation into a networked public innovation utility.

Another critical dimension will be the **deepening integration of incubation with research, manufacturing, and policy systems**. Incubators will increasingly operate alongside technology transfer offices, translational research centers, and manufacturing readiness facilities, creating seamless pathways from discovery to deployment. Closer coordination with regulators, standards bodies, and procurement agencies will shorten time-to-market and reduce uncertainty for startups operating in regulated sectors. This convergence will be essential to support hardware, biotech, and climate ventures that require extended validation cycles.

The future will also witness **greater financial sophistication** within incubation environments. Beyond grants and seed funding, incubators will manage blended finance models combining public funds, corporate capital, philanthropic contributions, and venture investments. Structured venture studios, co-creation funds, and outcome-linked financing mechanisms will enable sustained support for high-risk, high-impact innovations. Performance-based funding allocation and portfolio analytics will professionalize incubator management and enhance accountability.

Finally, incubation in India will increasingly emphasize **global integration and societal impact**. Cross-border incubator partnerships, international co-development programs, and global market access platforms will become standard components of incubation strategy. Simultaneously, impact measurement frameworks—covering healthcare outcomes, environmental sustainability, employment generation, and regional development—will shape program design and evaluation.

In essence, the future of incubation in India lies in its transformation from supportive infrastructure to strategic innovation governance. Incubators will function as national capability platforms—aligning science, entrepreneurship, industry, and policy to produce scalable technologies, globally competitive enterprises, and solutions aligned with India's long-term socio-economic priorities.

## ECOSYSTEM MAPPING: STRUCTURE OF THE INDIAN INCUBATION LANDSCAPE

Ecosystem mapping provides a systemic view of how incubation in India is organized, interconnected, and operationalized across institutions, sectors, and geographies. Rather than functioning as isolated entities, Indian incubators today form a multi-layered innovation architecture in which universities, government agencies, research organizations, industry partners, investors, and service providers interact through formal and informal networks. Mapping this ecosystem is essential to understand resource flows, capability distribution, and startup development pathways.

At the foundational layer are **knowledge and talent generators**—universities, medical institutes, agricultural universities, national laboratories, and engineering colleges. These institutions supply human capital, research outputs, and early-stage ideas. University and research-based incubators are embedded here, acting as first points of conversion where academic work is transformed into prototypes, patents, and spin-off ventures.

The second layer consists of **sectoral and mission-driven incubators**, including bio-incubators, med-tech hubs, electronics and AI centers, agritech incubators, and clean-tech platforms. These entities provide domain-specific infrastructure, regulatory guidance, and translational mentoring. They are often linked to national missions and thematic programs and serve as technology maturation platforms where startups move from laboratory proof to application-ready solutions.

The third layer is formed by **acceleration and market-access platforms**—corporate accelerators, venture studios, industry-linked incubators, and export-oriented hubs. These structures emphasize customer validation, pilot deployments, manufacturing linkages, and scale-up readiness. They integrate startups with supply chains, procurement systems, and global partners.

Cross-cutting all layers are **enabling institutions**: technology transfer offices, funding agencies, angel and venture networks, IP facilitation centers, testing and certification bodies, and policy support units. These actors regulate knowledge flows, capital mobilization, compliance pathways, and partnership formation. National digital platforms and incubator consortia further bind the ecosystem by standardizing processes, disseminating best practices, and coordinating multi-institutional programs.

Geographically, the Indian incubation ecosystem has evolved from metro-centric clusters to a **distributed national grid**. Incubators are now embedded in tier-2 and tier-3 cities, rural innovation centers, medical colleges, and agricultural universities. This spatial diversification enables localized problem-solving, regional entrepreneurship, and inclusive innovation while remaining connected to national and global opportunity structures.

Ecosystem mapping thus reveals incubation not as a collection of buildings, but as an interconnected capability system—one that channels ideas into enterprises, enterprises into industries, and industries into socio-economic transformation.

## INDIAN INCUBATOR PROFILES: TYPOLOGIES AND STRATEGIC ROLES

Indian incubators can be broadly profiled according to their institutional anchoring, sectoral orientation, and strategic mandate. These profiles highlight how different incubator models contribute distinctively to the national innovation agenda.

**University-anchored incubators** form the largest and most diverse group. Located within technical universities, life-science institutes, and multidisciplinary campuses, they emphasize student entrepreneurship, faculty spin-offs, and research translation. Their strengths lie in early-stage idea nurturing, low-cost experimentation, interdisciplinary mentoring, and sustained talent pipelines. These incubators are central to embedding entrepreneurship within education and normalizing startup creation as a scholarly and professional pathway.

**Government-supported and mission-mode incubators** are designed to advance strategic national priorities such as healthcare self-reliance, biotechnology innovation, electronics manufacturing, and sustainable agriculture. Their defining features include non-dilutive funding access, structured national programs, and alignment with public R&D infrastructure. They frequently act as implementing agencies for innovation policies, bridging ministries, academia, and startups through coordinated development frameworks.

**Bio-incubators and deep-tech centers** represent high-infrastructure, high-specialization profiles. They host wet labs, clean rooms, clinical validation units, pilot manufacturing facilities, and regulatory support cells. These incubators focus on long-cycle ventures and emphasize translational research, intellectual property creation, and technology readiness progression. Their strategic contribution lies in enabling indigenous product development in pharmaceuticals, diagnostics, medical devices, agri-biotech, and industrial biotechnology.

**Corporate and industry-linked incubators** function as market integration platforms. Anchored by large enterprises or industrial consortia, they emphasize co-creation, pilot deployment, and commercialization partnerships. Startups in these incubators gain early customer access, product validation environments, and scale-up pathways. These profiles are particularly influential in hardware, manufacturing, mobility, healthcare delivery, and enterprise technology.

**Regional and social innovation incubators** focus on context-specific challenges such as rural healthcare, agricultural productivity, water management, waste valorization, and inclusive digital services. Their impact is measured not only in financial returns, but in social outcomes, regional development, and technology diffusion.

Together, these profiles demonstrate that the Indian incubation ecosystem is no longer monolithic. It is a diversified institutional landscape in which different incubator types perform complementary roles—idea generation, technology translation, market integration, and societal deployment. This structural diversity is one of India's greatest strategic assets, enabling the country to supportovedly support mass entrepreneurship while simultaneously building deep scientific and technological capability.

## KEY CONCEPTS & DEFINITIONS

**Incubator**: An institutional platform that supports very early-stage ventures by providing physical infrastructure, technical facilities, mentorship, business development services, and ecosystem access over an extended period, with the objective of transforming ideas into viable, investment-ready enterprises.

**Accelerator**: A time-bound, cohort-based startup support program focused on rapidly scaling validated startups through intensive mentoring, customer access, investment preparation, and strategic partnerships, typically culminating in investor demo days.

**Innovation Hub**: A collaborative ecosystem space that integrates universities, industry, government, investors, and startups to promote open innovation, applied research, skill development, and venture creation across a region or sector.

**Bio-Incubator**: A specialized incubator equipped with wet laboratories, bioprocessing facilities, regulatory support, and translational expertise to support biotechnology, biomedical, pharmaceutical, and agri-biotech startups.

**Deep-Tech Startup**: A venture built on advanced scientific or engineering innovation (e.g., biotechnology, AI, advanced materials, robotics) characterized by long development cycles, high technical risk, and strong intellectual property foundations.

**Technology Transfer Office (TTO)**: An institutional unit responsible for identifying, protecting, managing, and commercializing intellectual property arising from research organizations through licensing, spin-offs, and industry partnerships.

**Research-to-Market Translation**: The structured process of converting academic or laboratory discoveries into protected technologies, validated products, and scalable enterprises.

**Proof of Concept (PoC)**: Early experimental validation demonstrating the technical feasibility of a concept or invention before full-scale development.

**Technology Readiness Level (TRL)**: A standardized framework used to assess the maturity of a technology, ranging from basic principles (TRL 1) to fully operational systems (TRL 9).

**Manufacturing Readiness Level (MRL)**: A scale measuring the maturity of manufacturing processes, from laboratory-scale feasibility to full-rate production capability.

**Milestone-Based Incubation**: An incubation approach in which continued support is linked to the achievement of predefined technical, commercial, and organizational development targets.

**Non-Dilutive Funding**: Financial support such as grants, fellowships, and challenge funds that do not require equity ownership in the startup.

**Venture Spin-Off**: A startup company formed to commercialize intellectual property generated within a university, research institute, or corporate R&D unit.

**Industry–Academia Partnership**: Structured collaboration between educational or research institutions and industry for co-development, validation, licensing, and commercialization of technologies.
**Ecosystem Orchestration**: The strategic coordination of multiple innovation actors—incubators, investors, corporations, universities, and regulators—to create efficient startup development and scale-up pathways.
**Incubation Pipeline**: The staged progression of a startup from ideation through validation, incubation, acceleration, and scale-up.
**Investment Readiness**: The degree to which a startup demonstrates validated technology, credible markets, regulatory awareness, financial clarity, and governance maturity suitable for external capital.
**Translational Infrastructure**: Shared facilities such as pilot plants, testing labs, clinical validation centers, and prototyping units that bridge laboratory research and commercial deployment.

---

**Case Study 1: BIRAC–BioNEST Bio-Incubators — Building India's Biotech Startup Backbone**

The Biotechnology Industry Research Assistance Council (BIRAC) initiated the Bio-Networking and Entrepreneurship Support (BioNEST) program to create a nationwide grid of bio-incubators embedded within universities, medical institutes, and research organizations. The objective was to lower entry barriers for life-science entrepreneurship by providing shared wet laboratories, pilot facilities, regulatory support, and early-stage funding access.

BioNEST incubators operate as translational platforms, supporting startups in diagnostics, vaccines, medical devices, agricultural biotechnology, and industrial biotechnology. Startups are provided modular laboratory access, BIRAC grant linkage, mentorship from scientists and industry experts, and structured pathways toward clinical validation and commercialization. These incubators played a particularly visible role during national healthcare challenges by enabling rapid development of indigenous diagnostic kits, bioprocess solutions, and med-tech innovations.

**Impact:** BioNEST has institutionalized bio-incubation across India, expanded biotech entrepreneurship beyond major metros, and demonstrated how public infrastructure combined with structured incubation can produce scalable, nationally relevant technologies.

---

**Case Study 2: University-Based Incubation — Translating Campus Research into Startups**

A leading Indian technical university established a multidisciplinary incubation center to integrate student innovation, faculty research, and industry collaboration within a single venture-building framework. The incubator focused on converting laboratory outputs into intellectual property, proof-of-concept prototypes, and spin-off companies. Strong integration with the university's Technology Transfer Office ensured early IP protection, structured licensing, and transparent equity frameworks.

The incubator introduced student startup fellowships, faculty entrepreneurship policies, and industry-sponsored innovation challenges. Life-science and engineering startups received access to advanced laboratories, clinical collaborators, and pilot manufacturing facilities, alongside business mentoring and investor readiness programs. Over time, several incubated ventures progressed from campus projects to funded startups, with some entering national accelerator programs and securing corporate partnerships.

**Impact:** The initiative embedded entrepreneurship into academic culture, strengthened research-to-market pipelines, and demonstrated the strategic value of university incubators in building sustainable regional innovation ecosystems.

---

**Case Study 3: Corporate-Linked Accelerator Model — From Incubation to Market Integration**

A major Indian healthcare and technology enterprise partnered with a national incubator to launch a sector-focused accelerator supporting startups in digital health, medical devices, and diagnostics. The program selected ventures that had completed early validation and required industry access, regulatory guidance, and scale-up pathways. Startups received structured mentoring from corporate R&D teams, access to hospital and industry pilot sites, and co-development opportunities.

The accelerator emphasized real-world deployment over demo-centric outcomes. Startups refined products through field testing, integrated compliance requirements into design cycles, and developed enterprise-grade business models. Several ventures progressed to commercial pilots, licensing agreements, and strategic investments, significantly shortening their time-to-market.

**Impact:** This model illustrated how industry-linked incubation and acceleration can convert promising startups into deployable enterprises, aligning innovation with market demand, manufacturing readiness, and long-term commercial partnerships.

---

## REVIEW QUESTIONS AND EXERCISES

## REVIEW QUESTIONS

1. Explain the role of incubation in improving startup survival and commercialization outcomes.
2. Differentiate between incubators, accelerators, and innovation hubs with respect to objectives, duration, and impact.

3. Why are bio-incubators and deep-tech support systems structurally different from conventional incubators?
4. Discuss the strategic importance of government and university incubators in the Indian context.
5. How do Technology Transfer Offices strengthen incubation ecosystems?
6. Analyze the role of industry–academia partnerships in accelerating research-to-market translation.
7. What are the key elements of effective funding, mentorship, and infrastructure models within incubators?
8. Why are national and global networks critical for incubator performance and startup scalability?
9. Examine how admission and evaluation criteria influence the quality and impact of an incubator's startup portfolio.
10. Describe the emerging trends that will shape the future of incubation in India.

## EXERCISES AND APPLICATION TASKS

1. **Ecosystem Mapping Exercise:** Select a university or region and map its incubation ecosystem, identifying incubators, funding agencies, research centers, corporate partners, and regulatory bodies.
2. **Comparative Analysis Task:** Compare a general incubator and a bio-incubator in terms of infrastructure, mentoring needs, funding patterns, and development timelines.
3. **Startup–Incubator Fit Assessment:** Develop a framework to evaluate which type of incubator (university, government, corporate, or bio-incubator) would be most suitable for a hypothetical med-tech startup.
4. **Policy Design Activity:** Propose a mission-driven incubator model aligned to a national priority (e.g., antimicrobial resistance, climate resilience, or digital health).
5. **Case Development Assignment:** Identify an Indian incubator and prepare a brief case describing its structure, strategic focus, success stories, and challenges.

# CHAPTER-12

# CASE STUDIES & SUCCESS STORIES

**Abstract**: This chapter presents a comprehensive collection of real-world case studies and success stories that illuminate the diverse pathways of entrepreneurial development across sectors, stages, and geographies. It explores Indian startup success narratives, university spin-offs, bio-startups and health-tech ventures, social and sustainable enterprises, and growth-stage startup journeys to demonstrate how innovation is translated into scalable impact. Alongside success cases, the chapter critically examines startup failures and turnaround stories, highlighting strategic missteps, resilience mechanisms, and restructuring approaches that convert setbacks into renewed growth. Dedicated sections on women-led and rural entrepreneurship showcase inclusive innovation models, while global benchmark startups provide comparative insights into international best practices. The chapter synthesizes cross-case learnings to extract ecosystem-level lessons related to policy support, funding dynamics, technology transfer, leadership, and market execution. It concludes with a forward-looking roadmap for entrepreneurs, outlining emerging opportunities, capability requirements, and strategic priorities necessary for building future-ready ventures in an increasingly knowledge-driven and sustainability-oriented economy.

**Keywords:** Startup case studies, Indian startup ecosystem, university spin-offs, bio-startups, health-tech entrepreneurship, social enterprises, sustainable innovation, growth-stage startups

## 12.1 INDIAN STARTUP SUCCESS NARRATIVES

India's startup ecosystem has emerged as one of the most dynamic and resilient innovation landscapes globally, driven by a convergence of demographic advantage, digital infrastructure, policy support, and a rapidly expanding consumer market. Indian startup success narratives illustrate how locally grounded problem-solving, when combined with scalable technology and adaptive business models, can generate ventures of global relevance. These stories span sectors such as fintech, edtech, health-tech, agritech, biotechnology, e-commerce, and deep-tech, reflecting the diversity and depth of entrepreneurial activity in the country (Fig 12.1).

A defining feature of Indian startup success is **frugal innovation**—the ability to design cost-effective, scalable solutions tailored to resource-constrained and heterogeneous markets. Companies in digital payments, logistics, telemedicine, and online education have demonstrated how platform-based models can democratize access to services while maintaining commercial viability. The rapid adoption of mobile technologies, cloud computing, and AI-driven analytics has enabled startups to leapfrog traditional infrastructure limitations and directly address high-impact societal challenges such as financial inclusion, healthcare accessibility, and rural connectivity.

Policy initiatives such as **Startup India**, **Digital India**, **Atal Innovation Mission**, and the expansion of biotechnology and semiconductor missions have further strengthened the entrepreneurial pipeline. These frameworks have reduced entry barriers, facilitated intellectual property protection, expanded incubator and accelerator networks, and improved access to early-stage funding. Indian success stories frequently highlight the catalytic role of academic institutions, government-supported incubators, and corporate partnerships in transforming laboratory concepts and grassroots innovations into venture-backed enterprises.

Indian startup narratives also underscore the importance of **market intimacy and rapid iteration**. Successful founders typically demonstrate deep contextual understanding of user behavior, price sensitivity, and regulatory environments. This has encouraged business models centered on vernacular platforms, hyperlocal services, asset-light logistics, and outcome-based healthcare solutions. Continuous experimentation, pivoting, and customer co-creation have been instrumental in achieving product–market fit within complex and evolving markets.

Another hallmark of Indian success cases is the **progression from domestic validation to global scaling**. Many ventures initially focus on solving uniquely Indian problems—such as low-cost diagnostics, micro-credit, or smallholder agriculture—but subsequently refine their technologies and processes to serve emerging markets across Asia, Africa, and Latin America. This outward scaling reinforces India's position not merely as a consumer market, but as a global innovation exporter.

Leadership and organizational culture feature prominently across Indian startup success stories. Founding teams often combine technical depth with operational agility and ecosystem engagement. High-performing startups invest early in governance structures, strategic hiring, and data-driven decision systems to manage rapid growth. Their journeys highlight the transition from founder-centric operations to professionally managed, innovation-oriented organizations capable of sustaining scale.

Collectively, Indian startup success narratives demonstrate that impactful entrepreneurship in India is not solely defined by valuation milestones, but by the creation of **scalable, inclusive, and technology-enabled solutions**. These cases provide practical insights into opportunity recognition, resource mobilization, regulatory navigation, and long-term value creation, forming a critical knowledge base for aspiring entrepreneurs, academic institutions, and policymakers seeking to strengthen the national innovation ecosystem.

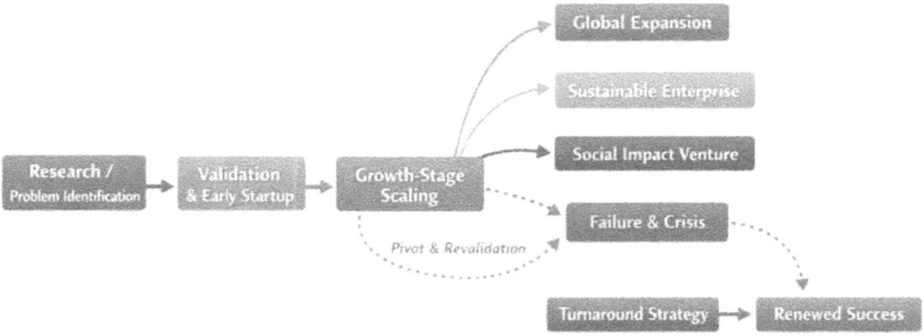


**Figure 12.1: Startup Lifecycle Pathways – From Idea to Impact.** This figure illustrates the non-linear evolution of startups from research and problem identification through validation and growth-stage scaling, highlighting multiple possible trajectories including global expansion, sustainable enterprise development, and social impact ventures. It also incorporates failure and crisis phases with feedback loops for pivot, revalidation, and turnaround strategies, emphasizing that entrepreneurial journeys are dynamic processes shaped by experimentation, resilience, and strategic realignment rather than a single linear path to success.

## 12.2 UNIVERSITY SPIN-OFF CASE STUDIES

University spin-offs represent a critical interface between academic research and market-driven innovation. In the Indian context, these ventures have increasingly become engines of deep-tech, biotechnology, health-tech, clean-tech, and advanced materials development, translating laboratory discoveries into commercially viable products and services. University spin-off case studies highlight how knowledge institutions are evolving from being primarily centers of education and research to becoming active contributors to national innovation, entrepreneurship, and economic development.

Indian universities, IITs, NITs, IISERs, central universities, and specialized research institutes have established technology transfer offices, incubation centers, and entrepreneurship cells that systematically support the journey from idea to enterprise. These structures facilitate intellectual property protection, prototype development, regulatory navigation, and early-stage funding access. Successful spin-off cases often originate from funded research projects, doctoral work, or interdisciplinary faculty–student collaborations, underscoring the importance of a strong research ecosystem as the foundation of sustainable academic entrepreneurship.

University spin-off narratives reveal the strategic importance of **technology readiness progression**—moving innovations from proof-of-concept to validated prototypes and eventually to market-ready solutions. This transition typically involves industry mentoring, proof-of-value pilots, and co-development partnerships. Case studies demonstrate that spin-offs performing well are those that integrate scientific rigor with early customer discovery, ensuring that technical novelty is aligned with genuine market needs.

Another prominent dimension of these cases is the role of **institutional and policy support**. Government-backed initiatives such as incubator grants, innovation fellowships, and seed funding schemes have significantly lowered commercialization risk. Universities that offer structured entrepreneurship programs, flexible IP policies, and incentive mechanisms for faculty engagement show higher rates of successful spin-off formation and survival. These success stories illustrate how supportive governance frameworks transform academic culture from publication-centric to impact-oriented.

University spin-off case studies also emphasize the challenge of **founder transition and team formation**. Academic founders often excel in research depth but require complementary entrepreneurial, regulatory, and business development expertise. Successful ventures therefore assemble hybrid leadership teams that blend scientific credibility with execution capability. This collaborative model enables spin-offs to secure investor confidence, navigate compliance landscapes, and scale beyond pilot markets.

Importantly, Indian university spin-offs increasingly address **national priority sectors**, including affordable healthcare, indigenous biotechnologies, renewable energy, smart manufacturing, and agri-innovation. Their trajectories highlight how academic entrepreneurship can contribute to self-reliance, import substitution, and technology sovereignty while remaining globally competitive.

**EXAMPLES**:

**1. Ather Energy – IIT Madras (Electric Mobility & Energy Systems)**

Founded by IIT Madras alumni and incubated at IIT Madras Research Park, Ather Energy originated from campus-based engineering research focused on battery management systems and electric vehicle design. What began as a student innovation project evolved into one of India's most prominent electric two-wheeler companies.

**Key success factors:**

- Strong institutional incubation and prototyping support
- Deep engineering integration (battery, software, IoT, vehicle design)
- Strategic industry partnerships and venture capital funding
- Indigenous technology development aligned with national clean mobility goals

**Learning insight:** University ecosystems can successfully nurture hardware-intensive, capital-heavy startups when supported by robust research infrastructure and industry-linked incubation.

**2. Agnikul Cosmos – IIT Madras (Space Technology & Launch Systems)**

Agnikul Cosmos is a space-tech spin-off incubated at the National Centre for Combustion Research, IIT Madras. The company develops indigenous small satellite launch vehicles and operates India's first private launchpad at Sriharikota.

**Key success factors:**

- Direct translation of aerospace and propulsion research into venture formation
- Access to advanced testing facilities and ISRO collaboration
- Policy enabling environment for private space enterprises
- Mission-driven deep-tech positioning

**Learning insight:** Long-term academic research capability, when coupled with regulatory facilitation and mission-mode funding, can generate globally competitive deep-tech enterprises.

### 3. Sea6 Energy – IIT Madras (Biotechnology & Sustainable Biofuels)

Sea6 Energy emerged from marine biotechnology research at IIT Madras, focusing on large-scale seaweed cultivation and biorefinery platforms for biofuels, animal nutrition, and biochemicals.

**Key success factors:**

- Strong IP base from funded academic research
- International pilot projects and industrial collaborations
- Alignment with sustainability and blue-economy priorities
- Multidisciplinary academic–industry founding team

**Learning insight:** Biotechnology spin-offs benefit significantly from long-term institutional research programs and international translational partnerships.

### 4. Bugworks Research – C-CAMP, Bengaluru (Biotechnology & Drug Discovery)

Bugworks Research was established in 2014 and was incubated at the Centre for Cellular and Molecular Platforms (C-CAMP), Bengaluru, a national life science innovation hub. The company was founded by scientists with strong academic research backgrounds and focuses on the discovery of novel antibiotics to combat multi-drug-resistant (MDR) and extensively drug-resistant (XDR) bacterial infections. Bugworks leverages cutting-edge structural biology, computational drug design, and translational microbiology to develop first-in-class antibacterial candidates. The venture has received support from global health organizations, government funding agencies, and international pharmaceutical collaborators, reflecting its strong translational and clinical relevance.

**Key success factors**:

- Incubation within a specialized national life-science translational ecosystem (C-CAMP)
- Strong linkage between academic science and applied drug discovery
- Access to advanced shared research infrastructure and regulatory mentoring
- Global partnerships and non-dilutive funding support

- Clear focus on an unmet global health priority (antimicrobial resistance)

**Learning insight**: Bugworks illustrates that impactful "university-origin" ventures do not always spin directly out of a single campus, but often emerge from inter-institutional research ecosystems such as C-CAMP that aggregate academic science, clinical networks, and industry translation capabilities.

**5. Strand Life Sciences – IISc Bengaluru (Genomics & Precision Medicine)**

Strand Life Sciences originated from computational biology and genomics research at IISc. It became one of India's earliest bioinformatics-driven enterprises, delivering genomic diagnostics, clinical decision tools, and precision medicine platforms.

**Key success factors:**

- Early mover advantage in bioinformatics commercialization
- Integration of computer science, biology, and clinical data
- Strong university–industry talent pipeline
- Progressive shift from services to IP-driven platforms

**Learning insight:** University environments are particularly powerful for creating interdisciplinary spin-offs that merge data science with life sciences.

Overall, university spin-off case studies provide a blueprint for transforming intellectual capital into socioeconomic value. They demonstrate that when universities cultivate innovation infrastructure, industry linkages, and entrepreneurial mindsets, they become powerful launchpads for high-impact startups. These narratives offer actionable lessons on research commercialization, venture formation, and ecosystem integration for institutions and aspiring academic entrepreneurs alike.

## 12.3 BIO-STARTUP AND HEALTH-TECH CASES

Bio-startups and health-tech ventures represent one of the most knowledge-intensive and socially consequential segments of the entrepreneurial ecosystem. These enterprises operate at the intersection of life sciences, clinical medicine, engineering, and data technologies, transforming advances in biotechnology, diagnostics, medical devices, and digital health into solutions that improve healthcare accessibility, affordability, and outcomes. Case studies in this domain highlight how scientific innovation, when coupled with regulatory strategy and clinical validation, can translate into scalable healthcare impact.

Indian bio-startup and health-tech success cases commonly originate from unmet clinical needs such as late disease detection, high treatment costs, limited rural healthcare access, antimicrobial resistance, and chronic disease burden. Ventures in diagnostics, biologics, medical devices, and digital therapeutics illustrate the shift from conventional product-centric models to

**integrated healthcare platforms** that combine hardware, wet-lab innovation, and AI-enabled analytics. These cases demonstrate how startups leverage genomics, biosensors, imaging, nanotechnology, and computational biology to develop precision-oriented and preventive healthcare solutions.

A defining feature of successful bio-startups is the emphasis on **translational research and validation pipelines**. Unlike software ventures, bio-enterprises must navigate multi-stage development pathways involving proof-of-concept, preclinical studies, clinical trials, regulatory approvals, and post-market surveillance. Case studies show that startups that embed regulatory planning, quality management systems, and clinician partnerships early in their lifecycle are significantly more resilient and investable. Close collaboration with hospitals, CROs, and public research institutes accelerates technology maturation and builds clinical credibility.

Health-tech cases further illustrate the power of **digital convergence**. AI-assisted radiology platforms, telemedicine ecosystems, wearable biosensors, and remote patient monitoring systems exemplify how software can extend the reach of biological and medical innovation. Startups operating in this space frequently adopt hybrid business models—combining B2B hospital solutions, B2G public health programs, and direct-to-consumer diagnostics—to achieve both scalability and public health relevance.

Another recurring pattern is the rise of **mission-driven bio-entrepreneurship**. Many successful Indian bio-startups align with national priorities such as affordable diagnostics, indigenous medical devices, vaccine and biologics development, antimicrobial resistance mitigation, and chronic disease management. These ventures often secure a mix of venture capital, strategic corporate investment, and non-dilutive government or global health grants, reflecting the blended financing nature of the life-science startup ecosystem.

Bio-startup and health-tech cases also emphasize the importance of **interdisciplinary founding teams**. High-performing ventures integrate molecular biologists, clinicians, biomedical engineers, regulatory professionals, and data scientists into unified execution units. This cross-functional structure enables rapid iteration across discovery, validation, manufacturing, and market deployment, which is critical in shortening time-to-impact without compromising safety or compliance.

**EXAMPLES**:

### 1. Eyestem Research – Bengaluru (Cell Therapy & Regenerative Medicine)

Eyestem Research is a Bengaluru-based biotechnology startup focused on developing **cell-based therapies for retinal degenerative diseases**, including age-related macular degeneration. The company works on human retinal pigment epithelial (RPE) cell therapies and advanced biologics aimed at restoring vision.

**Key success factors:**

- Strong translational research foundation in regenerative medicine
- Emphasis on GMP-compliant manufacturing and clinical pipelines
- Engagement with ophthalmology research centers and global collaborators
- Long-term vision aligned with high-unmet clinical need

**Learning insight:** Regenerative medicine startups require deep scientific specialization, early regulatory planning, and long-horizon investment strategies.

**2. String Bio – Bengaluru (Industrial Biotechnology & Synthetic Biology)**

String Bio applies **synthetic biology and microbial fermentation platforms** to convert greenhouse gases and agricultural residues into high-value proteins and biochemicals for nutrition and industrial use.

**Key success factors:**

- Advanced metabolic engineering and bioprocess development
- Strong IP portfolio and industrial pilot facilities
- Partnerships with global agri-food and sustainability-focused corporations
- Positioning within climate-tech and bioeconomy missions

**Learning insight:** Industrial biotech ventures demonstrate how bio-startups can scale from lab biology to industrial biomanufacturing ecosystems.

**3. Molbio Diagnostics – Goa/Bengaluru (Molecular Diagnostics & Point-of-Care Testing)**

Molbio Diagnostics developed the widely deployed **Truenat™ real-time PCR platform**, enabling rapid, portable, and affordable molecular testing for infectious diseases including tuberculosis and COVID-19

**Key success factors:**

- Indigenous platform innovation in molecular diagnostics
- Extensive clinical validation and regulatory clearances
- Strong manufacturing integration and public health deployment
- Alignment with national disease surveillance programs

**Learning insight:** Diagnostic startups achieve scale when innovation is tightly integrated with public health systems and local manufacturing.

**4. Niramai Health Analytix – Bengaluru (AI-enabled Breast Cancer Screening)**

Niramai developed **Thermalytix™, an AI-driven, radiation-free breast cancer screening solution** using thermal imaging and machine learning algorithms.

**Key success factors:**

- Fusion of biomedical science, AI, and clinical oncology

- Non-invasive, low-cost screening tailored for low-resource settings
- Strong clinical partnerships and large-scale validation studies
- Recognition by global health and innovation platforms

**Learning insight:** Health-tech success increasingly lies in combining biological signals with AI for scalable preventive healthcare.

**5. Achira Labs – Bengaluru (Microfluidics & Rapid Diagnostics)**

Achira Labs focuses on **microfluidic chip-based diagnostic platforms** for rapid detection of infectious diseases, antimicrobial resistance, and biomarkers at the point of care.

**Key success factors:**

- Advanced lab-on-chip technology
- Strong university and C-CAMP ecosystem linkage
- Focus on portable, low-cost diagnostic formats
- Emphasis on regulatory compliance and manufacturability

**Learning insight:** Lab-on-chip bio-startups exemplify how miniaturization and biosensing can decentralize diagnostics.

**6. Forus Health – Bengaluru (Ophthalmic Medical Devices & Digital Health)**

Forus Health developed **portable ophthalmic imaging devices** integrated with telemedicine platforms to enable early eye disease detection in remote settings.

**Key success factors:**

- Engineering-driven medical device innovation
- Integration with cloud-based screening platforms
- Extensive field deployment in rural and semi-urban healthcare
- Public–private healthcare collaborations

**Learning insight:** Medical device startups gain impact when hardware innovation is embedded within service delivery and digital health ecosystems.

**7. MedGenome – Bengaluru (Genomics & Precision Medicine)**

MedGenome is one of India's largest genomics-driven health-tech companies, delivering **NGS-based diagnostics, rare disease testing, and oncology profiling services**.

**Key success factors:**

- Strong genomics infrastructure and clinical bioinformatics
- International quality certifications and global collaborations
- Integration of diagnostics, research services, and data platforms
- Focus on rare diseases and precision oncology

**Learning insight:** Genomics startups illustrate how bioinformatics and molecular medicine can drive precision healthcare markets.

Collectively, these case studies demonstrate that successful bio-startups and health-tech enterprises are not merely technology creators but **healthcare system integrators**. They build robust innovation pipelines, engage deeply with clinical stakeholders, and operate within stringent ethical and regulatory frameworks. For aspiring entrepreneurs, these narratives provide essential lessons on long-cycle innovation management, evidence-based commercialization, and the strategic integration of biology with digital technologies to build sustainable healthcare ventures.

## 12.4 SOCIAL AND SUSTAINABLE ENTERPRISES

Social and sustainable enterprises represent a vital dimension of the entrepreneurial ecosystem, where innovation is driven not only by commercial opportunity but also by the imperative to generate measurable social and environmental impact. These ventures operate at the intersection of business, public welfare, and sustainability, addressing persistent challenges such as poverty, healthcare inequity, education access, clean energy, water security, waste management, and climate resilience. Case studies in this domain illustrate how purpose-driven entrepreneurship can produce scalable, financially viable models while advancing the United Nations Sustainable Development Goals (SDGs).

Indian social and sustainable enterprises are distinguished by their **context-responsive innovation**. Rather than importing standardized solutions, these ventures are built around deep engagement with local communities, informal economies, and resource-constrained environments. They frequently employ frugal engineering, decentralized delivery models, and inclusive design principles to ensure affordability, usability, and long-term adoption. This community-embedded approach transforms beneficiaries into co-creators, strengthening both impact outcomes and business sustainability.

A core feature of successful social enterprises is the integration of **triple-bottom-line thinking**—simultaneous pursuit of economic viability, social equity, and environmental stewardship. Enterprises in renewable energy, sustainable agriculture, waste valorization, low-cost healthcare, and skill development exemplify how revenue-generating operations can coexist with mission-aligned impact metrics. Many operate through hybrid organizational structures, combining for-profit ventures with foundations, cooperatives, or impact investment frameworks to balance scale with social accountability.

Social enterprise case studies also highlight the strategic importance of **innovative business models**. Pay-as-you-go services, micro-franchising, outcome-based financing, carbon credit integration, and public–private partnerships enable these ventures to penetrate underserved markets that traditional commercial models often overlook. Such enterprises demonstrate that last-mile delivery challenges can be addressed through decentralized production, digital monitoring platforms, and local entrepreneur networks.

Sustainability-oriented ventures increasingly leverage **technology-enabled impact**. IoT-based clean energy systems, AI-supported precision agriculture, blockchain-enabled supply chain traceability, and bio-based material innovations illustrate how advanced technologies are being deployed to improve resource efficiency, transparency, and resilience. These cases emphasize that sustainable entrepreneurship is no longer peripheral but is becoming central to industrial innovation and national development strategies. Leadership narratives in social enterprises often reveal a strong commitment to **ethical governance and stakeholder integration**. Successful founders cultivate partnerships with governments, NGOs, academic institutions, and international development agencies to build legitimacy, access scale pathways, and influence policy ecosystems. Measurement of impact through structured social return on investment (SROI), ESG frameworks, and life-cycle assessments is increasingly embedded within organizational decision-making.

**EXAMPLES**:

**1. SELCO India – Bengaluru (Decentralized Clean Energy & Livelihoods)**

SELCO India is one of India's most respected social enterprises, providing **decentralized solar energy solutions** to underserved households, healthcare centers, and micro-enterprises.

**Impact focus:**

- Affordable clean energy access
- Livelihood enhancement and rural entrepreneurship
- Health and education infrastructure electrification

**Key success factors:**

- User-centric product customization
- Innovative financing models with banks and MFIs
- Strong field-service networks
- Integration of technology with community needs

**Learning insight:** Sustainable enterprises succeed when technology deployment is integrated with local economic ecosystems.

**2. Aravind Eye Care System – Tamil Nadu (Sustainable Healthcare Delivery Model)**

Aravind Eye Care System pioneered a **high-volume, low-cost ophthalmic care model**, performing millions of cataract surgeries while remaining financially self-sustaining.

**Impact focus:**

- Elimination of preventable blindness
- Cross-subsidy-based inclusive healthcare
- Indigenous medical manufacturing (Aurolab)

**Key success factors:**

- Process innovation and operational excellence
- Tiered pricing and outreach camps
- Strong training and replication models
- Integration of service, manufacturing, and research

**Learning insight:** Social impact can be scaled through operational innovation and system-level design.

### 3. Husk Power Systems – Bihar/Global (Biomass Energy & Climate Tech)

Husk Power Systems develops **biomass and hybrid renewable microgrids** using agricultural waste to supply clean electricity in rural and peri-urban regions.

**Impact focus:**

- Rural electrification
- Climate change mitigation
- Local employment generation

**Key success factors:**

- Waste-to-energy innovation
- Pay-per-use energy services
- Public–private partnerships
- International climate finance integration

**Learning insight:** Sustainable enterprises gain resilience when aligned with climate, agriculture, and rural development systems.

### 4. Phool.co – Kanpur (Circular Economy & Waste-to-Value Biotechnology)

Phool.co converts **temple flower waste into incense, bio-leather, and biodegradable materials**, preventing river pollution and creating livelihood opportunities for women.

**Impact focus:**

- Urban waste management
- River conservation
- Women employment and circular bioeconomy

**Key success factors:**

- Biotechnology-based waste valorization
- Strong brand storytelling
- Sustainable materials innovation
- ESG-aligned market positioning

**Learning insight:** Circular bioeconomy enterprises can create high-value markets from traditionally neglected waste streams.

**5. DeHaat – Patna/Gurugram (Agri-tech & Smallholder Empowerment)**
DeHaat is an integrated agri-platform providing **farm advisory, quality inputs, market linkages, and financial services** to smallholder farmers.
**Impact focus:**

- Farmer income enhancement
- Supply chain efficiency
- Climate-smart agriculture

**Key success factors:**

- Digital platform combined with physical service centers
- End-to-end agricultural value chain integration
- Data-driven crop advisory
- Strong rural entrepreneur networks

**Learning insight:** Social enterprises scale faster when technology platforms are embedded into grassroots delivery systems.

**6. Jaipur Rugs – Rajasthan (Artisan Livelihoods & Sustainable Manufacturing)**
Jaipur Rugs connects **rural artisans directly to global markets**, preserving traditional crafts while ensuring fair wages and decentralized production.
**Impact focus:**

- Rural employment and women empowerment
- Ethical supply chains
- Sustainable handcrafted manufacturing

**Key success factors:**

- Artisan-centric business model
- Transparent supply chain design
- Global design and branding strategy
- Skill development ecosystems

**Learning insight:** Sustainable enterprises thrive when heritage skills are integrated into modern value chains.

**7. Banyan Nation – Hyderabad (Recycled Plastics & Circular Economy)**
Banyan Nation produces **high-quality recycled plastics** from post-consumer waste for use in FMCG and industrial packaging.
**Impact focus:**

- Plastic waste reduction
- Formalization of waste-picking communities
- Circular manufacturing systems

**Key success factors:**

- Advanced polymer recycling technology
- Industry-grade quality standards
- Ethical sourcing networks
- Corporate sustainability partnerships

**Learning insight:** Environmental enterprises must align technical rigor with supply chain formalization to achieve impact at scale.

Collectively, social and sustainable enterprise cases demonstrate that entrepreneurship can serve as a powerful mechanism for systemic change. These ventures move beyond short-term problem-solving to design **regenerative and inclusive economic models** capable of addressing long-horizon challenges such as climate change, demographic transitions, and healthcare sustainability. For aspiring entrepreneurs, these narratives provide strategic insight into mission-led opportunity recognition, impact-oriented business design, and the integration of sustainability as a core driver of innovation and growth.

## 12.5 GROWTH-STAGE STARTUP JOURNEYS

Growth-stage startups represent the critical transition from early validation to large-scale execution. This phase is characterized by rapid market expansion, organizational restructuring, capital intensification, and the shift from founder-driven operations to professionally managed enterprises. Case studies of growth-stage journeys illustrate how startups evolve from experimental ventures into scalable organizations capable of sustaining competitive advantage, operational efficiency, and long-term value creation.

A defining challenge at the growth stage is the move from **product–market fit to scale readiness**. Successful startups in this phase invest heavily in strengthening their core business architecture—standardizing processes, formalizing governance, and building technology infrastructure that can support exponential user and transaction growth. Growth-stage narratives frequently highlight the importance of transitioning from ad hoc decision-making to data-driven strategic management, with emphasis on unit economics, customer lifetime value, and operational predictability.

Another central theme is **organizational scaling and leadership evolution**. As teams expand, founders must delegate authority, recruit specialized leadership (CXOs, domain heads, regulatory leads), and establish performance management systems. Growth-stage case studies demonstrate that startups that consciously invest in culture, compliance, and talent development are better positioned to avoid execution breakdowns, founder burnout, and internal misalignment.

Growth-stage journeys also showcase the strategic role of **capital structuring and partnerships**. Unlike seed-stage funding, growth capital is typically deployed toward market penetration, infrastructure expansion, international entry, and strategic acquisitions. These cases reveal how successful ventures balance venture capital, strategic corporate investments, debt instruments, and public funding to optimize both control and scalability. Partnerships with large enterprises, government programs, and global distributors often act as force multipliers during this stage.

Operational complexity increases substantially as startups enter multi-city, national, or global markets. Growth-stage narratives emphasize **supply chain robustness, regulatory compliance, cybersecurity, and customer experience management** as core pillars of sustainable scale. Startups in fintech, health-tech, logistics, edtech, and consumer platforms illustrate how technology-driven process automation and advanced analytics become indispensable in maintaining service quality at volume.

Importantly, growth-stage journeys are rarely linear. Many successful startups encounter growth plateaus, unit economics stress, leadership conflicts, or market disruptions. Case studies demonstrate that resilience at this stage depends on the ability to reconfigure business models, prune non-core verticals, and realign strategies without destabilizing the organizational core.

**EXAMPLES**:

**1. Flipkart – E-commerce & Digital Infrastructure**

Flipkart's journey from a small online bookstore to one of India's largest e-commerce platforms exemplifies growth-stage transformation. As the company scaled, it built proprietary logistics (Ekart), payment systems, seller platforms, and data-driven supply chain technologies.

**Growth-stage transitions:**

- Shift from marketplace validation to national logistics infrastructure
- Professionalization of leadership and governance
- Strategic acquisitions (Myntra, PhonePe – early stage)
- Large-scale capital deployment and compliance frameworks

**Learning insight:** Growth requires building ecosystems, not just products.

**2. Zomato – Consumer Platform to Multi-vertical Enterprise**

Zomato evolved from a restaurant discovery platform into a multi-service food-tech company integrating delivery, cloud kitchens, hyperlocal logistics, and B2B supply platforms.

**Growth-stage transitions:**

- Expansion from information platform to transaction-led business
- Development of large-scale logistics operations
- International market experimentation
- Public market readiness and corporate restructuring

**Learning insight:** Growth-stage startups must re-architect business models to support operationally intensive services.

**3. Byju's – Edtech Platform to Global Learning Company**

Byju's scaled from an Indian test-prep venture into a global edtech enterprise through aggressive technology investment, content production, and international acquisitions.

**Growth-stage transitions:**

- Shift from localized education services to digital learning platforms
- Creation of global content and R&D units
- Strategic mergers and acquisitions
- Rapid organizational expansion and governance complexity

**Learning insight:** Growth-stage scaling introduces integration and governance challenges that require institutional maturity.

**4. Zerodha – Fintech Scaling with Capital Efficiency**

Zerodha grew from a small discount brokerage into India's largest retail stockbroking platform through a technology-first, bootstrapped growth strategy.

**Growth-stage transitions:**

- Platform engineering for millions of concurrent users
- Regulatory and cybersecurity strengthening
- Creation of ecosystem ventures (Rainmatter)
- Institutionalization without heavy external capital

**Learning insight:** Not all growth-stage journeys are capital intensive; process excellence and product trust can drive scale.

**5. Delhivery – Logistics Tech to National Infrastructure Company**

Delhivery's scale-up journey reflects the operational demands of growth-stage logistics startups. The company built national warehousing, last-mile delivery, freight services, and AI-enabled routing systems.

**Growth-stage transitions:**

- Asset and workforce expansion across India
- Technology-driven logistics optimization
- Compliance and risk management systems
- Evolution into a publicly listed logistics enterprise

**Learning insight:** Growth-stage startups must master operational depth as much as technological innovation.

**6. PharmEasy – Digital Health to Integrated Healthcare Platform**

PharmEasy scaled from an online pharmacy to an integrated healthcare ecosystem including diagnostics, chronic care management, and digital health services.

**Growth-stage transitions:**

- Strengthening regulatory and quality frameworks
- Mergers and acquisitions (diagnostics and pharmacy networks)
- Expansion into chronic care and telehealth
- National fulfillment and cold-chain logistics

**Learning insight:** Health-tech scale-ups must synchronize technology growth with regulatory discipline and service reliability.

Collectively, growth-stage startup journeys provide entrepreneurs with a pragmatic understanding of scale dynamics. They reveal that scaling is not merely about acquiring users or revenue acceleration, but about building **institutional capability**—systems, people, and partnerships that can sustain innovation and competitiveness over the long term. These cases form a critical knowledge base for founders preparing to navigate the complex transformation from startup to enduring enterprise.

## 12.6 STARTUP FAILURE AND TURNAROUND STORIES

While success narratives offer inspiration, failure and turnaround stories provide some of the most valuable entrepreneurial learning. A significant proportion of startups do not fail because of weak ideas, but due to premature scaling, flawed business models, regulatory misalignment, cash-flow mismanagement, leadership gaps, or inability to adapt to market realities. Case studies in this section examine how ventures either exited unsuccessfully or strategically restructured to reclaim relevance, offering critical insights into risk management, resilience, and organizational learning.

Startup failure cases reveal recurring systemic patterns. Common contributors include misreading customer demand, overdependence on venture capital without sustainable unit economics, weak product differentiation, and underestimation of operational complexity. In technology-driven sectors, additional challenges such as long development cycles, regulatory delays, and technology–market mismatch often accelerate venture collapse. These narratives emphasize that innovation without disciplined execution rarely sustains commercial viability.

Turnaround stories, in contrast, highlight the strategic recalibration mechanisms that enable ventures to survive disruption. These include pivoting business models, exiting unviable verticals, restructuring cost frameworks, changing leadership teams, renegotiating investor relationships, and redefining core value propositions. Growth-stage retrenchment, although often perceived as failure, frequently becomes a catalyst for organizational maturity and renewed strategic focus.

Indian startup turnaround cases particularly illustrate the importance of **contextual agility**. Shifts in regulation, consumer behavior, and competitive landscapes require startups to continuously reassess their assumptions. Ventures that successfully recover demonstrate strong internal governance, data-driven diagnostics, and the ability to make difficult decisions—such as shutting down popular but unprofitable products or downsizing to restore sustainability.

Another key theme is the role of **entrepreneurial resilience and learning culture**. Turnaround founders tend to institutionalize failure analysis, customer rediscovery, and rapid experimentation. These organizations move from growth-at-all-costs strategies to models emphasizing capital efficiency, operational discipline, and long-term value creation. Psychological resilience, stakeholder transparency, and ecosystem engagement are often decisive in regaining credibility with investors, employees, and partners.

## EXAMPLES: STARTUP FAILURE CASES

### 1. Stayzilla – Travel-tech Platform (Shutdown)

Stayzilla, once a well-funded online accommodation booking platform, shut down operations despite strong brand recall.

**Primary failure drivers:**

- Unsustainable unit economics
- High customer acquisition costs
- Cash-flow stress and funding dependency
- Legal and operational complexity in fragmented markets

**Learning insight:** Growth without a clear profitability pathway significantly increases failure risk.

### 2. Dazo – Food-tech Startup (Shutdown)

Dazo, a Bengaluru-based food delivery startup, failed during the highly competitive food-tech expansion phase.

**Primary failure drivers:**

- Aggressive scaling without operational readiness
- High burn rate and logistics inefficiencies
- Inability to differentiate in a crowded market

**Learning insight:** Execution discipline is as critical as innovation.

### 3. TinyOwl – Hyperlocal Food Delivery (Acquired/Effectively Failed)

TinyOwl expanded rapidly across Indian cities but later collapsed under operational and financial strain.

**Primary failure drivers:**

- Premature geographic expansion
- Weak unit economics
- Investor confidence erosion
- Organizational overstretch

**Learning insight:** Premature scaling is one of the most frequent causes of startup collapse.

### 4. AskMe – E-commerce & Local Search Platform (Shutdown)

AskMe attempted to build a hybrid marketplace and hyperlocal services platform but shut down after funding and operational challenges.

**Primary failure drivers:**

- Strategic diffusion
- High infrastructure cost
- Weak monetization strategy

- Market competition pressure

**Learning insight:** Strategic clarity and focus are essential to survival.

## EXAMPLES: TURNAROUND AND PIVOT STORIES

### 1. OYO – Hospitality Platform (Repeated Strategic Restructuring)

OYO experienced severe setbacks due to aggressive expansion, regulatory challenges, and quality control failures. It undertook major restructuring, exited unviable geographies, rationalized properties, strengthened compliance, and rebuilt operational controls.

**Turnaround actions:**

- Market exits and portfolio pruning
- Cost restructuring
- Regulatory alignment
- Centralized quality management systems

**Learning insight:** Turnarounds often require contraction before renewed growth.

### 2. Paytm – Payments Company to Financial Services Ecosystem (Regulatory Reset and Pivot)

Paytm repeatedly restructured its business model following regulatory shifts affecting wallets, payments banks, and fintech compliance.

**Turnaround actions:**

- Diversification beyond wallets
- Strengthening regulatory and compliance frameworks
- Expansion into merchant services, lending, and wealth-tech

**Learning insight:** Regulatory adaptability is a survival competency in fintech.

### 3. InMobi – Mobile Advertising Platform (Strategic Pivot)

InMobi initially struggled with product focus and international competition. It pivoted from consumer apps to enterprise-grade mobile advertising and data platforms.

**Turnaround actions:**

- Exit from non-core consumer verticals
- Enterprise product realignment
- Deep investment in AI-driven advertising systems

**Learning insight:** Strategic refocusing is often more powerful than relentless expansion.

### 4. Snapdeal – E-commerce Platform (Downscaling and Refocus)

After losing ground to competitors, Snapdeal exited multiple verticals, downsized aggressively, and repositioned itself as a value-commerce platform.

**Turnaround actions:**

- Workforce rationalization

- Technology and seller platform restructuring
- Focus on price-sensitive segments

**Learning insight:** Survival sometimes depends on redefining ambition and rebuilding fundamentals.

Collectively, startup failure and turnaround stories reframe failure not as an endpoint but as a data-rich phase of entrepreneurial evolution. They equip aspiring founders with practical frameworks for early warning detection, crisis response, strategic pivoting, and ethical shutdowns. In an increasingly volatile innovation economy, the ability to navigate failure constructively is a defining competence of sustainable entrepreneurship.

## 12.7 WOMEN AND RURAL ENTREPRENEURSHIP CASES

Women-led and rural enterprises represent a rapidly expanding and strategically significant segment of the entrepreneurial ecosystem. These ventures challenge conventional startup archetypes by embedding innovation within grassroots contexts, household economies, and community-based production systems. Case studies in this section highlight how women entrepreneurs and rural innovators are transforming local challenges into scalable business opportunities, contributing directly to inclusive growth, livelihood generation, and socio-economic resilience.

Women entrepreneurship cases demonstrate the impact of **gender-inclusive innovation systems**. Women-led ventures frequently emerge in healthcare, education, nutrition, agri-business, handicrafts, clean energy, and digital services—sectors closely linked to community welfare and human development. These narratives reveal how women founders leverage experiential knowledge, social networks, and empathy-driven design to create user-centric products and services. Successful cases often showcase the catalytic role of self-help groups (SHGs), microfinance institutions, university incubators, and government programs in enabling access to capital, mentoring, and markets.

Rural entrepreneurship cases underscore the role of **local resource mobilization and decentralized enterprise models**. Startups operating in rural contexts harness agricultural by-products, traditional skills, renewable energy sources, and indigenous knowledge systems to build ventures rooted in sustainability and circular economy principles. These enterprises frequently adopt cluster-based production, cooperative ownership, and micro-entrepreneur franchise models to scale impact while retaining local value creation.

Both women-led and rural ventures highlight the importance of **capability-building ecosystems**. Training in financial literacy, digital platforms, quality certification, and branding enables grassroots enterprises to integrate into national and global value chains. Case studies demonstrate how technology—particularly mobile platforms, digital payments, telemedicine, and agri-advisory systems—acts as a powerful equalizer, reducing geographic and gender-based access barriers.

Leadership trajectories in these cases reveal distinctive entrepreneurial dynamics. Women and rural founders often balance enterprise growth with social responsibilities, community engagement, and impact accountability. Their journeys emphasize trust-building, participatory governance, and incremental scaling strategies that prioritize stability and stakeholder inclusion over rapid valuation-driven expansion.

## EXAMPLES: WOMEN ENTREPRENEURSHIP

### 1. Biocon – Kiran Mazumdar-Shaw (Biopharmaceuticals & Biotechnology)

Biocon, founded by Kiran Mazumdar-Shaw, is India's most globally recognized women-led biotechnology enterprise. It evolved from a small enzyme manufacturing unit into a multinational biopharmaceutical company specializing in biosimilars, insulin, and novel biologics.

**Impact dimensions:**

- Affordable biologics and insulin access
- Indigenous biopharma innovation
- Global regulatory-compliant manufacturing

**Learning insight:** Women-led ventures can scale from domestic biotech startups to globally competitive science enterprises when supported by strong R&D and governance systems.

### 2. Niramai Health Analytix – Geetha Manjunath (Health-tech & AI Diagnostics)

ounded by Dr. Geetha Manjunath, Niramai developed **AI-driven thermal naging technology** for non-invasive breast cancer screening, particularly ted for low-resource and rural environments.

**act dimensions:**

- Early cancer detection
- Women-centric healthcare innovation
- Deployment in semi-urban and rural settings

**ng insight:** Women entrepreneurs are driving preventive and inclusive re innovation by aligning technology with accessibility.

### AR Cosmetics – Vineeta Singh (Consumer Products & Women-anding)

R Cosmetics grew from a niche cosmetics startup into a major Indian brand built around digital-first marketing, domestic manufacturing, and focused product design.

**t dimensions:**

- Women-led brand-building
- Indigenous product development
- Employment generation in retail and manufacturing

**Learning insight:** Women entrepreneurship extends beyond social sectors into high-growth consumer innovation markets.

**4. Lijjat Papad – Shri Mahila Griha Udyog Lijjat Papad (Women Cooperative Enterprise)**

Lijjat Papad is one of India's oldest and most successful women-led cooperative enterprises, providing livelihoods to tens of thousands of women through decentralized food production.

**Impact dimensions:**

- Rural and urban women employment
- Cooperative ownership model
- Long-term brand sustainability

**Learning insight:** Women-centered cooperative entrepreneurship can achieve scale, resilience, and social transformation simultaneously.

**EXAMPLES: RURAL ENTREPRENEURSHIP**

**5. Amul – Gujarat Cooperative Milk Marketing Federation (Dairy & Rural Industrialization)**

Amul transformed India's dairy sector by organizing millions of rural farmers into cooperatives, enabling value addition, cold-chain integration, and global dairy exports.

**Impact dimensions:**

- Farmer income enhancement
- Rural industrialization
- National nutrition security

**Learning insight:** Rural entrepreneurship can reshape national economic structures through cooperative business design.

**6. DeHaat – Rural Agri-entrepreneurship Platform**

DeHaat empowers rural micro-entrepreneurs to operate agricultural service centers delivering advisory, inputs, and market linkages to small farmers.

**Impact dimensions:**

- Village-level entrepreneurship
- Digital agriculture platforms
- Climate-smart farming systems

**Learning insight:** Rural entrepreneurship scales when digital platforms integrate with physical village ecosystems.

**7. MittiCool – Gujarat (Rural Innovation & Sustainable Products)**

MittiCool, founded by a rural innovator, produces non-electric clay refrigerators and eco-friendly earthenware, supporting sustainable living and rural manufacturing.

**Impact dimensions:**

- Sustainable household innovation
- Rural artisan livelihoods
- Climate-resilient product design

**Learning insight:** Grassroots innovation can create nationally recognized sustainable enterprises.

**8. Rang De – Rural Fintech & Social Investment Platform**

Rang De connects urban social investors with rural entrepreneurs, women-led SHGs, and micro-enterprises through structured impact finance.

**Impact dimensions:**

- Rural enterprise financing
- Women micro-entrepreneur empowerment
- Livelihood entrepreneurship

**Learning insight:** Financial inclusion is foundational to rural entrepreneurship sustainability.

Collectively, women and rural entrepreneurship cases reposition entrepreneurship as a mechanism of **structural inclusion** rather than elite opportunity. They demonstrate that high-impact ventures can emerge beyond metropolitan startup hubs, generating innovation from the grassroots level. These narratives provide essential insights into inclusive venture design, decentralized business models, and ecosystem interventions required to unlock the entrepreneurial potential of women and rural communities.

## 12.8 GLOBAL BENCHMARK STARTUPS

Global benchmark startups provide valuable reference models for entrepreneurs by demonstrating how innovation ecosystems across different countries nurture high-impact, globally scalable ventures. These case studies extend learning beyond national boundaries, offering insights into advanced commercialization strategies, regulatory navigation, funding architectures, technology leadership, and organizational design. Examining such benchmarks allows entrepreneurs to contextualize their ventures within international standards of competitiveness, governance, and innovation velocity.

Global benchmark startups are typically characterized by their **strong research integration, early global orientation, and platform-centric business models**. Many originate from world-class universities or national research programs and rapidly establish international partnerships. Their narratives often highlight how early investment in intellectual property, global compliance frameworks, and cross-border talent acquisition creates durable competitive advantage.

A prominent feature across benchmark cases is the ability to **translate breakthrough technologies into dominant market platforms**. Startups in artificial intelligence, biotechnology, space technology, fintech, and clean energy illustrate how sustained R&D investment and iterative market testing enable companies to move from niche innovation to global category leadership. These cases underscore the importance of continuous innovation pipelines rather than one-time technological success.

Global benchmark stories also reveal sophisticated approaches to **capital strategy and ecosystem leverage**. These ventures effectively combine venture capital, government innovation funding, strategic corporate partnerships, and international market access programs. Their growth trajectories frequently involve international acquisitions, standard-setting participation, and large-scale infrastructure build-outs, reflecting a high degree of institutional maturity even at relatively young organizational ages.

Another recurring dimension is **regulatory and ethical leadership**. Particularly in sectors such as health-tech, fintech, and climate technology, global startups succeed by proactively engaging with regulators, building transparent data governance systems, and embedding sustainability metrics into core operations. This anticipatory approach reduces friction during global expansion and strengthens long-term trust.

For Indian and emerging-market entrepreneurs, global benchmark startups serve not as templates for imitation, but as **strategic learning laboratories**. They demonstrate how clarity of mission, disciplined execution, deep technological moats, and international mindset can transform startups into enduring global enterprises. These narratives enable founders to benchmark their readiness across technology, compliance, capital, and culture dimensions as they prepare for international scale.

**EXAMPLES**:

**1. Moderna – USA (Biotechnology & mRNA Therapeutics)**

Moderna transformed from a research-driven biotech startup into a global biopharmaceutical leader by pioneering **mRNA-based therapeutic and vaccine platforms**.

**Benchmark dimensions:**

- Platform-based biotechnology innovation
- Long-term R&D investment before commercial success
- Rapid translation of research into global manufacturing during COVID-19
- Strong IP, regulatory, and clinical trial ecosystems

**Learning insight:** Deep-science startups require patient capital, platform thinking, and regulatory integration to achieve global impact.

**2. Tesla – USA (Clean Energy, EVs & Advanced Manufacturing)**

Tesla benchmarked how startups can disrupt established automotive and energy industries through **vertical integration, proprietary manufacturing, and software-driven systems.**

**Benchmark dimensions:**

- End-to-end technology ownership
- Continuous product and manufacturing innovation
- Brand-led global market creation
- Integration of clean energy and AI-driven mobility

**Learning insight:** Global startups achieve dominance when technology, manufacturing, and customer experience are systemically unified.

**3. SpaceX – USA (Commercial Space & Launch Systems)**

SpaceX redefined the global space industry by commercializing **reusable launch vehicles and private orbital services.**

**Benchmark dimensions:**

- Radical cost innovation through reusability
- Government–startup collaboration (NASA, DoD)
- Long-cycle engineering and mission-oriented culture
- Rapid prototyping and test-driven development

**Learning insight:** Mission-driven startups can transform capital-intensive sectors through deep engineering integration and ecosystem alignment.

**4. Stripe – Ireland/USA (Global Fintech Infrastructure)**

Stripe built a global developer-centric payments and financial services infrastructure powering millions of businesses worldwide.

**Benchmark dimensions:**

- API-first, platform-oriented architecture
- Early international expansion
- Regulatory and compliance mastery
- Continuous ecosystem product expansion

**Learning insight:** Platform thinking and regulatory readiness are foundational for globally scalable fintech enterprises.

**5. ByteDance – China (AI Platforms & Algorithmic Media)**

ByteDance leveraged **AI-driven content recommendation engines** to build globally dominant platforms such as TikTok.

**Benchmark dimensions:**

- Core algorithmic innovation
- Rapid internationalization
- Data-driven product iteration
- Strong consumer technology branding

**Learning insight:** Global digital leaders emerge from relentless data-centric innovation and product experimentation.

**6. DeepMind – UK (Artificial Intelligence & Scientific Computing)**
DeepMind advanced AI from academic research into transformative applications in healthcare, protein structure prediction, and energy optimization.
**Benchmark dimensions:**

- Research-first commercialization
- Strong academic integration
- Ethical AI leadership
- Platform application across scientific domains

**Learning insight:** AI startups can achieve benchmark status when research excellence is institutionalized within commercial organizations.

**7. Beyond Meat – USA (Sustainable Food & Bio-innovation)**
Beyond Meat pioneered large-scale commercialization of **plant-based protein technologies**, reshaping global food systems.
**Benchmark dimensions:**

- Food biotechnology innovation
- Sustainability-driven consumer markets
- Global manufacturing partnerships
- Brand positioning around climate impact

**Learning insight:** Sustainability-focused startups can generate global consumer movements when innovation aligns with environmental narratives.

These global benchmark startups provide aspirational yet practical reference points for entrepreneurs seeking to build internationally competitive ventures. They demonstrate that global success is not a function of geography alone, but of systematic innovation, disciplined scaling, and mission-oriented leadership.

## 12.9 LESSONS LEARNED FROM THE ECOSYSTEM

Synthesizing insights from Indian success stories, university spin-offs, bio-startups, social enterprises, growth-stage journeys, failures, and global benchmarks reveals a set of recurring ecosystem-level lessons. These lessons move beyond individual ventures to illuminate how entrepreneurial systems function, where they fail, and how they can be strengthened to consistently produce high-impact, sustainable startups.

A primary lesson is that **entrepreneurship is fundamentally ecosystem-dependent**. Successful startups rarely emerge in isolation; they are products of interconnected networks involving universities, incubators, investors, industry partners, regulators, and early adopters. Regions that institutionalize collaboration—through research parks, innovation missions, public–private partnerships, and sector-focused accelerators—demonstrate higher venture survival rates and faster commercialization cycles. The ecosystem's maturity often matters as much as the founder's ingenuity.

Another critical insight concerns the balance between **innovation depth and execution discipline**. Across cases, technological novelty alone is insufficient. Startups that endure are those that integrate robust product development with market validation, regulatory planning, financial controls, and scalable operations. Ecosystem mechanisms that emphasize mentoring, pilot access, clinical or industrial validation, and customer discovery significantly improve startup readiness and capital efficiency.

The cases also underscore the importance of **patient, diversified capital**. Deep-tech, biotech, and sustainability ventures require long development timelines and blended financing structures. Ecosystems that combine venture capital with grants, mission-linked public funding, corporate venture arms, and global partnerships create risk buffers that enable founders to pursue breakthrough innovation without premature commercialization pressure.

A recurring ecosystem-level challenge is **premature scaling**. Many failures originate from rapid expansion unsupported by unit economics, governance systems, or operational maturity. Successful ecosystems counteract this by promoting milestone-based funding, scale-readiness assessments, and structured growth programs. This reinforces the lesson that scale should be treated as a strategic phase, not as a default objective.

Another key learning relates to **talent and leadership pipelines**. High-performing ecosystems invest not only in startup formation but in continuous founder education, CXO development, and technical workforce training. University–industry mobility, entrepreneur-in-residence models, and executive mentorship networks consistently emerge as critical success enablers. Leadership evolution is as vital as product evolution.

The ecosystem perspective further highlights the growing centrality of **ethics, compliance, and sustainability**. Startups operating in healthcare, fintech, climate-tech, and data-driven sectors increasingly succeed by embedding governance, impact metrics, and regulatory engagement into their core strategies. Ecosystems that normalize these practices early reduce systemic risk and increase global credibility.

Finally, cross-case analysis demonstrates that resilient ecosystems cultivate a **learning-oriented entrepreneurial culture**—one that normalizes experimentation, destigmatizes failure, and institutionalizes knowledge transfer. Turnaround stories and shutdowns, when openly analyzed, strengthen the next generation of ventures by improving decision frameworks, risk literacy, and strategic realism.

Collectively, these lessons indicate that the ultimate competitive advantage of a startup nation or region lies not in isolated unicorns, but in the design of a **self-renewing entrepreneurial ecosystem**—one capable of repeatedly converting knowledge into innovation, innovation into enterprises, and enterprises into sustained societal and economic value.

## 12.10 FUTURE ROADMAP FOR ENTREPRENEURS

The future of entrepreneurship will be shaped by the convergence of deep technologies, global sustainability imperatives, demographic transitions, and digitally integrated markets. As innovation cycles shorten and competitive landscapes intensify, entrepreneurs must move beyond opportunity-driven venture creation toward **capability-driven, mission-oriented enterprise building**. This section outlines a strategic roadmap to guide future entrepreneurs in navigating emerging realities and building resilient, globally relevant ventures.

A central pillar of the future roadmap is the shift toward **deep-tech and science-led entrepreneurship**. Advances in artificial intelligence, synthetic biology, genomics, advanced materials, quantum computing, space technology, and clean energy are redefining value creation. Future entrepreneurs will need to engage more deeply with research ecosystems, build strong intellectual property portfolios, and design longer-horizon innovation pipelines. Collaboration with universities, national laboratories, and corporate R&D centers will become indispensable for sustaining technological relevance.

Another defining direction is the mainstreaming of **sustainability and climate entrepreneurship**. Ventures addressing renewable energy, circular bioeconomy, water systems, sustainable agriculture, carbon management, and green manufacturing will no longer be peripheral but central to industrial and investment agendas. Entrepreneurs must integrate life-cycle thinking, ESG frameworks, and impact metrics into business design, positioning sustainability not as compliance, but as a driver of competitiveness and market differentiation.

The future roadmap also emphasizes **platform and ecosystem entrepreneurship**. Startups will increasingly function as orchestrators of multi-stakeholder systems rather than standalone product companies. Digital health platforms, agri-innovation networks, fintech infrastructures, and smart manufacturing ecosystems will demand capabilities in API architecture, data governance, partnership strategy, and regulatory co-creation. Entrepreneurs will need to design ventures that scale through networks, not merely through internal expansion.

A fourth priority area is **global-first venture design**. From inception, startups must consider international standards, cross-border compliance, multicultural markets, and globally distributed talent. Emerging-market entrepreneurs, in particular, can leverage cost-efficient innovation, frugal engineering, and digital delivery to build solutions for global south and developed markets alike. Strategic internationalization, not opportunistic expansion, will define future competitiveness.

Equally critical is the evolution of **entrepreneurial leadership and organizational architecture**. Future founders must cultivate hybrid competencies spanning technology literacy, ethical governance, financial engineering, and systems thinking. Organizational structures will shift toward agile, modular, and AI-augmented teams. Continuous founder upskilling, professional management integration, and evidence-based decision systems will be non-negotiable for long-term sustainability.

The roadmap further calls for a reorientation toward **resilient entrepreneurship**. Entrepreneurs must design ventures capable of absorbing regulatory shifts, technological disruptions, and global shocks. This requires diversified revenue models, robust compliance frameworks, cybersecurity preparedness, and scenario-based strategic planning. Failure literacy and turnaround readiness will become core entrepreneurial skills.

Finally, the future entrepreneur will operate within a **learning-driven ecosystem**. Proactive engagement with incubators, accelerators, corporate innovation programs, and policy platforms will be essential. Entrepreneurs who systematically leverage ecosystem resources, contribute back through mentorship and collaboration, and participate in collective innovation initiatives will shape not only their own success, but the evolution of the broader entrepreneurial environment.

In conclusion, the future roadmap for entrepreneurs is defined by depth over speed, systems over silos, and impact over isolation. Those who integrate scientific rigor, sustainable value creation, global orientation, and adaptive leadership into their ventures will be best positioned to build enterprises that endure, scale responsibly, and contribute meaningfully to economic and societal transformation.

## KEY CONCEPTS & DEFINITIONS

**Startup Case Study**: A structured, evidence-based analysis of a startup's origin, strategy, execution, challenges, and outcomes, used to extract practical and theoretical insights into entrepreneurial processes.

**Entrepreneurial Ecosystem**: An interconnected network of institutions, individuals, capital providers, policies, and support organizations that collectively enable the creation, growth, and sustainability of startups.

**University Spin-off**: A venture formed to commercialize technologies, intellectual property, or research outcomes developed within a university or public research institution.

**Bio-startup**: A science-driven enterprise applying biotechnology, life sciences, or biomedical engineering to develop products or services in healthcare, agriculture, industry, or environment.

**Health-tech Venture**: A startup integrating healthcare services with digital technologies, medical devices, diagnostics, or data platforms to improve clinical outcomes and system efficiency.

**Social Enterprise**: An organization that applies entrepreneurial strategies to address social or environmental problems while maintaining financial sustainability.

**Sustainable Enterprise**: A venture designed around long-term environmental stewardship, responsible resource utilization, and economic viability, aligned with sustainability and ESG principles.

**Growth-stage Startup**: A venture that has achieved product–market fit and is focused on scaling operations, markets, infrastructure, and organizational capacity.

**Scale-up Phase**: The transitional stage where startups systematically expand production, customer base, workforce, and geographic reach while institutionalizing governance and processes.

**Premature Scaling**: Rapid expansion before validating unit economics, operational readiness, or market stability, often leading to financial and organizational failure.

**Startup Failure**: The inability of a venture to achieve sustainable operations due to strategic, financial, technological, market, or leadership-related shortcomings.

**Turnaround Strategy**: A set of corrective actions—including restructuring, pivoting, leadership changes, and cost realignment—implemented to restore a struggling venture to viability.

**Pivot**: A deliberate strategic shift in product, market, technology, or business model based on validated learning and market feedback.

**Women Entrepreneurship**: Entrepreneurial activity led by women founders, often emphasizing inclusive innovation, community engagement, and gender-equitable economic development.

**Rural Entrepreneurship**: Venture creation rooted in rural contexts, leveraging local resources, agricultural systems, traditional skills, and decentralized business models.

**Global Benchmark Startup**: An internationally recognized venture that sets industry standards through technological leadership, scalable business models, and global market influence.

**Deep-tech Entrepreneurship**: Venture creation based on substantial scientific or engineering innovation requiring long development cycles, strong IP, and specialized infrastructure.

**Mission-driven Enterprise**: A startup structured around solving a clearly defined societal, environmental, or national-priority challenge alongside financial objectives.

**Triple Bottom Line**: A sustainability framework measuring organizational performance across three dimensions: economic viability, social impact, and environmental responsibility.

**Ecosystem Learning**: The collective process by which entrepreneurial communities generate, share, and institutionalize knowledge from successes, failures, and experiments.

**Institutionalization of Startups**: The transition from founder-centric operations to professionally managed organizations with formal governance, compliance, and scalable systems.

**Impact-driven Innovation**: Entrepreneurial activity intentionally designed to generate measurable societal or environmental benefits in addition to commercial returns.
**Resilient Entrepreneurship**: The capability of ventures to absorb shocks, adapt to change, and sustain operations under uncertainty, disruption, or crisis conditions.
**Commercialization Pathway**: The structured progression from idea and research to product development, validation, regulatory approval, market entry, and scale.
**Future-ready Venture**: A startup architected to remain competitive through continuous innovation, sustainability integration, global orientation, and adaptive leadership.

---

## REVIEW QUESTIONS AND EXERCISES

### A. Review Questions

1. Explain the importance of startup case studies in understanding entrepreneurial success beyond theoretical business models.
2. Discuss the key characteristics that distinguish Indian startup success narratives from those of developed innovation ecosystems.
3. Analyze the strategic role of universities and public research institutions in generating spin-off ventures.
4. Why are bio-startups and health-tech ventures considered fundamentally different from software-based startups in terms of development and commercialization?
5. Examine the significance of social and sustainable enterprises in achieving inclusive economic growth.
6. What organizational and strategic transitions define the growth-stage journey of startups?
7. Identify and explain the most common causes of startup failure highlighted in this chapter.
8. Critically evaluate how turnaround strategies enable ventures to recover from growth crises.
9. Discuss the unique challenges and opportunities associated with women-led and rural entrepreneurship.
10. Why are global benchmark startups valuable for emerging-market entrepreneurs?
11. Synthesize the ecosystem-level lessons derived from the diverse case studies presented in this chapter.
12. How does the future roadmap for entrepreneurs differ from traditional startup growth narratives?
13. Explain how mission-driven entrepreneurship influences innovation priorities and business model design.

14. Compare growth-oriented entrepreneurship with impact-driven entrepreneurship using examples from this chapter.
15. Discuss how entrepreneurial ecosystems can reduce premature scaling and improve startup survival rates.

**B. Short-Answer / Concept-Based Questions**

1. Define university spin-off and explain its relevance to national innovation systems.
2. What is meant by "growth-stage institutionalization"?
3. Differentiate between startup failure and strategic pivot.
4. What is triple-bottom-line entrepreneurship?
5. How does regulatory preparedness affect bio-startup scalability?
6. Explain the role of patient capital in deep-tech ventures.
7. What is ecosystem learning, and why is it critical?
8. List four leadership capabilities essential for growth-stage founders.

**C. Applied and Analytical Exercises**

**Exercise 1: Case Deconstruction:** Select any one startup case discussed in this chapter and analyze it under the following headings:

- Problem addressed
- Innovation and value proposition
- Ecosystem support
- Key growth challenges
- Strategic lessons for entrepreneurs

**Exercise 2: Failure Analysis Framework:** Choose a failed or struggling startup (Indian or global) and prepare a structured failure diagnosis report covering:

- Market and customer assumptions
- Financial and operational factors
- Leadership and governance issues
- External environment and regulatory influences
- Preventive measures that could have altered the outcome

**Exercise 3: Turnaround Strategy Design:** Design a turnaround plan for a hypothetical growth-stage startup facing declining revenues and high burn rate. Your plan should include:

- Immediate stabilization actions
- Strategic refocus or pivot options
- Organizational restructuring measures
- Long-term sustainability roadmap

**Exercise 4: Ecosystem Mapping:** Create an entrepreneurial ecosystem map for a chosen sector (biotech, health-tech, agritech, fintech, or clean-tech), identifying:

- Key institutions and stakeholders
- Funding sources
- Support mechanisms
- Policy and regulatory actors
- Gaps and opportunities

**Exercise 5: Inclusive Entrepreneurship Proposal:** Develop a concept note for a women-led or rural startup. Include:

- Social or economic problem addressed
- Innovation approach
- Business and impact model
- Ecosystem partners required
- Scaling strategy

**Exercise 6: Global Benchmark Comparison:** Compare one Indian startup with one global benchmark startup on:

- Technology strategy
- Funding and partnerships
- Scaling pathway
- Governance and sustainability approach
- Transferable lessons

### D. Project-Based Assignments

1. **Mini Case Study Report:** Prepare a 2,000-word documented case study on a startup not covered in this chapter, mapping its lifecycle, ecosystem support, and strategic inflection points.
2. **Startup Readiness Audit:** Develop a checklist-based tool to evaluate whether a startup is ready to transition from early stage to growth stage.
3. **Future Venture Blueprint:** Design a "future-ready startup model" aligned with the roadmap in Section 12.10, including technology, sustainability, governance, and ecosystem integration strategies.

------------------------------------------------------------------------------------------------
------------------------------------------------------------------------------------------------

# ABOUT THE AUTHOR

Dr. Gaurav Kumar is an Associate Professor and Head of the Department of Biotechnology & Bioengineering, School of Biosciences & Technology and Head, Institution's Innovation Council (IIC) at Galgotias University, India. He holds a PhD from IIT (BHU), Varanasi, and brings over twelve years of experience spanning bioengineering research, academic leadership, and innovation ecosystem development.

Dr. Kumar has authored more than 45 international research publications, holds multiple national and international patents, and has edited books with Springer Nature and CRC Press. In parallel with his academic career, he has played a central role in institutional innovation and entrepreneurship initiatives. As Head of IIC and former In-Charge of the Incubation Cell, he has led Ministry of Education and AICTE innovation programs, secured government funding for entrepreneurship development, coordinated national hackathons, and mentored numerous students to transform their ideas into registered startup ventures.

His work bridges technology innovation, startup incubation, and academic entrepreneurship, with hands-on involvement in ideation, product development, intellectual property, and early-stage commercialization. Through this book, Dr. Kumar brings together scholarly insight and real-world startup experience to guide students, educators, and aspiring entrepreneurs in building scalable, sustainable ventures.

www.ingramcontent.com/pod-product-compliance
Ingram Content Group UK Ltd.
Pitfield, Milton Keynes, MK11 3LW, UK
UKHW061431210126
10227UKWH00027B/446

9 789334 434460